How to write a research proposal, paper or thesis

Authored by: Dr. Robert V. Labaree

Compiled by: Dr. Azadeh Nemati

سرشناسه :	نعمتی، آزاده- ۱۳۵۴- گردآورنده Nemati, Azadeh
عنوان و نام پدیدآور :	How to write a research proposal, paper or thesis/ compiled Azadeh Nemati
مشخصات نشر :	شیراز: کوشا مهر، ۱۳۹۴= ۲۰۱۶ م.
مشخصات ظاهری :	۲۷۳ ص.
شابک :	۸-۱۷۵-۹۷۴-۹۶۴-۹۷۸
وضعیت فهرست نویسی :	فیپا
یادداشت :	انگلیسی.
آوانویسی عنوان :	هاو...
موضوع :	زبان انگلیسی —نگارش علمی و فنی
رده بندی کنگره :	۱۳۹۴ ۲ه۷ن/۱۴۷۵ PE
رده بندی دیویی :	۸۰۸/۰۶۶
شماره کتابشناسی ملی :	۴۱۸۳۳۰۹

انتشارات کوشامهر

مرکز نشر و پخش کتابهای دانشگاهی

شیراز، بلوار کریم خان زند، روبروی خیام، پاساژ مسعود، پلاک۳۳

تلفن: ۳۲۳۱۶۳۹۸ دورنگار: ۳۲۳۱۴۶۶۵

ناشر برگزیده سالهای ۷۴، ۷۶، ۷۹، ۸۰، ۸۱

خادم نشر سال ۷۷ و ۸۳

How to write a research proposal, paper or thesis

گردآوری و تألیف: دکتر آزاده نعمتی

ناشر: انتشارات کوشامهر

شمارگان: ۱۰۰۰

چاپ: واصف

نوبت چاپ: اول ۱۳۹۵

قیمت: ۱۷۰۰۰۰ ریال

شابک: ۸-۱۷۵-۹۷۴-۹۶۴-۹۷۸

Foreword

It was always my dream to write a book and guide my MA or PhD students while writing their academic papers, proposals, thesis and dissertations. I cannot remember what exactly I was looking for in the net that I came across some useful information about organizing the social science research paper. I contented the librarian to help me in referencing the materials. He gave me the email of Dr. Labaree. I again contacted him and asked for permission. His writing is what I had in mind to write. Surprisingly he is saying from my mouth. It is my honor and I am thankful to God for crossing the path with him. After some contacts he kindly sent me the following email and it was the story of this book:

Dr. Nemati—
I apologize for the delay in responding to you. It has been very busy at work.

I have no problem with you recompiling my online writing guide into a small booklet or brochure for students in your classes. Since I am the author of the work, I would appreciate any publication to say that I am the author and your name as the compiler of the book [i.e., Dr. Robert V. Labaree, author; Compiled by Dr. Azadeh Nemati]. If you choose to revise the text in any way, which you are welcome to do, then the booklet can say, Dr. Robert V. Labaree, author; Revised by Dr. Azadeh Nemati.

I am bound by the copyright laws of the United States and the intellectual property rules of the University so I hope this is satisfactory. Thank you again for finding my writing guide to be useful. Please stay in touch and let me know if your students find it useful, and, if there are any parts that could be improved.

--Robert
Dr. Robert V. Labaree
Political Science / International Relations Librarian
Von KleinSmid Center Library for International and Public Affairs
https://libraries.usc.edu/locations/vkc-library

USC University of
Southern California

Contents

Title .... page

Purpose of Guide................................... 7
1.Types of Research Designs 7
2.Design Flaws to Avoid.......................... 24
3.1. Choosing a Research Problem 27
4.Narrowing a Topic Idea 31
5.Broadening a Topic Idea...................... 33
6.Extending the Timeliness of a Topic Idea 34

2. Preparing to Write................................37
1.Academic Writing Style....................... 40
2. Choosing a Title................................. 46
3. Making an Outline 48
4. Paragraph Development....................... 51

3. The Abstract.......................................55
1.Executive Summary 57

4.The Introduction 61
1.The C.A.R.S. Model 65
2.Background Information....................... 68
3.The Research Problem/Question........... 71
4.Theoretical Framework........................ 75

5. The Literature Review 81
1.Citation Tracking 89
2.Content Alert Services 92
3. Evaluating Sources............................. 94
4. Primary Sources 98
5. Secondary Sources 99
6.Tiertiary Sources................................ 100
7.What Is Scholarly vs. Popular?........... 103

6.The Methodology 107
1.Qualitative Methods............................ 111
2.Quantitative Methods.......................... 117

Contents

Contents

7. The Results 123
  1.Using Non-Textual Elements 126

8. The Discussion 131
  2.Limitations of the Study 135

9. The Conclusion 141
  1.Appendices 145

10. Proofreading Your Paper 149
  1.Common Grammar Mistakes 152
  2.Writing Concisely 156

11. Citing Sources 161
  1.Avoiding Plagiarism 165
  2.Footnotes or Endnotes? 166
  3.Further Readings 168

12. Annotated Bibliography 171

13. Giving an Oral Presentation 177
  1.Dealing with Nervousness 181
  2.Using Visual Aids 183

14. Grading Someone Else's Paper 185

15. How to Manage Group Projects 189

16.Writing a Book Review 193
  1.Multiple Book Review Essay 200
  2.Reviewing Collected Essays 209

17. Writing a Case Study 219

18. Writing a Field Report 229
  1.About Informed Consent 237
  2.Writing Field Notes 239

19. Writing a Policy Memo 243

20. Writing a Research Proposal 251

21.Acknowledgements 259

Glossary of Research Terms 261

Contents

Organizing Your Social Sciences Research Paper: Purpose of Guide

1

Organizing Your Social Sciences Research Paper: Types of Research Designs

Introduction
Before beginning your paper, you need to decide how you plan to design the study.

The research design refers to the overall strategy that you choose to integrate the different components of the study in a coherent and logical way, thereby, ensuring you will effectively address the research problem; it constitutes the blueprint for the collection, measurement, and analysis of data. Note that your research problem determines the type of design you should use, not the other way around!

General Structure and Writing Style
The function of a research design is to ensure that the evidence obtained enables you to effectively address the research problem logically and as unambiguously as possible. In social sciences research, obtaining information relevant to the research problem generally entails specifying the type of evidence needed to test a theory, to evaluate a program, or to accurately describe and assess meaning related to an observable phenomenon.

With this in mind, a common mistake made by researchers is that they begin their investigations far too early, before they have thought critically about what information is required to address the study's research questions. Without attending to these design issues beforehand, the overall research problem will not be adequately addressed and any conclusions drawn will risk being weak and unconvincing. As a consequence, the overall validity of the study will be undermined.

Given this, the length and complexity of describing research designs in your paper can vary considerably, but any well-developed design will achieve the following:

1. Identify the research problem clearly and justify its selection, particularly in relation to any valid alternative designs that could have been used,
2. Review and synethesize previously published literature associated with the problem,
3. Clearly and explicitly specify hypotheses [i.e., research questions] central to the research problem,
4. Effectively describe the data which will be necessary for an adequate testing of the hypotheses and explain how such data will be obtained, and
5. Describe the methods of analysis to be applied to the data in determining whether or not the hypotheses are true or false.

NOTE: To search for scholarly resources on specific research designs and methods, use the SAGE Research Methods database. The database contains links to more than 175,000 pages of SAGE publisher's book, journal, and reference content on quantitative, qualitative, and mixed research methodologies. Also included is a collection of case studies of social research projects that can be used to help you better understand abstract or complex methodological concepts.

Action Research Design
Definition and Purpose

The essentials of action research design follow a characteristic cycle whereby initially an exploratory stance is adopted, where an understanding of a problem is developed and plans are made for some form of interventionary strategy. Then the intervention is carried out (the "action" in Action Research) during which time, pertinent observations are collected in various forms. The new interventional strategies are carried out, and this cyclic process repeats, continuing until a sufficient understanding of (or a valid implementation solution for) the problem is achieved. The protocol is iterative or cyclical in nature and is intended to foster deeper understanding of a given situation, starting with conceptualizing and particularizing the problem and moving through several interventions and evaluations.

What do these studies tell you?

1. This is a collaborative and adaptive research design that lends itself to use in work or community situations.
2. Design focuses on pragmatic and solution-driven research outcomes rather than testing theories.
3. When practitioners use action research, it has the potential to increase the amount they learn consciously from their experience; the action research cycle can be regarded as a learning cycle.
4. Action research studies often have direct and obvious relevance to improving practice and advocating for change.
5. There are no hidden controls or preemption of direction by the researcher.

What these studies don't tell you?

1. It is harder to do than conducting conventional research because the researcher takes on responsibilities of advocating for change as well as for researching the topic.
2. Action research is much harder to write up because it is less likely that you can use a standard format to report your findings effectively [i.e., data is often in the form of stories or observation].
3. Personal over-involvement of the researcher may bias research results.
4. The cyclic nature of action research to achieve its twin outcomes of action (e.g. change) and research (e.g. understanding) is time-consuming and complex to conduct.
5. Advocating for change requires buy-in from participants.

Case Study Design

Definition and Purpose

A case study is an in-depth study of a particular research problem rather than a sweeping statistical survey or comprehesive comparative inquiry. It is often used to narrow down a very broad field of research into one or a few easily researchable examples. The case study research design is also useful for testing whether a specific theory and model actually applies to phenomena in the real world. It is a useful design when not much is known about an issue or phenomenon.

What do these studies tell you?

1. Approach excels at bringing us to an understanding of a complex issue through detailed contextual analysis of a limited number of events or conditions and their relationships.

2. A researcher using a case study design can apply a variety of methodologies and rely on a variety of sources to investigate a research problem.
3. Design can extend experience or add strength to what is already known through previous research.
4. Social scientists, in particular, make wide use of this research design to examine contemporary real-life situations and provide the basis for the application of concepts and theories and the extension of methodologies.
5. The design can provide detailed descriptions of specific and rare cases.

What these studies don't tell you?
1. A single or small number of cases offers little basis for establishing reliability or to generalize the findings to a wider population of people, places, or things.
2. Intense exposure to the study of a case may bias a researcher's interpretation of the findings.
3. Design does not facilitate assessment of cause and effect relationships.
4. Vital information may be missing, making the case hard to interpret.
5. The case may not be representative or typical of the larger problem being investigated.
6. If the criteria for selecting a case is because it represents a very unusual or unique phenomenon or problem for study, then your intepretation of the findings can only apply to that particular case.

Causal Design
Definition and Purpose
Causality studies may be thought of as understanding a phenomenon in terms of conditional statements in the form, "If X, then Y." This type of research is used to measure what impact a specific change will have on existing norms and assumptions. Most social scientists seek causal explanations that reflect tests of hypotheses. Causal effect (nomothetic perspective) occurs when variation in one phenomenon, an independent variable, leads to or results, on average, in variation in another phenomenon, the dependent variable.

Conditions necessary for determining causality:
- Empirical association -- a valid conclusion is based on finding an association between the independent variable and the dependent variable.

- Appropriate time order -- to conclude that causation was involved, one must see that cases were exposed to variation in the independent variable before variation in the dependent variable.
- Nonspuriousness -- a relationship between two variables that is not due to variation in a third variable.
-

What do these studies tell you?
1. Causality research designs assist researchers in understanding why the world works the way it does through the process of proving a causal link between variables and by the process of eliminating other possibilities.
2. Replication is possible.
3. There is greater confidence the study has internal validity due to the systematic subject selection and equity of groups being compared.

What these studies don't tell you?
1. Not all relationships are casual! The possibility always exists that, by sheer coincidence, two unrelated events appear to be related [e.g., Punxatawney Phil could accurately predict the duration of Winter for five consecutive years but, the fact remains, he's just a big, furry rodent].
2. Conclusions about causal relationships are difficult to determine due to a variety of extraneous and confounding variables that exist in a social environment. This means causality can only be inferred, never proven.
3. If two variables are correlated, the cause must come before the effect. However, even though two variables might be causally related, it can sometimes be difficult to determine which variable comes first and, therefore, to establish which variable is the actual cause and which is the actual effect.

Cohort Design
Definition and Purpose
Often used in the medical sciences, but also found in the applied social sciences, a cohort study generally refers to a study conducted over a period of time involving members of a population which the subject or representative member comes from, and who are united by some commonality or similarity. Using a quantitative framework, a cohort study makes note of statistical occurrence within a specialized subgroup, united by same or similar characteristics that are relevant to the research problem being investigated, rather than studying statistical occurrence within the general population. Using a qualitative framework, cohort studies generally

gather data using methods of observation. Cohorts can be either "open" or "closed."

- Open Cohort Studies [dynamic populations, such as the population of Los Angeles] involve a population that is defined just by the state of being a part of the study in question (and being monitored for the outcome). Date of entry and exit from the study is individually defined, therefore, the size of the study population is not constant. In open cohort studies, researchers can only calculate rate based data, such as, incidence rates and variants thereof.
- Closed Cohort Studies [static populations, such as patients entered into a clinical trial] involve participants who enter into the study at one defining point in time and where it is presumed that no new participants can enter the cohort. Given this, the number of study participants remains constant (or can only decrease).

What do these studies tell you?

1. The use of cohorts is often mandatory because a randomized control study may be unethical. For example, you cannot deliberately expose people to asbestos, you can only study its effects on those who have already been exposed. Research that measures risk factors often relies upon cohort designs.
2. Because cohort studies measure potential causes before the outcome has occurred, they can demonstrate that these "causes" preceded the outcome, thereby avoiding the debate as to which is the cause and which is the effect.
3. Cohort analysis is highly flexible and can provide insight into effects over time and related to a variety of different types of changes [e.g., social, cultural, political, economic, etc.].
4. Either original data or secondary data can be used in this design.

What these studies don't tell you?

1. In cases where a comparative analysis of two cohorts is made [e.g., studying the effects of one group exposed to asbestos and one that has not], a researcher cannot control for all other factors that might differ between the two groups. These factors are known as confounding variables.
2. Cohort studies can end up taking a long time to complete if the researcher must wait for the conditions of interest to develop within the group. This also increases the chance that key variables change during the course of the study, potentially impacting the validity of the findings.

3. Due to the lack of randominization in the cohort design, its external validity is lower than that of study designs where the researcher randomly assigns participants.

Cross-Sectional Design
Definition and Purpose
Cross-sectional research designs have three distinctive features: no time dimension; a reliance on existing differences rather than change following intervention; and, groups are selected based on existing differences rather than random allocation. The cross-sectional design can only measure differences between or from among a variety of people, subjects, or phenomena rather than a process of change. As such, researchers using this design can only employ a relatively passive approach to making causal inferences based on findings.

What do these studies tell you?
1. Cross-sectional studies provide a clear 'snapshot' of the outcome and the characteristics associated with it, at a specific point in time.
2. Unlike an experimental design, where there is an active intervention by the researcher to produce and measure change or to create differences, cross-sectional designs focus on studying and drawing inferences from existing differences between people, subjects, or phenomena.
3. Entails collecting data *at* and *concerning* one point in time. While longitudinal studies involve taking multiple measures over an extended period of time, cross-sectional research is focused on finding relationships between variables at one moment in time.
4. Groups identified for study are purposely selected based upon existing differences in the sample rather than seeking random sampling.
5. Cross-section studies are capable of using data from a large number of subjects and, unlike observational studies, is not geographically bound.
6. Can estimate prevalence of an outcome of interest because the sample is usually taken from the whole population.
7. Because cross-sectional designs generally use survey techniques to gather data, they are relatively inexpensive and take up little time to conduct.

What these studies don't tell you?
1. Finding people, subjects, or phenomena to study that are very similar except in one specific variable can be difficult.
2. Results are static and time bound and, therefore, give no indication of a sequence of events or reveal historical or temporal contexts.

3. Studies cannot be utilized to establish cause and effect relationships.
4. This design only provides a snapshot of analysis so there is always the possibility that a study could have differing results if another time-frame had been chosen.
5. There is no follow up to the findings.

Descriptive Design
Definition and Purpose
Descriptive research designs help provide answers to the questions of who, what, when, where, and how associated with a particular research problem; a descriptive study cannot conclusively ascertain answers to why. Descriptive research is used to obtain information concerning the current status of the phenomena and to describe "what exists" with respect to variables or conditions in a situation.

What do these studies tell you?
1. The subject is being observed in a completely natural and unchanged natural environment. True experiments, whilst giving analyzable data, often adversely influence the normal behavior of the subject [a.k.a., the Heisenberg effect whereby measurements of certain systems cannot be made without affecting the systems].
2. Descriptive research is often used as a pre-cursor to more quantitative research designs with the general overview giving some valuable pointers as to what variables are worth testing quantitatively.
3. If the limitations are understood, they can be a useful tool in developing a more focused study.
4. Descriptive studies can yield rich data that lead to important recommendations in practice.
5. Appoach collects a large amount of data for detailed analysis.

What these studies don't tell you?
1. The results from a descriptive research cannot be used to discover a definitive answer or to disprove a hypothesis.
2. Because descriptive designs often utilize observational methods [as opposed to quantitative methods], the results cannot be replicated.
3. The descriptive function of research is heavily dependent on instrumentation for measurement and observation.

Experimental Design
Definition and Purpose
A blueprint of the procedure that enables the researcher to maintain control over all factors that may affect the result of an experiment. In doing this, the researcher attempts to determine or predict what may occur. Experimental

research is often used where there is time priority in a causal relationship (cause precedes effect), there is consistency in a causal relationship (a cause will always lead to the same effect), and the magnitude of the correlation is great. The classic experimental design specifies an experimental group and a control group. The independent variable is administered to the experimental group and not to the control group, and both groups are measured on the same dependent variable. Subsequent experimental designs have used more groups and more measurements over longer periods. True experiments must have control, randomization, and manipulation.

What do these studies tell you?
1. Experimental research allows the researcher to control the situation. In so doing, it allows researchers to answer the question, "What causes something to occur?"
2. Permits the researcher to identify cause and effect relationships between variables and to distinguish placebo effects from treatment effects.
3. Experimental research designs support the ability to limit alternative explanations and to infer direct causal relationships in the study.
4. Approach provides the highest level of evidence for single studies.

What these studies don't tell you?
1. The design is artificial, and results may not generalize well to the real world.
2. The artificial settings of experiments may alter the behaviors or responses of participants.
3. Experimental designs can be costly if special equipment or facilities are needed.
4. Some research problems cannot be studied using an experiment because of ethical or technical reasons.
5. Difficult to apply ethnographic and other qualitative methods to experimentally designed studies.

Exploratory Design
Definition and Purpose
An exploratory design is conducted about a research problem when there are few or no earlier studies to refer to or rely upon to predict an outcome. The focus is on gaining insights and familiarity for later investigation or undertaken when research problems are in a preliminary stage of investigation. Exploratory designs are often used to establish an understanding of how best to proceed in studying an issue or what methodology would effectively apply to gathering information about the issue.

The goals of exploratory research are intended to produce the following possible insights:

- Familiarity with basic details, settings, and concerns.
- Well grounded picture of the situation being developed.
- Generation of new ideas and assumptions.
- Development of tentative theories or hypotheses.
- Determination about whether a study is feasible in the future.
- Issues get refined for more systematic investigation and formulation of new research questions.
- Direction for future research and techniques get developed.

What do these studies tell you?

1. Design is a useful approach for gaining background information on a particular topic.
2. Exploratory research is flexible and can address research questions of all types (what, why, how).
3. Provides an opportunity to define new terms and clarify existing concepts.
4. Exploratory research is often used to generate formal hypotheses and develop more precise research problems.
5. In the policy arena or applied to practice, exploratory studies help establish research priorities and where resources should be allocated.

What these studies don't tell you?

1. Exploratory research generally utilizes small sample sizes and, thus, findings are typically not generalizable to the population at large.
2. The exploratory nature of the research inhibits an ability to make definitive conclusions about the findings. They provide insight but not definitive conclusions.
3. The research process underpinning exploratory studies is flexible but often unstructured, leading to only tentative results that have limited value to decision-makers.
4. Design lacks rigorous standards applied to methods of data gathering and analysis because one of the areas for exploration could be to determine what method or methodologies could best fit the research problem.

Historical Design
Definition and Purpose
The purpose of a historical research design is to collect, verify, and synthesize evidence from the past to establish facts that defend or refute a hypothesis. It uses secondary sources and a variety of primary documentary evidence, such as, diaries, official records, reports, archives, and non-textual

information [maps, pictures, audio and visual recordings]. The limitation is that the sources must be both authentic and valid.

What do these studies tell you?
1. The historical research design is unobtrusive; the act of research does not affect the results of the study.
2. The historical approach is well suited for trend analysis.
3. Historical records can add important contextual background required to more fully understand and interpret a research problem.
4. There is often no possibility of researcher-subject interaction that could affect the findings.
5. Historical sources can be used over and over to study different research problems or to replicate a previous study.

What these studies don't tell you?
1. The ability to fulfill the aims of your research are directly related to the amount and quality of documentation available to understand the research problem.
2. Since historical research relies on data from the past, there is no way to manipulate it to control for contemporary contexts.
3. Interpreting historical sources can be very time consuming.
4. The sources of historical materials must be archived consistentally to ensure access. This may especially challenging for digital or online-only sources.
5. Original authors bring their own perspectives and biases to the interpretation of past events and these biases are more difficult to ascertain in historical resources.
6. Due to the lack of control over external variables, historical research is very weak with regard to the demands of internal validity.
7. It is rare that the entirety of historical documentation needed to fully address a research problem is available for interpretation, therefore, gaps need to be acknowledged.

Longitudinal Design
Definition and Purpose
A longitudinal study follows the same sample over time and makes repeated observations. For example, with longitudinal surveys, the same group of people is interviewed at regular intervals, enabling researchers to track changes over time and to relate them to variables that might explain why the changes occur. Longitudinal research designs describe patterns of change and help establish the direction and magnitude of causal relationships. Measurements are taken on each variable over two or more distinct time

periods. This allows the researcher to measure change in variables over time. It is a type of observational study sometimes referred to as a panel study.

What do these studies tell you?

1. Longitudinal data facilitate the analysis of the duration of a particular phenomenon.
2. Enables survey researchers to get close to the kinds of causal explanations usually attainable only with experiments.
3. The design permits the measurement of differences or change in a variable from one period to another [i.e., the description of patterns of change over time].
4. Longitudinal studies facilitate the prediction of future outcomes based upon earlier factors.

What these studies don't tell you?

1. The data collection method may change over time.
2. Maintaining the integrity of the original sample can be difficult over an extended period of time.
3. It can be difficult to show more than one variable at a time.
4. This design often needs qualitative research data to explain fluctuations in the results.
5. A longitudinal research design assumes present trends will continue unchanged.
6. It can take a long period of time to gather results.
7. There is a need to have a large sample size and accurate sampling to reach representativness.

Meta-Analysis Design

Definition and Purpose

Meta-analysis is an analytical methodology designed to systematically evaluate and summarize the results from a number of individual studies, thereby, increasing the overall sample size and the ability of the researcher to study effects of interest. The purpose is to not simply summarize existing knowledge, but to develop a new understanding of a research problem using synoptic reasoning. The main objectives of meta-analysis include analyzing differences in the results among studies and increasing the precision by which effects are estimated. A well-designed meta-analysis depends upon strict adherence to the criteria used for selecting studies and the availability of information in each study to properly analyze their findings. Lack of information can severely limit the type of analyses and conclusions that can be reached. In addition, the more dissimilarity there is in the results among individual studies [heterogeneity], the more difficult it is to justify interpretations that govern a valid synopsis of results.

A meta-analysis needs to fulfill the following requirements to ensure the validity of your findings:

- Clearly defined description of objectives, including precise definitions of the variables and outcomes that are being evaluated;
- A well-reasoned and well-documented justification for identification and selection of the studies;
- Assessment and explicit acknowledgment of any researcher bias in the identification and selection of those studies;
- Description and evaluation of the degree of heterogeneity among the sample size of studies reviewed; and,
- Justification of the techniques used to evaluate the studies.

What do these studies tell you?

1. Can be an effective strategy for determining gaps in the literature.
2. Provides a means of reviewing research published about a particular topic over an extended period of time and from a variety of sources.
3. Is useful in clarifying what policy or programmitic actions can be justified on the basis of analyzing research results from multiple studies.
4. Provides a method for overcoming small sample sizes in individual studies that previously may have had little relationship to each other.
5. Can be used to generate new hypotheses or highlight research problems for future studies.

What these studies don't tell you?

1. Small violations in defining the criteria used for content analysis can lead to difficult to interpret and/or meaningless findings.
2. A large sample size can yield reliable, but not necessarily valid, results.
3. A lack of uniformity regarding, for example, the type of literature reviewed, how methods are applied, and how findings are measured within the sample of studies you are analyzing, can make the process of synthesis difficult to perform.
4. Depending on the sample size, the process of reviewing and synthesizing multple studies can be very time consuming.

Mixed-Method Design
Definition and Purpose
Mixed methods research represents more of an approach to examining a research problem than a methodology. Mixed method is characterized by a focus on research problems that require, 1) an examination of real-life contextual understandings, multi-level perspectives, and cultural influences; 2) an intentional application of rigorous quantitative research assessing

magnitude and frequency of constructs and rigorous qualitative research exploring the meaning and understanding of the constructs; and, 3) an objective of drawing on the strengths of quantitative and qualitative data gathering techniques to formulate a holistic interpretive framework for generating possible solutions or new understandings of the problem. Tashakkori and Creswell (2007) and other proponents of mixed methods argue that the design encompasses more than simply combining qualitative and quantitative methods but, rather, reflects a new "third way" epistemological paradigm that occupies the conceptual space between positivism and interpretivism.

What do these studies tell you?

1. Narrative and non-textual information can add meaning to numeric data, while numeric data can add precision to narrative and non-textual information.
2. Can utilize existing data while at the same time generating and testing a grounded theory approach to describe and explain the phenomenon under study.
3. A broader, more complex research problem can be investigated because the researcher is not constrained by using only one method.
4. The strengths of one method can be used to overcome the inherent weaknesses of another method.
5. Can provide stronger, more robust evidence to support a conclusion or set of recommendations.
6. May generate new knowledge new insights or uncover hidden insights, patterns, or relationships that a single methodological approach might not reveal.
7. Produces more complete knowledge and understanding of the research problem that can be used to increase the generalizability of findings applied to theory or practice.

What these studies don't tell you?

1. A researcher must be proficient in understanding how to apply multiple methods to investigating a research problem as well as be proficient in optimizing how to design a study that coherently melds them together.
2. Can increase the likelihood of conflicting results or ambiguous findings that inhibit drawing a valid conclusion or setting forth a recommended course of action [e.g., sample interview responses do not support existing statistical data].
3. Because the research design can be very complex, reporting the findings requires a well-organized narrative, clear writing style, and precise word choice.

4. Design invites collaboration among experts. However, merging different investigative approaches and writing styles requires more attention to the overall research process than studies conducted using only one methodological paradigm.
5. Concurrent merging of quantitative and qualitative research requires greater attention to having adequate sample sizes, using comparable samples, and applying a consistent unit of analysis. For sequential designs where one phase of qualitative research builds on the quantitative phase or vice versa, decisions about what results from the first phase to use in the next phase, the choice of samples and estimating reasonable sample sizes for both phases, and the interpretation of results from both phases can be difficult.
6. Due to multiple forms of data being collected and analyzed, this design requires extensive time and resources to carry out the multiple steps involved in data gathering and interpretation.

Observational Design
Definition and Purpose
This type of research design draws a conclusion by comparing subjects against a control group, in cases where the researcher has no control over the experiment. There are two general types of observational designs. In direct observations, people know that you are watching them. Unobtrusive measures involve any method for studying behavior where individuals do not know they are being observed. An observational study allows a useful insight into a phenomenon and avoids the ethical and practical difficulties of setting up a large and cumbersome research project.
What do these studies tell you?
1. Observational studies are usually flexible and do not necessarily need to be structured around a hypothesis about what you expect to observe [data is emergent rather than pre-existing].
2. The researcher is able to collect in-depth information about a particular behavior.
3. Can reveal interrelationships among multifaceted dimensions of group interactions.
4. You can generalize your results to real life situations.
5. Observational research is useful for discovering what variables may be important before applying other methods like experiments.
6. Observation research designs account for the complexity of group behaviors.

What these studies don't tell you?
1. Reliability of data is low because seeing behaviors occur over and over again may be a time consuming task and are difficult to replicate.
2. In observational research, findings may only reflect a unique sample population and, thus, cannot be generalized to other groups.
3. There can be problems with bias as the researcher may only "see what they want to see."
4. There is no possiblility to determine "cause and effect" relationships since nothing is manipulated.
5. Sources or subjects may not all be equally credible.
6. Any group that is knowingly studied is altered to some degree by the presence of the researcher, therefore, potentially skewing any data collected.

Philosophical Design
Definition and Purpose
Understood more as an broad approach to examining a research problem than a methodological design, philosophical analysis and argumentation is intended to challenge deeply embedded, often intractable, assumptions underpinning an area of study. This approach uses the tools of argumentation derived from philosophical traditions, concepts, models, and theories to critically explore and challenge, for example, the relevance of logic and evidence in academic debates, to analyze arguments about fundamental issues, or to discuss the root of existing discourse about a research problem. These overarching tools of analysis can be framed in three ways:
- Ontology -- the study that describes the nature of reality; for example, what is real and what is not, what is fundamental and what is derivative?
- Epistemology -- the study that explores the nature of knowledge; for example, by what means does knowledge and understanding depend upon and how can we be certain of what we know?
- Axiology -- the study of values; for example, what values does an individual or group hold and why? How are values related to interest, desire, will, experience, and means-to-end? And, what is the difference between a matter of fact and a matter of value?

What do these studies tell you?
1. Can provide a basis for applying ethical decision-making to practice.
2. Functions as a means of gaining greater self-understanding and self-knowledge about the purposes of research.

3. Brings clarity to general guiding practices and principles of an individual or group.
4. Philosophy informs methodology.
5. Refine concepts and theories that are invoked in relatively unreflective modes of thought and discourse.
6. Beyond methodology, philosophy also informs critical thinking about epistemology and the structure of reality (metaphysics).
7. Offers clarity and definition to the practical and theoretical uses of terms, concepts, and ideas.

What these studies don't tell you?

1. Limited application to specific research problems [answering the "So What?" question in social science research].
2. Analysis can be abstract, argumentative, and limited in its practical application to real-life issues.
3. While a philosophical analysis may render problematic that which was once simple or taken-for-granted, the writing can be dense and subject to unnecessary jargon, overstatement, and/or excessive quotation and documentation.
4. There are limitations in the use of metaphor as a vehicle of philosophical analysis.
5. There can be analytical difficulties in moving from philosophy to advocacy and between abstract thought and application to the phenomenal world.

Sequential Design
Definition and Purpose

Sequential research is that which is carried out in a deliberate, staged approach [i.e. serially] where one stage will be completed, followed by another, then another, and so on, with the aim that each stage will build upon the previous one until enough data is gathered over an interval of time to test your hypothesis. The sample size is not predetermined. After each sample is analyzed, the researcher can accept the null hypothesis, accept the alternative hypothesis, or select another pool of subjects and conduct the study once again. This means the researcher can obtain a limitless number of subjects before making a final decision whether to accept the null or alternative hypothesis. Using a quantitative framework, a sequential study generally utilizes sampling techniques to gather data and applying statistical methods to analze the data. Using a qualitative framework, sequential studies generally utilize samples of individuals or groups of individuals [cohorts] and use qualitative methods, such as interviews or observations, to gather information from each sample.

What do these studies tell you?
1. The researcher has a limitless option when it comes to sample size and the sampling schedule.
2. Due to the repetitive nature of this research design, minor changes and adjustments can be done during the initial parts of the study to correct and hone the research method.
3. This is a useful design for exploratory studies.
4. There is very little effort on the part of the researcher when performing this technique. It is generally not expensive, time consuming, or workforce intensive.
5. Because the study is conducted serially, the results of one sample are known before the next sample is taken and analyzed. This provides opportunities for continuous improvement of sampling and methods of analysis.

What these studies don't tell you?
1. The sampling method is not representative of the entire population. The only possibility of approaching representativeness is when the researcher chooses to use a very large sample size significant enough to represent a significant portion of the entire population. In this case, moving on to study a second or more specific sample can be difficult.
2. Because the sampling technique is not randomized, the design cannot be used to create conclusions and interpretations that pertain to an entire population. Generalizability from findings is limited.
3. Difficult to account for and interpret variation from one sample to another over time, particularly when using qualitative methods of data collection

2

Organizing Your Social Sciences Research Paper: Design Flaws to Avoid

Design Flaws to Avoid

The research design establishes the decision-making processes, conceptual structure of investigation, and methods of analysis used to address the central research problem of your study. Taking the time to develop a thorough research design helps to organize your thoughts, set the boundaries of your study, maximize the reliability of your findings, and avoid misleading or incomplete conclusions. Therefore, if any aspect of your research design is flawed or under-developed, the quality and reliability of your final results, as well as the overall value of your study, will be diminished.

In no particular order, here are some common problems to avoid when designing a research study.

- **Lack of Specificity** -- do not describe the investigative aspects of your study in overly-broad generalities. Avoid using vague qualifiers, such as, extremely, very, entirely, completely, etc. It's important that you design a study that describes the process of investigation in clear and concise terms. Otherwise, the reader cannot be certain what you intend to do.

- **Poorly Defined Research Problem** -- the starting point of most new research is to formulate a problem statement and begin the process of formulating questions to address that problem. Your paper should outline and explicitly delimit the problem and state what you intend to investigate since it will determine what research design you will use [research problem always precedes choice of design].

- **Lack of Theoretical Framework** -- the theoretical framework represents the conceptual foundation of your study. Therefore, your research design should include an explicit set of basic postulates or assumptions related to the research problem and an equally explicit set of logically derived hypotheses.

- **Significance** -- the research design must include a clear answer to the "So What?" question. Be sure you clearly articulate why your study is important and how it contributes to the larger body of literature about the topic being investigated.

- **Relationship between Past Research and Your Study** -- do not simply offer a summary description of prior research. Your literature review should include an explicit statement linking the results of prior research to the research you are about to undertake. This can be done, for example, by indentifying basic weaknesses in previous research studies and how your study helps to fill this gap in knowledge.

- **Contribution to the Field** -- in placing your study within the context of prior research, don't just note that a gap exists; be clear in describing how your study contributes to, or possibly challenges, existing assumptions or findings.

- **Provincialism** -- this refers to designing a narrowly applied scope, geographical area, sampling, or method of analysis that unduly restricts your ability to create meaningful outcomes and, by extension, obtaining results that are relevant and possibly transferable to understanding phenomena in other settings.
- **Objectives, Hypotheses, or Questions** -- your research design should include one or more questions or hypotheses that you are attempting to answer about the research problem underpinning your study. They should be clearly articulated and closely tied to the overall aims of your paper. Although there is no rule regarding the number of questions or hypotheses associated with a research problem, most studies in the social sciences address between one and five.
- **Poor Method** -- the design must include a well-developed and transparent plan for how you intend to collect or generate data and how it will be analyzed.
- **Proximity Sampling** -- this refers to using a sample which is based not upon the purposes of your study, but rather, is based upon the proximity of a particular group of subjects. The units of analysis, whether they be persons, places, or things, must not be based solely on ease of access and convenience.
- **Techniques or Instruments** -- be clear in describing the techniques [e.g., semi-structured interviews] or instruments [e.g., questionnaire] used to gather data. Your research design should note how the technique or instrument will provide reasonably reliable data to answer the questions associated with the central research problem.
- **Statistical Treatment** -- in quantitative studies, you must give a complete description of how you will organize the raw data for analysis. In most cases, this involves describing the data through the measures of central tendencies like mean, median, and mode that help the researcher explain how the data are concentrated and, thus, leading to meaningful interpretations of key trends or patterns found within the data.
- **Vocabulary** -- research often contains jargon and specialized language that the reader is presumably familiar with. However, avoid overuse of technical or pseudo-technical terminology. Problems with vocabulary also can refer to the use of popular terms, cliche's, or culture-specific language that is inappropriate for academic writing.
- **Ethical Dilemmas** -- in the methods section of qualitative research studies, your design must document how you intend to minimize risk for participants [a.k.a., "respondents"] during stages of data

gathering while, at the same time, still being able to adequately address the research problem. Failure to do so can lead the reader to question the validity and objectivity of your entire study.

- **Limitations of Study** -- all studies have limitations. Your research design should anticipate and explain the reasons why these limitations exist and clearly describe the extent of missing data. It is important to include a statement concerning what impact these limitations may have on the validity of your results.

3

Organizing Your Social Sciences Research Paper: 1. Choosing a Research Problem

Definition

A research problem is the main organizing principle guiding the analysis of your paper. The problem under investigation offers us an occasion for writing and a focus that governs what we want to say. It represents the core subject matter of scholarly communication, and the means by which we arrive at other topics of conversations and the discovery of new knowledge and understanding.

Choosing a Research Problem / How to Begin

Do not expect that choosing a research problem to study will be a quick or easy task! You should be thinking about it right from the start of the course. **There are generally three ways you are asked to write about a research problem**: 1) your professor provides you with a general topic from which you study a particular aspect of; 2) your professor provides you with a list of possible topics; or, 3) your professor leaves it up to you to choose a topic and you only have to obtain his/her permission to write about it before beginning your investigation. Here are some strategies for getting started for each scenario.

I. How To Begin: You are given the topic to write about
Step 1: Identify concepts and terms that make up the topic statement.

For example, your professor wants the class to focus on the following research problem: "Is the European Union becoming a credible security actor with the ability to contribute to confronting global terrorism? The main concepts are: European Union, global terrorism, credibility [**hint**: focus on identifying proper nouns, nouns or noun phrases, and action verbs in the assignment description].

Step 2: Review related literature to help refine how you will approach focusing on the topic and finding a way to analyze it. You can begin by doing any or all of the following: reading through background information from materials listed in your course syllabus; searching the HOMER library catalog to find a recent book on the topic and, if appropriate, more specialized works about the topic; conducting a preliminary review of the research literature using multidisciplinary library databases such as ProQuest or Academic OneFile or subject-specific databases found here. Use the main concept terms you developed in Step 1 to retrieve relevant articles. This will help you refine and frame the research problem. Don't be surprised if you need to do this several times before you finalize how to approach writing about the topic.

NOTE: Always review the references cited by the authors in footnotes, endnotes, or a bibliography to help locate additional research on the topic. This is a strategy for looking back into the literature for related research studies. However, if you're having trouble at this point locating related research literature, **ask a librarian for help!**

ANOTHER NOTE: If you find an article from a journal that's particularly helpful, put quotes around the title of the article and paste it into Google Scholar. If the article record appears, look for a "cited by" reference followed by a number. This link indicates how many times other researchers have subsequently cited the article. This is a strategy for looking forward into the literature for related research studies.

Step 3: Since social science research papers are generally designed to get you to develop your own ideas and arguments, **look for sources that can help broaden, modify, or strengthen your initial thoughts and arguments** [for example, if you decide to argue that the European Union is ill prepared to take on responsibilities for broader global security because of the debt crisis in many EU countries, then focus on identifying sources that support as well as refute this position].

There are least four appropriate roles your related literature plays in helping you formulate how to begin your analysis:

- *Sources of criticism* -- frequently, you'll find yourself reading materials that are relevant to your chosen topic, but you disagree with the author's position. Therefore, one way that you can use a source is to describe the counter-argument, provide evidence from your review of the literature as to why the prevailing argument is unsatisfactory, and to discuss how your own view is more appropriate based upon your interpretation of the evidence.

- *Sources of new ideas* -- while a general goal in writing college research papers in the social sciences is to approach a research problem with some basic idea of what position you'd like to take and what grounds you'd like to stand upon, it is certainly acceptable [and often encouraged] to read the literature and extend, modify, and refine your own position in light of the ideas proposed by others. Just make sure that you cite the sources!

- *Sources for historical context* -- another role your related literature plays in helping you formulate how to begin your analysis is to place issues and events in proper historical context. This can help to demonstrate familiarity with developments in relevent scholarship about your topic, provide a means of comparing historical versus contemporary issues and events, and identifying key people, places, and things that had an important role related to the research problem.

- *Sources of interdisciplinary insight* -- an advantage of using databases like ProQuest or Academic OneFile to begin exploring your topic is that it covers publications from a variety of different disciplines. Another way to formulate how to study the topic is to look at it from different disciplinary perspectives. If the topic concerns immigration reform, for example, ask yourself, how do studies from sociological journals found by searching *Proquest* vary in their analysis from those in law journals. A goal in reviewing related literature is to provide a means of approaching a topic from multiple perspectives rather than the perspective offered from just one discipline.

NOTE: Remember to keep careful notes at every stage or utilize a citation management system like EndNotes or RefWorks. You may think you'll remember what you have searched and where you found things, but it's easy to forget or get confused.

Step 4: Assuming you've done an effective job of synthesizing and thinking about the results of our initial search for related literature, you're ready to prepare a detailed **outline for your paper** that lays the foundation for a more in-depth and focused review of relevant research literature [after consulting with a librarian, if needed!]. How will you know you haven't done an effective job of synthesizing and thinking about the results of our initial search for related literature? A good indication is that you start composing your paper outline and gaps appear in how you want to approach the study. This indicates the need to do further research on the research problem.

II. How To Begin: You are provided a list of possible topics to choose from

Step 1: I know what you're thinking--which topic from this list my professor has given me will be the easiest to find the most information on? An effective instructor should never include a topic that is so obscure or complex that no research is available to examine and from which to begin to design a study. Instead of searching for the path of least resistence, choose a topic that you find interesting in some way, or that is controversial and that you have a strong opinion about, or has some personal meaning for you. You're going to be working on your topic for quite some time, so choose one that you find interesting and engaging or that motivates you to take a position.

Once you've settled on a topic of interest from the list, follow Steps 1 - 4 listed above to further develop it into a research paper.

\\\\\\\\\\\\

III. How To Begin: Your professor leaves it up to you to choose a topic

Step 1: Under this scenario, the key process is turning an idea or general thought into a topic that can be configured into a research problem. When given an assignment where you choose the research topic, don't begin by thinking about what to write about, but rather, ask yourself the question, "What do I want to know?" Treat an open-ended assignment as an opportunity to learn about something that's new or exciting to you.

Step 2: If you lack ideas, or wish to gain focus, try some or all of the following strategies:

Review your course readings, particularly the suggested readings, for topic ideas. Don't just review what you've already read but jump ahead in the syllabus to readings that have not been covered yet.

Search the **HOMER** library catalog for a good, recent introductory book and, if appropriate, more specialized works related to the discipline area of the course [e.g., for the course SOCI 335, search for books on population and society].

Browse through some current journals in your subject discipline. Even if most of the articles are not relevant, you can skim through the contents quickly. You only need one to be the spark that begins the process of wanting to learn more about a topic. Consult a librarian and/or your professor about the core journals within your subject discipline.

Think about essays you have written for past classes and other coursework you have taken or academic lectures and programs you have attended.

Thinking back, what most interested you? What would you like to know more about?

Search online media sources, such as <u>CNN</u>, the <u>Los Angeles Times</u>, <u>Huffington Post</u>, or <u>Newsweek</u>, to see if your idea has been covered in the news. Use this coverage to refine your idea into something that you'd like to investigate further but in a more deliberate, scholarly way based on a particular problem that needs to be researched.

Step 3: To build upon your initial idea, use the suggestions under this tab to help narrow, broaden, or increase the timeliness of your idea so you can write it out as a research problem.

Once you are comfortable with having turned your idea into a research problem, follow Steps 1 - 4 listed in Part I above to further develop it into a research pape

4

Organizing Your Social Sciences Research Paper: Narrowing a Topic Idea

Importance of...

Whether assigned a general issue to investigate, you are given a list of problems to study, or you have to identify your own topic to investigate, it is important that the research problem the guides your study is not too broad, otherwise, it will be very difficult to adequately address the problem in the space and time allowed. You could experience a number of problems if your topic is too broad, including:

- You find too many information sources and, as a consequence, it is difficult to decide what to include or exclude or what are the most important.
- You find information that is too general and, as a consequence, it is difficult to develop a clear framework for understanding the research problem and the methods needed to analyze it.
- You find information that covers a wide variety of concepts or ideas that can't be integrated into one paper and, as a consequence, you easily trail off into unnecessary tangents.

Strategies for Narrowing the Research Topic

The most common challenge when beginning to write a research paper is narrowing down your topic. Even if your professor gives you a specific topic to study, it will almost never be so specific that you won't have to narrow it down at least to some degree [besides, grading fifty papers that are all about the exact same thing is very boring!].

A topic is too broad to be managable when you find that you have too many different, and oftentimes conflicting and only remotely related, ideas about how to investigate the research problem. Although you will want to start the writing process by considering a variety of different approaches to studying the research problem, you will need to narrow the focus of your investigation at some point. This way, you don't attempt to do too much in one paper.

Here are some strategies to help focus your topic into something more manageable:

- **Aspect** -- choose one lens through which to view the research problem, or look at just one facet of it [e.g., rather than studying the role of food in Eastern religious rituals; study the role of food in Hindu ceremonies, or, the role of one particular type of food among several religions].
- **Components** -- determine if your initial variables or unit of analyses can be broken into smaller parts, which can then be analyzed more precisely [e.g., a study of tobacco use among adolescents can focus on just chewing tobacco rather than all forms of usage or, rather than adolescents in general, focus on female adolescents in a certain age range who smoke].
- **Place** -- the smaller the area of analysis, the more narrow the focus [e.g., rather than study trade relations in West Africa, study trade relations between Niger and Cameroon].
- **Relationship** -- how do two or more different perspectives or variables relate to one another? [e.g., cause/effect, compare/contrast, contemporary/historical, group/individual, male/female, opinion/ reason, problem/solution].
- **Time** -- the shorter the time period, the more narrow the focus.
- **Type** -- focus your topic in terms of a specific type or class of people, places, or things [e.g., a study of traffic patterns near schools can focus only on SUVs, or just student drivers, or just the timing of stoplights in the area].
- **Combination** -- use two or more of the above strategies to focus your topic very narrowly.

NOTE: Apply one of the above first to determine if that gives you a manageable research problem to investigate; combining multiple strategies risks creating the opposite problem--your topic becomes too narrowly defined and you can't locate enough research or data to support your study.

5

Organizing Your Social Sciences Research Paper: Broadening a Topic Idea

Importance of...

It is important to adopt a flexible approach when choosing a topic to investigate. The goal when writing any research paper is to choose a research problem that is focused and time-limited. However, your starting point should not be so narrowly defined that you unnecessarily constrict your opportunity to investigate the topic thoroughly. A research problem that is too narrowly defined leads to any of the following:

- You don't find enough information and what you do find is tangential or irrelevant.
- You find information that is so specific that it can't lead to any significant conclusions.
- Your sources cover so few ideas that you can't expand them into a significant paper.
- The research problem is so case specific that it limits opportunities to generalize or apply the results to other contexts.

Strategies for Broadening the Research Topic

In general, an indication that a research problem is too narrowly defined is that you can't find any relevent or meaningful information about it. If this happens, don't immediately abandon your efforts to investigate the problem because it could very well be an excellent topic of study. A good way to begin is to look for parallels and opportunities for broader associations that apply to the initial research problem. A strategy for doing this is to ask yourself the basic six questions of who, what, where, when, how, and why.

Here is an example of how to apply the six questions strategy to broadening your topic. The research problem is to investigate ways to improve trade relations between Peru and Bolivia. Ask yourself:

- **Who?** -- are there other countries involved in the relations between these two countries that might want to challenge or encourage this relationship? Are there particular individuals or special interest groups [e.g., politicians, union leaders, etc.] promoting trade relations or trying to inhibit it? [remember to ask both the individual who question and the collective who question].

- **What?** -- what are the specific trading commodities you are examining? Are there commodities not currently traded between Peru and Bolivia that could be?
- **Where?** -- are there examples of other bi-lateral trade agreements that could model the potential for closer trade relations between Peru and Bolivia? Note that the question of where can also relate to spatial and geographical issues, such as, are there any barriers impeding transportation of goods?
- **When?** -- how long have these countries had or not had trade relations? How far into the future might a trade relationship last given other factors? When can relate to past issues as well as future areas of interest.
- **How?** -- how might Peru and Bolivia forge these ties in relation to, for example, long-standing internal conflicts within each country? Note that the how question can also be framed as, "In what way might...." [e.g., In what way might improved trade relations lead to other forms of economic exchanges between the two countries?].
- **Why?** -- what advantages can each country gain by pursuing active trade relations? Why might other countries be concerned about closer ties between these two countries? Asking why can raise the "So What?" question applied to your topic and provide a means of assessing significance.

Reflecting upon these six questions can help you formulate ways to expand the parameters of your initial research problem, providing an opportunity to obtain new ideas that can be investigated. Once you've found additional directions in which to procede with your topic, you can try narrowing it down again, if needed.

6

Organizing Your Social Sciences Research Paper: Extending the Timeliness of a Topic Idea

Importance of...

It is often the case that a research problem, even one assigned by your professor, interests you because it relates to a current issue in the news or it is something you have very recently experienced. Choosing a research problem that connects to current affairs is an excellent way to remain engaged in the topic; you feel a connection to the issue or event because it's happening now and a definitive outcome has yet to play itself out. However, you could experience a number of problems if your topic focuses on a very recent issue or event, including:

- It can be difficult to find scholarly sources and, as a consequence, your study may be considered less rigorous and valid because it does not cite research studies that provide in-depth analysis of the topic.

- Ironically, examination of a very recent event or issue may force you to draw upon historical precedents in order to effectively frame the research problem and, as a consequence, the scholarly sources supporting your paper ends up being more about the historical context than the current event or issue.

- The consequences or results of a current event or issue have yet to be determined and, therefore, your conclusions or any recommendations presented in your paper may be rendered less relevant as things unfold.

Strategies for Extending the Timeliness of the Research Topic

A clue indicating a topic is too current would be if the only information you find is from news service organizations, blogs, articles from popular magazines and newspapers, and other non-scholarly sources. Depending on the assignment, relying on non-scholarly sources may be acceptable. More frequently, though, professors will require you to cite scholarly research studies as part of your analysis. However, the nature of scholarly research in the social sciences [also referred to as "academic" or "peer-reviewed" research] is that papers submitted for publication frequently take more than a year between editorial review of the manuscript to when it is finally published. In response to this, many journal publishers provide access to what is termed "pre-prints." These are essentially online versions of the final draft of a manuscript and, thus, should not be considered the authoritive copy of an article. Given these issues, it will often be diffcult, or perhaps impossible, to locate scholarly research studies about a very current issue or event.

The obvious solution is to choose a different research problem to investigate. However, if the topic is of particular interest to you, **here are several strategies you can use to find scholarly or related research-level analysis of a very current issue or event:**

1. **Look for related literature that provide opportunities for comparative analysis.** For example, only now are scholarly research studies emerging that investigate the rise of ISIS and its impact on the Middle East. However, by reviewing the research literature about past terrorist movements, you can extrapolate key lessons learned or identify new ways of

understanding the central research problem associated with the current, on-going event.

2. **Locate opinions/statements of prominant authors and researchers**. Leading scholars are often called upon by news organizations, editors of leading newspapers and other media outlets, both in print and online, to comment and provide insight during and immediately after an event. For example, in the immediate aftermath of Hurricane Katrina, many prominant experts on disaster management and recovery were interviewed and asked to comment on how New Orleans should be rebuilt. Although these sources do not constitute a body of scholarly research, the writings of leading scholars can be considered authoritive because they represent the opinions and observations of experts who have gained in-depth knowledge on the topic as a result of conducting prior research.

3. **Identify research centers and special interest organizations that focus on studying current issues and events**. Research centers and special interest organizations often lead the effort to study and publish in-depth reports about a current issue or event. In the case of research centers, this is because their purpose is to bring together scholars and practitioners who have special expertise or interest in a particular subject area. The mission of many special interest groups is to attempt to influence policy or to promote a specific agenda. Note, that because many research institutes and special interest group organizations are privately funded, you must watch out for any bias in their analysis or recommendations. A good source for indentifying research centers and special interest organizations is the **Gale Directory Library** database.

4. **Look for Congressional Hearings and government agency reports**. Congress often holds hearings shortly after an important event [e.g., the Ebola outbreak] or a very new topic of interest. Although politically-driven, the testimony to Congress is often presented by leading scholars and experts in the field who provide detailed explanation and analysis of an issue. However, unlike the opinions of experts in media outlets, the testimony of witnesses at Congressional hearings are under oath. In addition to Congress, governmental agencies may issue reports produced by experts in the field. To locate Congressional hearings **GO HERE**. To locate documents issued by government agencies

Organizing Your Social Sciences Research Paper: 2. Preparing to Write

Things to Think About Before You Begin

After you have determined the type of research design you will use, but before you sit down and begin to organize your paper, there are few things you should consider doing that will help make the actual writing process go much smoother.

Make a Schedule

If your professor has not already created intermediary deadlines for completing the assignment, then drafting a schedule and noting deadlines on your personal calendar should be your first step. Drawing from key dates in your class syllabus as well as your own sense of much time you need to think about, research, organize, and write a paper, note key dates in your calendar when tasks should be completed. A helpful strategy is to work backwards from when the final paper due.

Choose specific dates of important steps along the way but focus on setting realistic goals, and then stick to them! Make sure to give yourself enough time to find out what resources are available to you [including meeting with a librarian, if needed], to choose a research problem to investigate, to select and read relevant research literature, to outline your paper, to organize the information you are going to cite in your paper, and to write your first and final drafts [and any necessary drafts in between]. Developing a personal assignment calendar will also help you manage your time in relation to work assigned in other classes.

Analyze the Assignment

Carefully analyze the assignment to determine what you are specifically being asked to do. Look for key terms, topics, subject areas, and/or issues that can help you develop a research problem that interests you. Be sure that you understand the type of paper you are being asked to write. Research papers discuss a topic in depth and cite to credible sources that can back up the evidence that you present in offering a particular perspective. However, there are many different ways this process can be achieved.

The way in which your professor may ask you to frame your analysis can include any of the following approaches:

- **Case study approach** -- explain the implications and unique characteristics of a complex research problem using a single bounded unit of analysis of study [e.g., an organization, behavior of doctors in an emergency room, a supreme court ruling, an event].
- **Comparison approach** -- compare and contrast two ideas, constructs, or tangible things with one another.
- **Definition approach** -- discuss in depth the cultural and associative meanings of, for example, a political theory, a policy proposal, or a controversial practice.
- **Descriptive approach** -- choose a subject that you know well and help others to understand it.
- **Evaluative appoach** -- assess a theoretical concept, issue, person, place, or thing in a critical way.
- **Exploratory approach** -- pursue a specific line of inquiry, often with the purpose of making recommendations for further research or to advocate and provide evidence for specific actions to be taken.
- **Interpretive approach** -- apply the theoretical knowledge gained in your coursework to a particular case study, such as, a business situation in a management course or a psychological case profile.
- **Narrative approach** -- write from a certain point of view, usually your own and written in the first person.
- **Persuasive approach** -- take a position in a scholarly argument and give the reader reasons based on evidence why they should agree with your position.
- **Policy memorandum approach** -- write short factual sentences devoid of emotion that summarize a situation to date, identify the main issue of concern, provide a breakdown of the elements of this main issue, and then recommend how to address the issue based on research about the topic.

NOTE: If for any reason you are unclear or confused about any aspect of the assignment, request clarification from your professor as soon as possible. Few professors will accept the excuse that, "I didn't understand the assignment" if you end up being upset about the grade you receive.

General Information
To make a paper readable:
- Use a 12 point standard font, such as, New Times Roman, Calibri, Geneva, Bookman, Helvetica, etc.
- Text should be double spaced on 8 1/2" x 11" white paper with one inch margins on all four sides.
- Number pages consecutively but never number the title page as page 1.

General mistakes to avoid:
- Start each new section on a new page--avoid orphan headings [insert a page break!].
- Dividing a table or figure--if possible, confine non-textual elements, such as a table or chart, to a single page.
- Submitting a paper with pages out of order.
- Not adhering to recommended page limits.

General stylistic and grammatical mistakes to avoid:
- Use normal prose with appropriate articles ["a," "the," "an"].
- Spell checkers and grammar checkers are helpful, but they don't catch everything. Always proofread and, if possible, get someone to do it for you before submitting your final paper.
- Indent the first line of each paragraph.
- If a paragraph is nearly a page or more longer, then it is probably too long for the reader to contemplate and should be divided into smaller paragraphs.
- Write in active voice when possible but note that some professors prefer a passive voice.
- Write out all abbreviations the first time they are used with parentheses around the abbreviation. Do not use too many abbreviations. They shorten the text but make it more difficult to read. Never start a sentence with an abbreviation.
- Do not use contractions in academic writing and do not start sentences with conjunctions (and, but, or) or numerals.
- Avoid informal wording, addressing the reader directly, and using jargon, slang terms, or superlatives unless they appear in direct quotes from other sources.

In all sections of your paper:
- Stay focused on the research problem you are investigating [follow the steps in this guide].
- Use paragraphs to separate each important point.
- Present your points in a logical order.

- Use present tense to report well accepted facts [e.g., "The Prime Minister of Bulgaria is Boyko Borissov."]
- Use past tense to describe specific results from your study [e.g., "Evidence shows that the impact of the invasion was magnified by events in 1989."]
- Avoid the use of superfluous non-textual elements [images/figures/charts/tables]; include only those necessary for presenting or enhancing an understanding of the results.

NOTE: These are general guidelines that apply to almost every paper you write in college. However, the specific format of your paper--how you arrange the title page, headings, subheadings, non-textual elements, citations, appendices, etc.--will be dictated by the writing style manual you are asked to use [e.g., APA, Chicago, MLA, or other].

1

Organizing Your Social Sciences Research Paper: Academic Writing Style

Definition

Academic writing refers to a particular style of expression that researchers use to define the intellectual boundaries of their disciplines and their areas of expertise. Characteristics of academic writing include a formal tone, use of the third-person rather than first-person perspective (usually), a clear focus on the research problem under investigation, and precise word choice. Like specialist languages adopted in other professions, such as, law or medicine, academic writing is designed to convey agreed meaning about complex ideas or concepts for a group of scholarly experts.

Importance of Good Academic Writing

Although the accepted form of academic writing in the social sciences can vary considerable depending on the methodological framework and intended audience, most research-level papers require careful attention to the following stylistic elements:

I. The Big Picture

Unlike fiction or journalistic writing, the overall structure of academic writing is formal and logical. It must be cohensive and possess a logically organized flow of ideas, which means that the various parts are connected to form a unified whole. There should be links between sentences and paragraphs so the reader is able to follow your argument and all sources are properly cited.

II. The Tone

Throughout your paper, it is important that you present the arguments of others fairly and with an appropriate narrative tone. When presenting a position or argument that you disagree with, describe this argument accurately and without loaded or biased language. In academic writing, the author is expected to investigate the research problem from an authoritative point of view. You should, therefore, state the strengths of your arguments confidently, using language that is neutral, not confrontational or dismissive.

III. The Language

Clear use of language is essential in academic writing. Well-structured paragraphs and clear topic sentences enable a reader to follow your line of thinking without difficulty. Your language should be concise, formal, and express precisely what you want it to mean. Avoid vague expressions that are not specific and precise enough for the reader to derive exact meaning ["they," "we," "people," "the organization," etc.], abbreviations like 'i.e.' ["in other words"], 'e.g.' ["for example"], and contractions, such as, "don't", "isn't", etc.

IV. Academic Conventions

Citing sources in the body of your paper and providing a list of references as either footnotes or endnotes is a very important aspect of academic writing. It is essential to always acknowledge the source of any ideas, research findings, data, or quoted text that you have used in your paper as a defense against allegations of plagiarism.

V. Evidence-Based Arguments

Your assignments often ask you to express your own point of view about the research problem you are investigating. However, what is valued in academic writing is that opinions are based on a sound understanding of the pertinent body of knowledge and academic debates that exist in your discipline. You need to support your opinion with evidence from scholarly sources. It should be an objective position presented as a logical argument. The quality of your evidence will determine the strength of your argument. The challenge is to convince the reader of the validity of your opinion through a well-documented, coherent, and logically structured piece of writing.

VI. Thesis-Driven Analysis

The writing is "thesis-driven," meaning that the starting point is a particular perspective, idea, or "thesis" applied to the chosen research problem, such as, establishing, proving, or disproving solutions to the questions posed for the topic; simply describing a topic without the research questions does not qualify as academic writing.

VII. Complexity and Higher-Order Thinking

One of the main functions of academic writing is to describe complex ideas as clearly as possible. Often referred to as higher-order thinking skills, these include cognitive processes that are used to comprehend, solve problems, and express concepts or that describe abstract ideas that cannot be easily acted out, pointed to, or shown with images.

Strategies for...

Understanding Academic Writing and Its Jargon

The very definition of jargon is language specific to a particular sub-group of people. Therefore, in modern university life, jargon represents the specific language and meaning assigned to words and phrases specific to a discipline or area of study. For example, the idea of being rational may hold the same general meaning in both political science and psychology, but its *application* to understanding and explaining phenomena within the research domain of a discipline may have subtle differences based upon how scholars in that discipline apply the concept to the theories and practice of their work. Given this, **it is important that specialist terminology [i.e., jargon] must be used accurately and applied under the appropriate conditions**. Subject-specific dictionaries are the best places to confirm the meaning of terms within the context of a specific discipline. These can be found by searching in the USC Libraries HOMER catalog. It is appropriate for you to use specialist language within your field of study, but avoid using such language when writing for non-academic or general audiences.

Problems with Opaque Writing

Traditional academic writing can utilize needlessly complex syntax or jargon that is stated out of context or is not well-defined. When writing, avoid these problems in particular:

1. Excessive use of specialized terminology. Yes, it is appropriate for you to use specialist language and a formal style of expression, but it does not mean using "big words" just for the sake of doing so. Overuse of complex or obscure words or writing complicated sentence constructions gives readers the impression that your paper is more about style than substance; it leads the reader to question if you really know what you are talking about. Focus on creating clear and elegant prose that minimizes reliance on specialized terminology.

2. Inappropriate use of specialized terminology. Because you are dealing with the concepts, research, and data of your subject, you need to use the technical language appropriate to the discipline. However, nothing will undermine the validity of your study quicker than the inappropriate application of a term or concept. Avoid using terms whose meaning you are unsure of--don't just guess or assume! Consult the meaning of terms in specialized, discipline-specific dictionaries. These can be found by searching the HOMER catalog, entering, for example, the phrase "sociology and dictionaries."

Other Problems to Avoid
In addition to understanding the use of specialized language, there are other aspects of academic writing in the social sciences that you should be aware of. These include:

- **Personal nouns**. Excessive use of personal nouns [e.g., I, me, you, us] may lead the reader to believe the study was overly subjective. Using these words may be interpreted as being done only to avoid presenting empirical evidence about the research problem.
- **Directives**. Avoid directives that demands the reader to "Do this" or "Do that." Directives should be framed as evidence-based recommendations or goals leading to specific outcomes.
- **Informal, conversational tone using slang and idioms**. Academic writing relies on excellent grammar and precise word structure. Your narrative should not include regional dialects or slang terms because they can be open to interpretation; be direct and concise.
- **Wordiness**. Focus on being concise, straightforward, and writing that does not have confusing language. By doing so, you help eliminate the possibility of the reader misinterpreting the research design and purpose of your study.
- **Vague expressions (e.g., "they," "we," "people," "the company," "that area," etc.)**. Being concise in your writing also includes avoiding vague references to persons, places, or things. While proofreading your paper, be sure to look for and edit any vague statements that lack context.
- **Numbered lists and bulleted items**. The use of bulleted items or lists should be used only if the narrative dictates a need for clarity. For example, it is fine to state, "The four main problems with hedge funds are:" and then list them 1, 2, 3, 4. However, in academic writing this must then be followed by detailed explanation and analysis of each item. Given this, the question you should ask

yourself while proofreading is: why begin with a list in the first place rather than just starting with systematic analysis of each item?

- **Descriptive writing**. Describing a research problem is an important means of contextualizing a study and, in fact, some description is needed because you can't assume the reader knows everything about the topic. However, the content of your paper should focus on methodology, the analysis and interpretation of findings, and their implications as they apply to the research problem and not background information and descriptions of tangential issues.
- **Personal experiences.** Drawing upon personal experience [e.g., traveling abroad; caring for someone with Alzheimer's disease] can be an effective way of engaging your readers in understanding the research problem. Use personal experience only as an example, though, because academic writing relies on evidence-based research. To do otherwise is simply story-telling.

NOTE: Rules concerning excellent grammar and precise word structure do not apply when quoting someone. If the quote is especially vague or hard to understand, consider paraphrasing it. Otherwise, a quote should be inserted in the text of your paper exactly as it was stated. If you believe the quote is important to understanding the meaning of the work as a whole, consider inserting the term "sic" in brackets after the quoted word or text to indicate that the quotation has been transcribed exactly as found in the original source, complete with any erroneous spelling or nonstandard expressions.

Structure and Writing Style
I. Improving Academic Writing

To improve your academic writing skills, you should focus your efforts on three key areas:

1. Clear Writing. Thinking about precedes writing about. Good writers spend sufficient time distilling information and reviewing major points from the literature they have reviewed before creating their work. Writing detailed outlines can help you clearly organize your thoughts. Effective academic writing begins with solid planning, so manage your time carefully.

2. Excellent Grammar. Needless to say, English grammar can be difficult and complex; even the best scholars take many years before thay have command of the major points of good grammar. Take the time to learn the major and minor points of good grammar. Spend time practicing writing and seek detailed feedback from professors. Take advantage of the **Writing Center** on campus if you need a lot of help. Proper punctuation and good

proofreading skills can significantly improve academic writing [see subtab for proofreading you paper].
Invest in and always refer to these three types of resources to help your grammar and writing skills:

- A good writing reference book, such as, Strunk and White's book, ***The Elements of Style*** or the ***St. Martin's Handbook***;
- A college-level dictionary, such as, ***Merriam-Webster's Collegiate Dictionary***;
- The latest edition of ***Roget's Thesaurus in Dictionary Form***.

3. Consistent Stylistic Approach. Whether your professor requires you to use MLA, APA or the Chicago Manual of Style, choose one style manual and stick to it. Each of these style manuals provide guidance on how to write out numbers, references, citations, footnotes, and lists. Consistent adherence to a style of writing helps with the narrative flow of your paper and improves its readability. Note that some disciplines require a particular style [e.g., education uses APA] so as you write more papers within your major, familiarity will improve.

II. Evaluating Quality of Writing

A useful approach for evaluating the quality of your academic writing is to consider the following issues from the perspective of the reader. While proofreading your final draft, critically assess the following elements in your writing.

- It is shaped around one clear research problem, and it explains what that problem is from the outset.
- Your paper tells the reader why the problem is important and why people should know about it.
- You have accurately and thoroughly informed the reader what has already been published about this problem or others related to it and noted important gaps in the research.
- You have provided evidence to support your argument that the reader finds convincing.
- The paper includes a description of how and why particular evidence was collected and analyzed, and why specific theoretical arguments or concepts were used.
- The paper is made up of paragraphs, each containing only one controlling idea.
- You indicate how each section of the paper addresses the research problem.
- You have considered counter-arguments or counter-examples where they are relevant.

- Arguments, evidence, and their significance have been presented in the conclusion.
- Limitations of your research have been explained as evidence of the potential need for further study.
- The narrative flows in a clear, accurate, and well-organized way.

2

Organizing Your Social Sciences Research Paper: Choosing a Title

Definition

The title summarizes the main idea or ideas of your study. A good title contains the fewest possible words needed to adequately describe the contents and/or purpose of your research paper.

Importance of Choosing a Good Title

The title is without doubt the part of a paper that is read the most, and it is usually read first. If the title is too long it usually contains too many unnecessary words. Avoid language, such as, "A Study to Investigate the...," that is obvious or that does not help the reader understand the purpose of your paper. On the other hand, a title which is too short often uses words which are too general. For example, a paper with the title, "African Politics" is so non-specific it could be the title of a book. A good title will provide information about the focus of your research study.

Structure and Writing Style

The following parameters can be used to help you formulate a suitable research paper title:
1. The purpose of the research
2. The narrative tone of the paper [typically defined by the type of the research]
3. The methods used

The initial aim of a title is to capture the reader's attention and to draw attention to the research problem being investigated.

Create a Working Title

Typically, the final title you submit to your professor is created after the research is complete so that the title accurately captures what has been

done. The working title should be developed early in the research process because it can help anchor the focus of the study in much the same way the research problem does. Referring back to the working title can help you reorient yourself back to the main purpose of the study if you feel yourself drifting off on a tangent while writing.

The Final Title

Effective titles in academic research papers have several characteristics.

- Indicate accurately the subject and scope of the study,
- Avoid using abbreviations,
- Use words that create a positive impression and stimulate reader interest,
- Use current nomenclature from the field of study,
- Identify key variables, both dependent and independent,
- May reveal how the paper will be organized,
- Suggest a relationship between variables which supports the major hypothesis,
- Is limited to 10 to 15 substantive words,
- Does not include "study of," "analysis of" or similar constructions,
- Titles are usually in the form of a phrase, but can also be in the form of a question,
- If you use a quote as part of the title, the source of the quote is cited [usually using an asterisk and footnote],
- Use correct grammar and capitalization with all first words and last words capitalized, including the first word of a subtitle. All nouns, pronouns, verbs, adjectives, and adverbs that appear between the first and last words of the title are also capitalized, and
- In academic papers, rarely is a title followed by an exclamation mark. However, a title or subtitle can be in the form of a question.

The Subtitle

Subtitles are quite common in social science research papers. **Examples of why you may include a subtitle:**

1. **Explains or provides additional context**, e.g., "Linguistic Ethnography and the Study of Welfare Institutions as a Flow of Social Practices: The Case of Residential Child Care Institutions as Paradoxical Institutions." [Palomares, Manuel and David Poveda. *Text & Talk: An Interdisciplinary Journal of Language, Discourse and Communication Studies* 30 (January 2010): 193-212]

2. **Adds substance to a literary, provocative, or imaginative title or quote**, e.g., "Listen to What I Say, Not How I Vote": Congressional Support for the President in Washington and at Home." [Grose, Christian R. and Keesha M. Middlemass. *Social Science Quarterly* 91 (March 2010): 143-167]

3. **Qualifies the geographic scope of the research**, e.g., "The Geopolitics of the Eastern Border of the European Union: The Case of Romania-Moldova-Ukraine." [Marcu, Silvia. *Geopolitics* 14 (August 2009): 409-432]

4. **Qualifies the temporal scope of the research**, e.g., "A Comparison of the Progressive Era and the Depression Years: Societal Influences on Predictions of the Future of the Library, 1895-1940." [Grossman, Hal B. *Libraries & the Cultural Record* 46 (2011): 102-128]

5. **Focuses on investigating the ideas, theories, or work of a particular individual**, e.g., "A Deliberative Conception of Politics: How Francesco Saverio Merlino Related Anarchy and Democracy." [La Torre, Massimo. *Sociologia del Diritto* 28 (January 2001): 75 - 98]

6. **Identifies the methodology used**, e.g. "Student Activism of the 1960s Revisited: A Multivariate Analysis Research Note." [Aron, William S. *Social Forces* 52 (March 1974): 408-414]

3

Organizing Your Social Sciences Research Paper: Making an Outline

Definition

An outline is a formal system used to develop a framework for thinking about what the eventual contents and organization of your paper should be. An outline helps you predict the overall structure and flow of a paper

Importance of...

Writing papers in college requires you to come up with sophisticated, complex, and sometimes very creative ways of structuring your ideas. Taking the time to draft an outline can help you determine whether your ideas connect to each other, what order of ideas works best, where gaps in your thinking may exist, or whether you have sufficient evidence to support each of your points.

A good outline is important because:

- You will be **much less likely to get writer's block** because an outline will show where you're going and what the next step is.

- It will help you **stay organized and focused** throughout the writing process and helps ensure a proper coherence [flow of ideas] in your final paper. However, the outline should be viewed as a guide, not a straitjacket.
- **A clear, detailed outline ensures** that you always have something to help re-calibrate your writing should you feel yourself drifting into subject areas unrelated to the research problem.
- **The outline can be key to staying motivated.** You can put together an outline when you're excited about the project and everything is clicking; making an outline is never as overwhelming as sitting down and beginning to write a twenty page paper without any sense of where it is going.
- **An outline help you organize multiple ideas about a topic.** Most research problems can be analyzed in any number of inter-related ways; an outline can help you sort out which modes of analysis are most appropriate or ensure the most robust findings.
- An outline not only helps you organize your thoughts but can also **serve as a schedule for when certain aspects of your writing should be accomplished.** Review the assignment and incorporate when certain tasks are due. If your professor has not created specific deadlines for handing in your writing, think about your own writing style in relation to other assignments and include this in your outline.

Structure and Writing Style
I. General Approaches

There are two general approaches you can take when writing an outline for your paper:

The **topic outline** consists of short phrases. This approach is useful when you are dealing with a number of different issues that could be arranged in a variety of different ways in your paper. Due to short phrases having more content than using simple sentences, they create better content from which to build your paper.

The **sentence outline** is done in full sentences. This approach is useful when your paper focuses on complex issues in detail. The sentence outline is also useful because sentences themselves have many of the details in them needed to build a paper and it allows you to include those details in the sentences instead of having to create an outline of short phrases that goes on page after page.

II. Steps to Making the Outline

A strong outline details each topic and subtopic in your paper, organizing these points so that they build your argument toward an evidence-based conclusion. Writing an outline will also help you focus on the task at hand and avoid unnecessary tangents, logical fallacies, and underdeveloped paragraphs.

1. **Identify the research problem**. The research problem is the focal point from which the rest of the outline flows. Try to sum up the point of your paper in one sentence or phrase. It also can be key to deciding what the title of your paper should be.

2. **Identify the main categories**. What main points will you analyze? The introduction describes all of your main points; the rest of your paper can be spent developing those points.

3. **Create the first category**. What is the first point you want to cover? If the paper centers around a complicated term, a definition can be a good place to start. For a paper about a particular theory, giving the general background on the theory can be a good place to begin.

4. **Create subcategories**. After you have followed these steps, create points under it that provide support for the main point. The number of categories that you use depends on the amount of information that you are trying to cover. There is no right or wrong number to use.

Once you have developed the basic outline of the paper, organize the contents to match the standard format of a research paper as described in this guide.

III. Things to Consider When Writing an Outline

- **There is no rule dictating which approach is best**. Choose either a topic outline or a sentence outline based on which one you believe will work best for you. However, once you begin developing an outline, it's helpful to stick to only one approach.

- **Both topic and sentence outlines use** Roman and Arabic numerals along with capital and small letters of the alphabet arranged in a consistent and rigid sequence. A rigid format should be used especially if you are required to hand in your outline.

- **Although the format of an outline is rigid, it shouldn't make you inflexible about how to write your paper.** Often when you start investigating a research problem [i.e., reviewing the research literature], especially if you are unfamiliar with the topic, you should anticipate the likelihood your analysis could go in different directions. If your paper changes focus, or you need to add new sections, then feel free to reorganize the outline.

- **If appropriate, organize the main points of your outline in chronological order**. In papers where you need to trace the history or chronology of events or issues, it is important to arrange your outline in the same manner, knowing that it's easier to re-arrange things now than when you've almost finished your paper.
- **For a standard research paper of 15-20 pages, your outline should be no more than four pages in length**. It may be helpful as your are developing your outline to also jot down a tentative list of references.

4

Organizing Your Social Sciences Research Paper: Paragraph Development

Definition

A paragraph is a group of related sentences that support one main idea. In general, paragraphs consist of three parts: the topic sentence, body sentences, and the concluding or the bridge sentence to the next paragraph or section. Paragraphs show where the subdivisions of a research paper begin and end and, thus, help the reader see the organization of the essay and grasp its main points.

Importance of Constructing Good Paragraphs

Paragraphs are the building blocks of papers. Without well-written paragraphs that flow logically from one idea to the next and that inform and help support in some meaningful way the central research problem being investigated, your paper will not be viewed as credible and, well, you'll probably receive a poor grade.

Here are some suggestions for troubleshooting common problems associated with developing paragraphs:

1. **The paragraph has no controlling idea**. Imagine each paragraph as having three general layers of text. The core content is in the middle. It includes all the evidence you need to make the point. However, this evidence needs to be introduced by a topic sentence in some way or your readers don't know what to do with all the evidence you have given them. Therefore, the

beginning of the paragraph explains the controlling idea of the paragraph. The last part of the paragraph tells the reader how the paragraph relates to the broader argument and often provides a transition to the next idea. Once you have mastered the use of topic sentences, you may decide that the topic sentence for a particular paragraph really should not be the first sentence of the paragraph. This is fine—the topic sentence can actually go at the beginning, middle, or end of a paragraph; what's important is that it is there to inform readers what the main idea of the paragraph is and how it relates back to the broader thesis of your paper.

2. **The paragraph has more than one controlling idea**. This is the most common reason why a paragraph is too long. If a paragraph is more than a page long, it likely contains more than one controlling idea. In this case, consider eliminating sentences that relate to the second idea, with the thought that maybe they don't really inform and help support the central research problem, or split the paragraph into two or more paragraphs, each with only one controlling idea.

3. **Transitions are needed within the paragraph**. You are probably familiar with the idea that transitions may be needed between paragraphs or sections in a paper. Sometimes they are also helpful within the body of a single paragraph. Within a paragraph, transitions are often single words or short phrases that help to establish relationships between ideas and to create a logical progression of those ideas in a paragraph. This is especially true within paragraphs that discuss multiple examples or discuss complex ideas, issues, or concepts.

Structure and Writing Style
I. General Structure

Most paragraphs in an essay parallel the general three-part structure of each section of a research paper and, by extension, the overall research paper, with an introduction, a body that includes facts and analysis, and a conclusion. You can see this structure in paragraphs whether they are narrating, describing, comparing, contrasting, or analyzing information. Each part of the paragraph plays an important role in communicating the meaning you intend to covey to the reader.

Introduction: the first section of a paragraph; should include the topic sentence and any other sentences at the beginning of the paragraph that give background information or provide a transition.

Body: follows the introduction; discusses the controlling idea, using facts, arguments, analysis, examples, and other information.

Conclusion: the final section; summarizes the connections between the information discussed in the body of the paragraph and the paragraph's controlling idea. For long paragraphs, you may also want to include a bridge sentence that introduces the next paragraph or section of the paper.

NOTE: This general structure does not imply that you should not be creative in your writing. Arranging where each element goes in a paragraph can make a paper more engaging for the reader. However, do not be too creative in experimenting with the narrative flow of paragraphs. To do so may distract from the main arguments of your research and weaken the quality of your academic writing.

II. Development and Organization

Before you can begin to determine what the composition of a particular paragraph will be, you must consider what is the most important idea that you are trying to convey to your reader. This is the "controlling idea," or the thesis statement from which you compose the remainder of the paragraph. In other words, your paragraphs should remind your reader that there is a recurrent relationship between your controlling idea and the information in each paragraph. The research problem functions like a seed from which your paper, and your ideas, will grow. The whole process of paragraph development is an organic one—a natural progression from a seed idea to a full-blown research study where there are direct, familial relationships in the paper between all of your controlling ideas and the paragraphs which derive from them.

The decision about what to put into your paragraphs begins with brainstorming about how you want to pursue the research problem. There are many techniques for brainstorming; whichever one you choose, this stage of paragraph development cannot be skipped because it lays a foundation for developing a set of paragraphs [representing a section of the paper] that describes a specific element of your overall analysis.

Given these factors, **every paragraph in a paper should be**:

- **Unified**—All of the sentences in a single paragraph should be related to a single controlling idea [often expressed in the topic sentence of the paragraph].
- **Clearly related to the research problem**—The sentences should all refer to the central idea, or the thesis, of the paper.
- **Coherent**—The sentences should be arranged in a logical manner and should follow a definite plan for development.
- **Well-developed**—Every idea discussed in the paragraph should be adequately explained and supported through evidence and details that work together to explain the paragraph's controlling idea.

There are many different ways you can organize a paragraph. However, the organization you choose will depend on the controlling idea of the paragraph. Ways to organize a paragraph include:

- **Narrative**: Tell a story. Go chronologically, from start to finish.
- **Descriptive**: Provide specific details about what something looks or feels like. Organize spatially, in order of appearance, or by topic.
- **Process**: Explain step by step how something works. Perhaps follow a sequence—first, second, third.
- **Classification**: Separate into groups or explain the various parts of a topic.
- **Illustrative**: Give examples and explain how those examples prove your point

Organizing Your Social Sciences Research Paper: 3. The Abstract

Definition

An abstract summarizes, usually in one paragraph of 300 words or less, the major aspects of the entire paper in a prescribed sequence that includes: 1) the overall purpose of the study and the research problem(s) you investigated; 2) the basic design of the study; 3) major findings or trends found as a result of your analysis; and, 4) a brief summary of your interpretations and conclusions.

Importance of a Good Abstract

Sometimes your professor will ask you to include an abstract, or general summary of your work, with your research paper. **The abstract allows you to elaborate upon each major aspect of the paper and helps readers decide whether they want to read the rest of the paper.** Therefore, enough key information [e.g., summary results, observations, trends, etc.] must be included to make the abstract useful to someone who may want to examine your work.

How do you know when you have enough information in your abstract?

A simple rule-of-thumb is to imagine that you are another researcher doing a similar study. Then ask yourself: if your abstract was the only part of the paper you could access, would you be happy with the amount of information presented there? Does it tell the whole story about your study? If the answer is "no" then the abstract likely needs to be revised.

Structure and Writing Style

I. Types of Abstracts

To begin, you need to determine which type of abstract you should include with your paper. There are four general types.

Critical Abstract

A critical abstract provides, in addition to describing main findings and information, a judgement or comment about the study's validity, reliability, or completeness. The researcher evaluates the paper and often compares it with other works on the same subject. Critical abstracts are generally 400-500 words in length due to the additional interpretive commentary. These types of abstracts are used infrequently.

Descriptive Abstract

A descriptive abstract indicates the type of information found in the work. It makes no judgments about the work, nor does it provide results or conclusions of the research. It does incorporate key words found in the text and may include the purpose, methods, and scope of the research. Essentially, the descriptive abstract only describes the work being summarized. Some researchers consider it an outline of the work, rather than a summary. Descriptive abstracts are usually very short, 100 words or less.

Informative Abstract

The majority of abstracts are informative. While they still do not critique or evaluate a work, they do more than describe it. A good informative abstract acts as a surrogate for the work itself. That is, the researcher presents and explains all the main arguments and the important results and evidence in the paper. An informative abstract includes the information that can be found in a descriptive abstract [purpose, methods, scope] but it also includes the results and conclusions of the research and the recommendations of the author. The length varies according to discipline, but an informative abstract is usually no more than 300 words in length.

Highlight Abstract

A highlight abstract is specifcally written to attract the reader's attention to the study. No pretence is made of there being either a balanced or complete picture of the paper and, in fact, incomplete and leading remarks may be used to spark the reader's interest. In that a highlight abstract cannot stand independent of its associated article, it is not a true abstract and, therefore, rarely used in academic writing.

II. Writing Style

Use the active voice when possible, but note that much of your abstract may require passive sentence constructions. Regardless, write your abstract using concise, but complete, sentences. Get to the point quickly and **always use the past tense** because you are reporting on research that has been completed.

Although it is the first section of your paper, the abstract, by definition, should be written last since it will summarize the contents of your entire paper. To begin composing your abstract, take whole sentences or key phrases from each section and put them in a sequence that summarizes the paper. Then revise or add connecting phrases or words to make it cohensive and clear. Before handing in your final paper, check to make sure that the information in the abstract completely agrees with what your have written in the paper.

The abstract SHOULD NOT contain:
- Lengthy background information,
- References to other literature [say something like, "current research shows that..." or "studies have indicated..."],
- Using ellipticals [i.e., ending with "..."] or incomplete sentences,
- Abbreviations, jargon, or terms that may be confusing to the reader, and
- Any sort of image, illustration, figure, or table, or references to them

1

Organizing Your Social Sciences Research Paper: Executive Summary

Definition

An executive summary is a thorough overview of a research report or other type of document that synthesizes key points for its readers, saving them time and preparing them to understand the study's overall content. It is a separate, stand-alone document of sufficient detail and clarity to ensure that the reader can completely understand the contents of the main research study. An executive summary can be anywhere from 1-10 pages long depending on the length of the report, or it can be the summary of more than one document [e.g., papers submitted for a group project].

Importance of a Good Executive Summary

Although an executive summary is similar to an abstract in that they both summarize the contents of a research study, there are several key differences. With research abstracts, the author's recommendations are rarely included, or if they are, they are implicit rather than explicit. Recommendations are generally not stated in academic abstracts because scholars operate in a discursive environment, where debates, discussions, and dialogs are meant to precede the implementation of any new research findings. The conceptual nature of much academic writing also means that recommendations arising from the findings are widespread and not easily or usefully encapsulated.

Executive summaries are used mainly when a research study has been developed for an organizational partner, funding entity, or other external group that participated in the research. In such cases, the research report and executive summary are often written for policy makers outside of academe, while abstracts are written for the academic community. Professors, therefore, assign the writing of executive summaries so students can practice sythesizing and writing about the contents of comprehensive research studies for external stakeholder groups.

When preparing to write, keep in mind that:
- An executive summary is not an abstract.
- An executive summary is not an introduction.
- An executive summary is not a preface.
- An executive summary is not a random collection of highlights.

Structure and Writing Style
I. Writing an Executive Summary
Read the Entire Document
This may go without saying, but it is critically important that you read your entire research study thoroughly from start to finish before beginning to write the executive summary. Take notes as you go along, highlighting important statements of fact, key findings, and recommended courses of action. This will better prepare you for how to organize and summarize your study. Remember this is not a brief abstract of 300 words or less but, essentially, a mini-paper of your paper, with a focus on recommendations.

Isolate the Major Points Within the Original Document
Choose which parts of the document are the most important to those who will read it. These points must be included within the executive summary in order to provide a thorough and complete explanation of what the document is trying to convey.

Separate the Main Sections
Closely examine each section of the original document and discern the main differences in each. After you have a firm understanding about what each section offers in respect to the other sections, write a few sentences for each section describing the main ideas. Although the format may vary, the main sections of an executive summary likely will include the following:
- The opening statement, brief background information,

- The purpose of research study,
- Method of data gathering and analysis,
- Overview of findings, and,
- A description of each recommendation, accompanied by a justification. Note that the recommendations are sometimes quoted verbatim from the research study.

Combine the Information

Use the information gathered to combine them into an executive summary that is no longer than 10% of the original document. Be concise! The purpose is to provide a brief explanation of the entire document with a focus on the recommendations that have emerged from your research. How you word this will likely differ depending on your audience and what they care most about. If necessary, selectively incorporate bullet points for emphasis and brevity.

Re-read the Executive Summary

After you've completed your executive summary, let it sit for a while before coming back to re-read it. Check to make sure that the summary will make sense as a separate document from the full research study. By taking some time before re-reading it, you allow yourself to see the summary with unbiased eyes.

II. Common Mistakes to Avoid

Length of the Executive Summary

As a general rule, the correct length of an executive summary is that it meets the criteria of no more pages than 10% of the number of pages in the original document, with an upper limit of no more than ten pages. This requirement keeps the document short enough to be read by your audience, but long enough to allow it to be a complete, stand-alone synopsis.

Cutting and Pasting

With the exception of specific recommendations made in the study, do not simply cut and paste whole sections of the original document into the executive summary. You should paraphrase information from the longer document. Avoid taking up space with excessive subtitles and lists, unless they are absolutely necessary for the reader to have a complete understanding of the original document.

Consider the Audience

Although unlikely to be required by your professor, there is the possibility that more than one executive summary will have to be written for a given document [e.g., one for policy-makers, one for private industry, one for philanthropists]. This may only necessitate the rewriting of the conclusion, but it could require rewriting the entire summary in order to fit the needs of the reader. If necessary, be sure to consider the types of audiences who may benefit from your study and make adjustments accordingly.

Clarity in Writing

One of the biggest mistakes you can make is related to the clarity of your executive summary. Always note that your audience [or audiences] are likely seeing your research study for the first time. The best way to avoid a disorganized or cluttered executive summary is to write it after the study is completed. Always follow the same strategies for proofreading that you would for any research paper.

Use Strong and Positive Language

Don't weaken your executive summary with passive, imprecise language. The executive summary is a stand-alone document intended to convince the reader to make a decision concerning whether to implement the recommendations you make. Once convinced, it is assumed that the full document will provide the details needed to implement the recommendations. Although you should resist the temptation to pad your summary with pleas or biased statements, do pay particular attention to ensuring that a sense of urgency is created in the implications, recommendations, and conclusions presented in the executive summary. Be sure to target readers who are likely to implement the recommendations.

Organizing Your Social Sciences Research Paper: 4.The Introduction

Definition

The introduction leads the reader from a general subject area to a particular field of research. It establishes the context and significance of the research being conducted by summarizing current understanding and background information about the topic, stating the purpose of the work in the form of the research problem supported by a hypothesis or a set of questions, briefly explaining the methodological approach used to examine the research problem, highlighting the potential outcomes your study can reveal, and outlining the remaining structure of the paper.

Importance of a Good Introduction

Think of the introduction as a mental road map that must answer for the reader these four questions:

1. What was I studying?
2. Why was this topic important to investigate?
3. What did we know about this topic before I did this study?
4. How will this study advance new knowledge or new ways of understanding?

A well-written introduction is important because, quite simply, you never get a second chance to make a good first impression. The opening paragraphs of your paper will provide your readers with their initial impressions about the logic of your argument, your writing style, the overall quality of your research, and, ultimately, the validity of your findings and conclusions. A vague, disorganized, or error-filled introduction will create a negative impression, whereas, a concise, engaging, and well-written introduction will lead your readers to think highly of your analytical skills, your writing style, and your research approach.

Structure and Writing Style

I. Structure and Approach

The introduction is the broad beginning of the paper that answers three important questions for the reader:

1. What is this?
2. Why should I read it?
3. What do you want me to think about / consider doing / react to?

Think of the structure of the introduction as an inverted triangle of information. Organize the information so as to present the more general aspects of the topic early in the introduction, then narrow your analysis to more specific topical information that provides context, finally arriving at your research problem and the rationale for studying it and, whenever possible, a description of the potential outcomes your study can reveal.

These are general phases associated with writing an introduction:

1. Establish an area to research by:
   - Highlighting the importance of the topic, and/or
   - Making general statements about the topic, and/or
   - Presenting an overview on current research on the subject.
2. Identify a research niche by:
   - Opposing an existing assumption, and/or
   - Revealing a gap in existing research, and/or
   - Formulating a research question or problem, and/or
   - Continuing a disciplinary tradition.
3. Place your research within the research niche by:
   - Stating the intent of your study,
   - Outlining the key characteristics of your study,
   - Describing important results, and
   - Giving a brief overview of the structure of the paper.

NOTE: Even though the introduction is the first main section of a research paper, it is often useful to finish the introduction late in the writing process because the structure of the paper, the reporting and analysis of results, and the conclusion will have been completed. Reviewing and, if necessary, rewriting the introduction ensures that it correctly matches the overall structure of your final paper.

II. Delimitations of the Study

Delimitations refer to those characteristics that limit the scope and define the conceptual boundaries of your research. This is determined by the conscious exclusionary and inclusionary decisions you make about how to investigate the research problem. In other words, not only should you tell the reader what it is you are studying and why, but you must also acknowledge why you rejected alternative approaches that could have been used to examine the topic.

Obviously, the first limiting step was the choice of research problem itself. However, implicit are other, related problems that could have been chosen but were rejected. These should be noted in the conclusion of your introduction. For example, a delimitating statement could read, "Although many factors can be understood to impact the likelihood young people will vote, this study will focus only on socioeconomic factors related to the need to work full-time while in school." The point is not to document every possible delimiting factor, but to highlight why obvious issues related to the research problem were not addressed.

Examples of delimitating choices would be:
- The key aims and objectives of your study,
- The research questions that you address,
- The variables of interest [i.e., the various factors and features of the phenomenon being studied],
- The method(s) of investigation,
- The time period your study covers, and
- Any relevant alternative theoretical frameworks that could have been adopted.

Review each of these decisions. Not only do you clearly establish what you intend to accomplish in your research, but you should also include a declaration of what the study does not intend to cover. In the latter case, your exclusionary decisions should be based upon criteria understood as, "not interesting"; "not directly relevant"; "too problematic because..."; "not feasible," and the like. Make this reasoning explicit!

NOTE: Delimitations refer to the initial choices made about the broader, overall design of your study and should not be confused with documenting the limitiations of your study discovered after the research has been completed.

ANOTHER NOTE: Do not view delimitating statements as admitting to an inherent failing or shortcoming in your research. They are an accepted element of academic writing intended to keep the reader focused on the research problem by explicitly defining the conceptual boundaries and scope of your study. It addresses any critical questions in the reader's mind of, "Why the hell didn't the author examine this?"

III. The Narrative Flow

Issues to keep in mind that will help the narrative flow in your introduction:
- **Your introduction should clearly identify the subject area of interest**. A simple strategy to follow is to use key words from your

title in the first few sentences of the introduction. This will help focus the introduction on the topic at the appropriate level and ensures that you get to the subject matter quickly without losing focus, or discussing information that is too general.

- **Establish context by providing a brief and balanced review of the pertinent published literature that is available on the subject.** The key is to summarize for the reader what is known about the specific research problem before you did your analysis. This part of your introduction should not represent a comprehensive literature review. It consists of a general review of the important, foundational research literature [with citations] that lays a foundation for understanding key elements of the research problem. See the drop-down menu under this tab for "Background Information" regarding types of contexts.

- **Clearly state the hypothesis that you investigated**. When you are first learning to write in this format it is okay, and actually preferable, to use a past statement like, "The purpose of this study was to...." or "We investigated three possible mechanisms to explain the...."

- **Why did you choose this kind of research study or design?** Provide a clear statement of the rationale for your approach to the problem studied. This will usually follow your statement of purpose in the last paragraph of the introduction.

IV. Engaging the Reader
The overarching goal of your introduction is to make your readers want to read your paper. The introduction should grab your reader's attention. Strategies for doing this can be to:
1. Open with a compelling story,
2. Include a strong quotation or a vivid, perhaps unexpected anecdote,
3. Pose a provocative or thought-provoking question,
4. Describe a puzzling scenario or incongruity, or
5. Cite a stirring example or case study that illustrates why the research problem is important.

NOTE: Choose only one strategy for engaging your readers; avoid giving an impression that your paper is more flash than substance.

1

Organizing Your Social Sciences Research Paper: The C.A.R.S. Model

Introduction

The Creating a Research Space [C.A.R.S.] Model was developed by John Swales based upon his analysis of journal articles representing a variety of discipline-based writing practices. His model attempts to explain and describe the organizational pattern of writing the introduction to scholarly research studies. Following the CARS Model is useful because it can help you to: 1) begin the writing process [getting started is often the most difficult task]; 2) understand the way in which an introduction sets the stage for the rest of your paper; and, 3) assess how the introduction fits within the larger scope of your study.

The model assumes that writers follow a general organizational pattern in response to two types of challenges ["competitions"] relating to establishing a presence within a particular domain of research: 1) the competition to create a rhetorical space and, 2) the competition to attract readers into that space. The model proposes three actions [Swales calls them "moves"], accompanied by specific steps, that reflect the development of an effective introduction for a research paper. These "moves" and steps can be used as a template for writing the introduction to your own social sciences research papers.

The Model
Creating a Research Space
Move 1: Establishing a Territory [the situation]

This is generally accomplished in two ways: by demonstrating that a general area of research is important, critical, interesting, problematic, relevant, or otherwise worthy of investigation and by introducing and reviewing key sources of prior research in that area to show where gaps exist or where prior research has been inadequate in addressing the research problem.

The steps taken to achieve this would be:

- Step 1 -- Claiming importance of, and/or [writing action = describing the research problem and providing evidence to support why the topic is important to study]
- Step 2 -- Making topic generalizations, and/or [writing action = providing statements about the current state of knowledge, consensus, practice or description of phenomena]

- Step 3 -- Reviewing items of previous research [writing action = synthesize prior research that further supports the need to study the research problem; this is not a literature review but more a reflection of key studies that have touched upon but perhaps not fully addressed the topic]

Move 2: Establishing a Niche [the problem]

This action refers to making a clear and cogent argument that your particular piece of research is important and possesses value. This can be done by indicating a specific gap in previous research, by challenging a broadly accepted assumption, by raising a question, a hypothesis, or need, or by extending previous knowledge in some way.

The steps taken to achieve this would be:

- Step 1a -- Counter-claiming, or [writing action = introduce an opposing viewpoint or perspective or identify a gap in prior research that you believe has weakened or undermined the prevailing argument]
- Step 1b -- Indicating a gap, or [writing action = develop the research problem around a gap or understudied area of the literature]
- Step 1c -- Question-raising, or [writing action = similar to gap identification, this involves presenting key questions about the consequences of gaps in prior research that will be addressed by your study. For example, one could state, "Despite prior observations of voter behavior in local elections in urban Detroit, it remains unclear why do some single mothers choose to avoid...."]
- Step 1d -- Continuing a tradition [writing action = extend prior research to expand upon or clarify a research problem. This is often signaled with logical connecting terminology, such as, "hence," "therefore," "consequently," "thus" or language that indicates a need. For example, one could state, "Consequently, these factors need to examined in more detail...." or "Evidence suggests an interesting correlation, therefore, it is desirable to survey different respondents...."]

Move 3: Occupying the Niche [the solution]

The final "move" is to announce the means by which your study will contribute new knowledge or new understanding in contrast to prior research on the topic. This is also where you describe the remaining organizational structure of the paper.

The steps taken to achieve this would be:

- Step 1a -- Outlining purposes, or [writing action = answering the "So What?" question. Explain in clear language the objectives of your study]

- Step 1b -- Announcing present research [writing action = describe the purpose of your study in terms of what the research is going to do or accomplish. In the social sciences, the "So What?" question still needs to addressed]
- Step 2 -- Announcing principle findings [writing action = present a brief, general summary of key findings written, such as, "The findings indicate a need for...," or "The research suggests four approaches to...."]
- Step 3 -- Indicating article structure [writing action = state how the remainder of your paper is organized]

Writing Tip

Swales showed that establishing a research niche [move 2] is often signaled by specific terminology that expresses a contrasting viewpoint, a critical evaluation of gaps in the literature, or a perceived weakness in prior research. The purpose of using these words is to draw a clear distinction between perceived deficiencies in previous studies and the research you are presenting that is intended to help resolve these deficiencies. Below is a table of common words used by authors.

Contrast	Quantity	Verbs	Adjectives
albeit	few	challenge	difficult
although	handful	deter	dubious
but	less	disregard	elusive
howbeit	little	exclude	inadequate
however	no	fail	incomplete
nevertheless	none	hinder	inconclusive
notwithstanding	not	ignore	inefficacious
unfortunately		lack	ineffective
whereas		limit	inefficient
yet		misinterpret	questionable
		neglect	scarce
		obviate	uncertain
		omit	unclear
		overlook	unconvincing
		prevent	unproductive
		question	unreliable
		restrict	unsatisfactory

NOTE: You may prefer not to adopt a negative stance in your writing when placing it within the context of prior research. In such cases, an alternative approach is to utilize a neutral, contrastive statement that expresses a new perspective without giving the appearance of trying to diminish the validity of other people's research.

Examples of how this can be achieved include the following statements, with A representing the findings of prior research, B representing your research problem, and X representing one or more variables that have been investigated.

- The research has focused on A, rather than on B...
- Research into A can be useful but to counterbalance X, it is important to consider B...
- These studies have emphasized A, as opposed to B...
- While prior studies have examined A, it may be preferable to contemplate the impact of B...
- After consideration of A, it is important to also recognize B...
- The study of A has been exhaustive, but changing circumstances related to X support the need for revisiting B...
- Although considerable research has been devoted to A, less attention has been paid to B...
- This research offers insight into the need for A, though consideration of B is also helpful...

2

Organizing Your Social Sciences Research Paper: Background Information

Definition

Background information identifies and describes the history and nature of a well-defined research problem with reference to the existing literature. The background information should indicate the root of the problem being studied, its scope, and the extent to which previous studies have successfully investigated the problem, noting, in particular, where gaps exist that your study attempts to address. Introductory background information differs from a literature review in that it places the research problem in proper context rather than provide a thorough examining pertinent literature.

Importance of Having Enough Background Information

Background information expands upon the key points stated in your introduction but is not intended to be the main focus of the paper. Sufficient background information helps your reader determine if you have a basic understanding of the research problem being investigated and promotes confidence in the overall quality of your analysis and findings. This information provides the reader with the essential context needed to understand the research problem and its significance.

Depending on the problem being studied, forms of contextualization may include one or more of the following:

- **Cultural** -- placed within the learned behavior of specific groups of people.
- **Economic** -- of or relating to systems of production and management of material wealth and/or business activities.
- **Gender** -- located within the behavioral, cultural, or psychological traits typically associated with being male or female.
- **Historical** -- the time in which something takes place or was created and how that influences how you interpret it.
- **Philosophical** -- clarification of the essential nature of being or of phenomena as it relates to the research problem.
- **Physical/Spatial** -- reflects the space around something and how that influences how you see it.
- **Political** -- concerns the environment in which something is produced indicating it's public purpose or agenda.
- **Social** -- the environment of people that surrounds something's creation or intended audience, reflecting how the people around something use and interpret it.
- **Temporal** -- reflects issues or events of, relating to, or limited by time.

Background information can also include summaries of important, relevant research studies. The key is to summarize for the reader what is known about the specific research problem before you conducted your analysis. This is accomplished with a general review of the foundational research literature (with citations) that report findings that inform your study's aims and objectives.

NOTE: Research studies cited as part of the background information of your introduction should not include very specific, lengthy explanations. This should be discussed in greater detail in your literature review section.

Structure and Writing Style

Providing background information in the Introduction of a research paper serves as a bridge that links the reader to the topic of your study. But precisely how long and in-depth this bridge should be is largely dependent upon how much information you think the reader will need to know in order to fully understand the topic being discussed and to appreciate why the issues you are investigating are important.

From another perspective, the length and detail of background information also depends on the degree to which you need to demonstrate to your professor how much you understand the research problem. Keep this in mind because providing pertinent background information can be an effective way to demonstrate that you have a clear grasp of key issues and concepts underpinning your overall study. Don't try to show off, though! And, avoid stating the obvious.

Given that the structure and writing style of your background information can vary depending upon the complexity of your research and/or the nature of the assignment, **here are some questions to consider while writing this part of your introduction**:

1. Are there concepts, terms, theories, or ideas that may be unfamiliar to the reader and, thus, require additional explanation?
2. Are there historical elements that need to be explored in order to provide needed context, to highlight specific people, issues, or events, or to lay a foundation for understanding the emergence of a current issue or event?
3. Are there theories, concepts, or ideas borrowed from other disciplines or academic traditions that may be unfamiliar to the reader?
4. Is the research study unusual in a way that requres additional explanation, such as, 1) your study uses a method of analysis never applied before; 2) your study investigates a very esoteric or complex research problem; or, 3) your study relies upon analyzing unique texts or documents, such as archival materials or primary documents like diaries or personal letters, that do not represent the established body of source literature on the topic.

Almost all introductions to a research problem require some contextualizing, but **the scope and breadth of background information varies depending on your assumption about the reader's level of prior knowledge**. Despite this assessment, however, background information should be brief and succienct; save any elaboration of critical points or in-depth discussion of key issues for the literature review section of your paper.

3

Organizing Your Social Sciences Research Paper: The Research Problem/Question

Definition

A research problem is a statement about an area of concern, a condition to be improved upon, a difficulty to be eliminated, or a troubling question that exists in scholarly literature, in theory, or in practice that points to the need for meaningful understanding and deliberate investigation. In some social science disciplines the research problem is typically posed in the form of one or more questions. A research problem does not state how to do something, offer a vague or broad proposition, or present a value question.

Importance of...

The purpose of a problem statement is to:

1. **Introduce the reader to the importance of the topic being studied**. The reader is oriented to the significance of the study and the research questions or hypotheses to follow.
2. **Place the problem into a particular context** that defines the parameters of what is to be investigated.
3. **Provide the framework for reporting the results** and indicates what is probably necessary to conduct the study and explain how the findings will present this information.

So What!

In the social sciences, the research problem establishes the means by which you must answer the "So What" question. The "So What" question refers to a research problem surviving the relevancy test [the quality of a measurement procedure that provides repeatability and accuracy]. Note that answering the "So What" question requires a commitment on your part to not only show that you have researched the material, but that you have thought about its significance.

To survive the "So What" question, problem statements should possess the following attributes:

- Clarity and precision [a well-written statement does not make sweeping generalizations and irresponsible statements],

- Demonstrate a researchable topic or issue [i.e., feasibility of conducting the study is based upon access to information that can be effectively acquired, interpreted, synthesized, and understood],
- Identification of what would be studied, while avoiding the use of value-laden words and terms,
- Identification of an overarching question or small set of questions accompanied by key factors or variables,
- Identification of key concepts and terms,
- Articulation of the study's boundaries or parameters or limitations,
- Some generalizability in regards to applicability and bringing results into general use,
- Conveyance of the study's importance, benefits, and justification [i.e., regardless of the type of research, it is important to demonstrate that the research is not trivial],
- Does not have unnecessary jargon or overly complex sentence constructions; and,
- Conveyance of more than the mere gathering of descriptive data providing only a snapshot of the issue or phenomenon under investigation.

Structure and Writing Style

I. Types and Content

There are four general conceptualizations of a research problem in the social sciences:

1. **Casuist Research Problem** -- this type of problem relates to the determination of right and wrong in questions of conduct or conscience by analyzing moral dilemmas through the application of general rules and the careful distinction of special cases.
2. **Difference Research Problem** -- typically asks the question, "Is there a difference between two or more groups or treatments?" This type of problem statement is used when the researcher compares or contrasts two or more phenomena.
3. **Descriptive Research Problem** -- typically asks the question, "what is...?" with the underlying purpose to describe a situation, state, or existence of a specific phenomenon.
4. **Relational Research Problem** -- suggests a relationship of some sort between two or more variables to be investigated. The underlying purpose is to investigate qualities/characteristics that are connected in some way.

A problem statement in the social sciences should contain:

- A lead-in that helps ensure the reader will maintain interest over the study,
- A declaration of originality [e.g., mentioning a knowledge void, that will be supported by the literature review],
- An indication of the central focus of the study [establishing the boundaries of analysis], and
- An explanation of the study's significance or the benefits to be derived from an investigating the research problem.

II. Sources of Problems for Investigation

Indentifying a problem to study can be challenging, not because there's a lack of issues that could be investigated, but due to pursuing a goal of formulating an academically relevant and researchable problem that is unique and does not simply duplicate the work of others. To facilitate how you might select a problem from which to build a research study, consider these sources of inspiration:

Deductions from Theory

This relates to deductions made from social philosophy or generalizations embodied in life in society that the researcher is familiar with. These deductions from human behavior are then fitted within an empirical frame of reference through research. From a theory, the researcher can formulate a research problem or hypothesis stating the expected findings in certain empirical situations. The research asks the question: "What relationship between variables will be observed if theory aptly summarizes the state of affairs?" One can then design and carry out a systematic investigation to assess whether empirical data confirm or reject the hypothesis, and hence, the theory.

Interdisciplinary Perspectives

Identifying a problem that forms the basis for a research study can come from academic movements and scholarship originating in disciplines outside of your primary area of study. A review of pertinent literature should include examining research from related disciplines that can reveal new avenues of exploration and analysis. An interdisciplinary approach to selecting a research problem offers an opportunity to construct a more comprehensive understanding of a very complex issue that any single discipline may be able to provide.

Interviewing Practitioners

The identification of research problems about particular topics can arise from formal or informal discussions with practitioners who provide insight into new directions for future research and how to make research findings more relevant to practice. Discussions with experts in the field, such as, teachers, social workers, health care providers, lawyers, business leaders, etc., offers the chance to identify practical, "real world" problems that may be understudied or ignored within academic circles. This approach also provides some practical knowledge which may help in the process of designing and conducting your study.

Personal Experience

Your everyday experiences can give rise to worthwhile problems for investigation. Think critically about your own experiences and/or frustrations with an issue facing society, your community, your neighborhood, your family, or your personal life. This can be derived, for example, from deliberate observations of certain relationships for which there is no clear explanation or witnessing an event that appears harmful to a person or group or that is out of the ordinary.

Relevant Literature

The selection of a research problem can be derived from an extensive and thorough review of pertinent research associated with your overall area of interest. This may reveal where gaps exist in our understanding of a topic. Research may be conducted to: 1) fill such gaps in knowledge; 2) evaluate if the methodologies employed in prior studies can be adapted to solve other problems; or, 3) determine if a similar study could be conducted in a different subject area or applied to different study sample [i.e., different groups of people]. Also, authors frequently conclude their studies by noting implications for further research; this can also be a valuable source of new problems to investigate.

III. What Makes a Good Research Statement?

A good problem statement begins by introducing the broad area in which your research is centered and then gradually leads the reader to the more narrow questions you are posing. The statement need not be lengthy but a good research problem should incorporate the following features:

1. Compelling topic

Simple curiosity is not a good enough reason to pursue a research study. The problem that you choose to explore must be important to you, your readers, and to a larger community you share. The problem chosen must be one that motivates you to address it.

2. Supports multiple perspectives

The problem most be phrased in a way that avoids dichotomies and instead supports the generation and exploration of multiple perspectives. A general rule of thumb is that a good research problem is one that would generate a variety of viewpoints from a composite audience made up of reasonable people.

3. Researchable

It seems a bit obvious, but you don't want to find yourself in the midst of investigating a complex research project and realize that you don't have much to draw on for your research. Choose research problems that can be supported by the resources available to you. Not sure? Seek out help from a librarian!

NOTE: Do not confuse a research problem with a research topic. A topic is something to read and obtain information about whereas a problem is something to be solved or framed as a question that must be answered.

IV. Mistakes to Avoid

Beware of circular reasoning! Don't state that the research problem as simply the absence of the thing you are suggesting. For example, if you propose the following: "The problem in this community is that there is no hospital."

This only leads to a research problem where:

- The **need** is for a hospital
- The **objective** is to create a hospital
- The **method** is to plan for building a hospital, and
- The **evaluation** is to measure if there is a hospital or not.

This is an example of a research problem that fails the "So What?" test. In this example, the problem **does not reveal the relevance** of why you are investigating the fact there is no hospital in the community [e.g., there's a hospital in the community ten miles away]; it **does not elucidate the significance** of why one should study the fact there is no hospital in the community [e.g., that hospital in the community ten miles away has no emergency room]; and, the research problem does not offer an intellectual pathway towards **adding new knowledge or clarifying prior knowledge** [e.g., the county in which there is no hospital already conducted a study about the need for a hospital]

4

Organizing Your Social Sciences Research Paper: Theoretical Framework

Definition

Theories are formulated to explain, predict, and understand phenomena and, in many cases, to challenge and extend existing knowledge within the limits of critical bounding assumptions. The theoretical framework is the structure that can hold or support a theory of a research study. The theoretical framework introduces and describes the theory that explains why the research problem under study exists.

Importance of Theory

A theoretical framework consists of concepts and, together with their definitions and reference to relevant scholarly literature, existing theory that is used for your particular study. The theoretical framework must demonstrate an understanding of theories and concepts that are relevant to the topic of your research paper and that relate to the broader areas of knowledge being considered.

The theoretical framework is most often not something readily found within the literature. You must review course readings and pertinent research studies for theories and analytic models that are relevant to the research problem you are investigating. The selection of a theory should depend on its appropriateness, ease of application, and explanatory power.

The theoretical framework strengthens the study in the following ways:

1. An explicit statement of theoretical assumptions permits the reader to evaluate them critically.
2. The theoretical framework connects the researcher to existing knowledge. Guided by a relevant theory, you are given a basis for your hypotheses and choice of research methods.
3. Articulating the theoretical assumptions of a research study forces you to address questions of why and how. It permits you to intellectually transition from simply describing a phenomenon you have observed to generalizing about various aspects of that phenomenon.
4. Having a theory helps you identify the limits to those generalizations. A theoretical framework specifies which key variables influence a phenomenon of interest and highlights the need to examine how those key variables might differ and under what circumstances.

By virtue of its application nature, good theory in the social sciences is of value precisely because it fulfills one primary purpose: to explain the meaning, nature, and challenges associated with a phenomenon, often experienced but unexplained in the world in which we live, so that we may use that knowledge and understanding to act in more informed and effective ways.

Strategies for Developing the Theoretical Framework
I. Developing the Framework
Here are some strategies to develop of an effective theoretical framework:
1. **Examine your thesis title and research problem**. The research problem anchors your entire study and forms the basis from which you construct your theoretical framework.
2. **Brainstorm about what you consider to be the key variables in your research**. Answer the question, "What factors contribute to the presumed effect?"
3. **Review related literature** to find how scholars have addressed your research question.
4. **List the constructs and variables** that might be relevant to your study. Group these variables into independent and dependent categories.
5. **Review key social science theories** that are introduced to you in your course readings and choose the theory that can best explain the relationships between the key variables in your study [note the Writing Tip on this page].
6. **Discuss the assumptions or propositions** of this theory and point out their relevance to your research.

A theoretical framework is used to limit the scope of the relevant data by focusing on specific variables and defining the specific viewpoint [framework] that the researcher will take in analyzing and interpreting the data to be gathered. It also facilitates the understanding of concepts and variables according to given definitions and builds new knowledge by validating or challenging theoretical assumptions.

II. Purpose
Think of theories as the conceptual basis for understanding, analyzing, and designing ways to investigate relationships within social systems. To that end, the following roles served by a theory can help guide the development of your framework.
- Means by which new research data can be interpreted and coded for future use,
- Response to new problems that have no previously identified solutions strategy,
- Means for identifying and defining research problems,
- Means for prescribing or evaluating solutions to research problems,
- Ways of discerning certain facts among the accumulated knowledge that are important and which facts are not,

- Means of giving old data new interpretations and new meaning,
- Means by which to identify important new issues and prescribe the most critical research questions that need to be answered to maximize understanding of the issue,
- Means of providing members of a professional discipline with a common language and a frame of reference for defining the boundaries of their profession, and
- Means to guide and inform research so that it can, in turn, guide research efforts and improve professional practice.

Structure and Writing Style

The theoretical framework may be rooted in a specific theory, in which case, your work is expected to test the validity of that existing theory in relation to specific events, issues, or phenomena. Many social science research papers fit into this rubric. For example, Peripheral Realism Theory, which categorizes perceived differences among nation-states as those that give orders, those that obey, and those that rebel, could be used as a means for understanding conflicted relationships among countries in Africa. A test of this theory could be the following: Does Peripheral Realism Theory help explain intra-state actions, such as, the disputed split between southern and northern Sudan that led to the creation of two nations?

However, you may not always be asked by your professor to test a specific theory in your paper, but to develop your own framework from which your analysis of the research problem is derived. Based upon the above example, it is perhaps easiest to understand the nature and function of a theoretical framework if it is viewed as an answer to two basic questions:

1. **What is the research problem/question?** [e.g., "How should the individual and the state relate during periods of conflict?"]
2. **Why is your approach a feasible solution?** [i.e., justify the application of your choice of a particular theory and explain why alternative constructs were rejected. I could choose instead to test Instrumentalist or Circumstantialists models developed among ethnic conflict theorists that rely upon socio-economic-political factors to explain individual-state relations and to apply this theoretical model to periods of war between nations].

The answers to these questions come from a thorough review of the literature and your course readings [summarized and analyzed in the next section of your paper] and the gaps in the research that emerge from the review process. With this in mind, **a complete theoretical framework will likely not emerge until after you have completed a thorough review of the literature**.

Just as a research problem in your paper requires contextualization and background information, a theory requires a framework for understanding its application to the topic being investigated. **When writing and revising this part of your research paper, keep in mind the following:**

- **Clearly describe the framework, concepts, models, or specific theories that underpin your study.** This includes noting who the key theorists are in the field who have conducted research on the problem you are investigating and, when necessary, the historical context that supports the formulation of that theory. This latter element is particularly important if the theory is relatively unknown or it is borrowed from another discipline.

- **Position your theoretical framework within a broader context of related frameworks, concepts, models, or theories.** As noted in the example above, there will likely be several concepts, theories, or models that can be used to help develop a framework for understanding the research problem. Therefore, note why the theory you've chosen is the appropriate one.

- **The present tense is used when writing about theory.** Although the past tense can be used to describe the history of a theory or the role of key theorists, the construction of your theoretical framwork is happening now.

- **You should make your theoretical assumptions as explicit as possible.** Later, your discussion of methodology should be linked back to this theoretical framework.

- **Don't just take what the theory says as a given!** Reality is never accurately represented in such a simplistic way; if you imply that it can be, you fundamentally distort a reader's ability to understand the findings that emerge. Given this, always note the limitiations of the theoretical framework you've chosen [i.e., what parts of the research problem require further investigation because the theory inadequately explains a certain phenomena].

Organizing Your Social Sciences Research Paper: 5. The Literature Review

Definition

A literature review surveys books, scholarly articles, and any other sources relevant to a particular issue, area of research, or theory, and by so doing, provides a description, summary, and critical evaluation of these works in relation to the research problem being investigated. Literature reviews are designed to provide an overview of sources you have explored while researching a particular topic and to demonstrate to your readers how your research fits within a larger field of study.

Importance of a Good Literature Review

A literature review may consist of simply a summary of key sources, but in the social sciences, a literature review usually has an organizational pattern and combines both summary and synthesis, often within specific conceptual categories. A summary is a recap of the important information of the source, but a synthesis is a re-organization, or a reshuffling, of that information in a way that informs how you are planning to investigate a research problem. The analytical features of a literature review might:

- Give a new interpretation of old material or combine new with old interpretations,
- Trace the intellectual progression of the field, including major debates,
- Depending on the situation, evaluate the sources and advise the reader on the most pertinent or relevant research, or
- Usually in the conclusion of a literature review, identify where gaps exist in how a problem has been researched to date.

The purpose of a literature review is to:

- Place each work in the context of its contribution to understanding the research problem being studied.

- Describe the relationship of each work to the others under consideration.
- Identify new ways to interpret prior research.
- Reveal any gaps that exist in the literature.
- Resolve conflicts amongst seemingly contradictory previous studies.
- Identify areas of prior scholarship to prevent duplication of effort.
- Point the way in fulfilling a need for additional research.
- Locate your own research within the context of existing literature [very important].

Types of Literature Reviews

It is important to think of knowledge in a given field as consisting of three layers. First, there are the primary studies that researchers conduct and publish. Second are the reviews of those studies that summarize and offer new interpretations built from and often extending beyond the primary studies. Third, there are the perceptions, conclusions, opinion, and interpretations that are shared informally that become part of the lore of field.

In composing a literature review, it is important to note that it is often this third layer of knowledge that is cited as "true" even though it often has only a loose relationship to the primary studies and secondary literature reviews. Given this, while literature reviews are designed to provide an overview and synthesis of pertinent sources you have explored, there are a number of approaches you could adopt depending upon the type of analysis underpinning your study.

Types of Literature Reviews

Argumentative Review

This form examines literature selectively in order to support or refute an argument, deeply imbedded assumption, or philosophical problem already established in the literature. The purpose is to develop a body of literature that establishes a contrarian viewpoint. Given the value-laden nature of some social science research [e.g., educational reform; immigration control], argumentative approaches to analyzing the literature can be a legitimate and important form of discourse. However, note that they can also introduce problems of bias when they are used to make summary claims of the sort found in systematic reviews [see below].

Integrative Review

Considered a form of research that reviews, critiques, and synthesizes representative literature on a topic in an integrated way such that new frameworks and perspectives on the topic are generated. The body of literature includes all studies that address related or identical hypotheses or research problems. A well-done integrative review meets the same standards as primary research in regard to clarity, rigor, and replication. This is the most common form of review in the social sciences.

Historical Review

Few things rest in isolation from historical precedent. Historical literature reviews focus on examining research throughout a period of time, often starting with the first time an issue, concept, theory, phenomena emerged in the literature, then tracing its evolution within the scholarship of a discipline. The purpose is to place research in a historical context to show familiarity with state-of-the-art developments and to identify the likely directions for future research.

Methodological Review

A review does not always focus on **what** someone said [findings], but **how** they came about saying what they say [method of analysis]. Reviewing methods of analysis provides a framework of understanding at different levels [i.e. those of theory, substantive fields, research approaches, and data collection and analysis techniques], how researchers draw upon a wide variety of knowledge ranging from the conceptual level to practical documents for use in fieldwork in the areas of ontological and epistemological consideration, quantitative and qualitative integration, sampling, interviewing, data collection, and data analysis. This approach helps highlight ethical issues which you should be aware of and consider as you go through your own study.

Systematic Review

This form consists of an overview of existing evidence pertinent to a clearly formulated research question, which uses pre-specified and standardized methods to identify and critically appraise relevant research, and to collect, report, and analyze data from the studies that are included in the review. Typically it focuses on a very specific empirical question, often posed in a cause-and-effect form, such as "To what extent does A contribute to B?"

Theoretical Review

The purpose of this form is to examine the corpus of theory that has accumulated in regard to an issue, concept, theory, phenomena. The theoretical literature review helps to establish what theories already exist, the relationships between them, to what degree the existing theories have been investigated, and to develop new hypotheses to be tested. Often this form is used to help establish a lack of appropriate theories or reveal that current theories are inadequate for explaining new or emerging research problems. The unit of analysis can focus on a theoretical concept or a whole theory or framework.

Structure and Writing Style
I. Thinking About Your Literature Review
The structure of a literature review should include the following:
- An overview of the subject, issue, or theory under consideration, along with the objectives of the literature review,
- Division of works under review into themes or categories [e.g. works that support a particular position, those against, and those offering alternative approaches entirely],
- An explanation of how each work is similar to and how it varies from the others,
- Conclusions as to which pieces are best considered in their argument, are most convincing of their opinions, and make the greatest contribution to the understanding and development of their area of research.

The critical evaluation of each work should consider:
- **Provenance** -- what are the author's credentials? Are the author's arguments supported by evidence [e.g. primary historical material, case studies, narratives, statistics, recent scientific findings]?
- **Methodology** -- were the techniques used to identify, gather, and analyze the data appropriate to addressing the research problem? Was the sample size appropriate? Were the results effectively interpreted and reported?
- **Objectivity** -- is the author's perspective even-handed or prejudicial? Is contrary data considered or is certain pertinent information ignored to prove the author's point?
- **Persuasiveness** -- which of the author's theses are most convincing or least convincing?
- **Value** -- are the author's arguments and conclusions convincing? Does the work ultimately contribute in any significant way to an understanding of the subject?

II. Development of the Literature Review
Four Stages
1. Problem formulation -- which topic or field is being examined and what are its component issues?
2. Literature search -- finding materials relevant to the subject being explored.
3. Data evaluation -- determining which literature makes a significant contribution to the understanding of the topic.

4. Analysis and interpretation -- discussing the findings and conclusions of pertinent literature.

Consider the following issues before writing the literature review: Clarify

If your assignment is not very specific about what form your literature review should take, seek clarification from your professor by asking these questions:

1. Roughly how many sources should I include?
2. What types of sources should I review (books, journal articles, websites; scholarly versus popular sources)?
3. Should I summarize, synthesize, or critique sources by discussing a common theme or issue?
4. Should I evaluate the sources?
5. Should I provide subheadings and other background information, such as definitions and/or a history?

Find Models

Use the exercise of reviewing the literature to examine how authors in your discipline or area of interest have composed their literature review sections. Read them to get a sense of the types of themes you might want to look for in your own research or to identify ways to organize your final review. The bibliography or reference section of sources you've already read are also excellent entry points into your own research.

Narrow the Topic

The narrower your topic, the easier it will be to limit the number of sources you need to read in order to obtain a good survey of relevant resources. Your professor will probably not expect you to read everything that's available about the topic, but you'll make your job easier if you first limit scope of the research problem. A good strategy is to begin by searching the HOMER catalog for books about the topic and review the table of contents for chapters that focuses on specific issues. You can also review the indexes of books to find references to specific issues that can serve as the focus of your research. For example, a book surveying the history of the Israeli-Palestinian conflict may include a chapter on the role Egypt has played in mediating the conflict, or look in the index for the pages where Egypt is mentioned in the text.

Consider Whether Your Sources are Current

Some disciplines require that you use information that is as current as possible. This is particularly true in disciplines in medicine and the sciences where research conducted becomes obsolete very quickly as new discoveries are made. However, when writing a review in the social sciences, a survey of the history of the literature may be required. In other words, a complete understanding the research problem requires you to deliberately examine how knowledge and perspectives have changed over time. Sort through other current bibliographies or literature reviews in the field to get a sense of what your discipline expects. You can also use this method to explore what is considered by scholars to be a "hot topic" and what is not.

III. Ways to Organize Your Literature Review

Chronological of Events

If your review follows the chronological method, you could write about the materials according to when they were published. This approach should only be followed if a clear path of research building on previous research can be identified and that these trends follow a clear chronological order of development. For example, a literature review that focuses on continuing research about the emergence of German economic power after the fall of the Soviet Union.

By Publication

Order your sources by publication chronology, then, only if the order demonstrates a more important trend. For instance, you could order a review of literature on environmental studies of brown fields if the progression revealed, for example, a change in the soil collection practices of the researchers who wrote and/or conducted the studies.

Thematic ["conceptual categories"]

Thematic reviews of literature are organized around a topic or issue, rather than the progression of time. However, progression of time may still be an important factor in a thematic review. For example, a review of the Internet's impact on American presidential politics could focus on the development of online political satire. While the study focuses on one topic, the Internet's impact on American presidential politics, it will still be organized chronologically reflecting technological developments in media. The only difference here between a "chronological" and a "thematic" approach is what is emphasized the most: the role of the Internet in presidential politics. Note however that more authentic thematic reviews tend to break away from chronological order. A review organized in this manner would shift between time periods within each section according to the point made.

Methodological

A methodological approach focuses on the methods utilized by the researcher. For the Internet in American presidential politics project, one methodological approach would be to look at cultural differences between the portrayal of American presidents on American, British, and French websites. Or the review might focus on the fundraising impact of the Internet on a particular political party. A methodological scope will influence either the types of documents in the review or the way in which these documents are discussed.

Other Sections of Your Literature Review

Once you've decided on the organizational method for your literature review, the sections you need to include in the paper should be easy to figure out because they arise from your organizational strategy. In other words, a chronological review would have subsections for each vital time period; a thematic review would have subtopics based upon factors that relate to the theme or issue. However, sometimes you may need to add additional sections that are necessary for your study, but do not fit in the organizational strategy of the body. What other sections you include in the body is up to you but include only what is necessary for the reader to locate your study within the larger scholarship framework.

Here are examples of other sections you may need to include depending on the type of review you write:

- **Current Situation**: information necessary to understand the topic or focus of the literature review.
- **History**: the chronological progression of the field, the literature, or an idea that is necessary to understand the literature review, if the body of the literature review is not already a chronology.
- **Selection Methods**: the criteria you used to select (and perhaps exclude) sources in your literature review. For instance, you might explain that your review includes only peer-reviewed articles and journals.
- **Standards**: the way in which you present your information.
- **Questions for Further Research**: What questions about the field has the review sparked? How will you further your research as a result of the review?

IV. Writing Your Literature Review

Once you've settled on how to organize your literature review, you're ready to write each section. When writing your review, keep in mind these issues.

Use Evidence

A literature review section is, in this sense, just like any other academic research paper. Your interpretation of the available sources must be backed up with evidence [citations] that demonstrates that what you are saying is valid.

Be Selective

Select only the most important points in each source to highlight in the review. The type of information you choose to mention should relate directly to the research problem, whether it is thematic, methodological, or chronological. Related items that provide additional information but that are not key to understanding the research problem can be included in a list of further readings.

Use Quotes Sparingly

Some short quotes are okay if you want to emphasize a point, or if what an author stated cannot be easily paraphrased. Sometimes you may need to quote certain terminology that was coined by the author, not common knowledge, or taken directly from the study. Do not use extensive quotes as a substitute for your own summary and interpretation of the literature.

Summarize and Synthesize

Remember to summarize and synthesize your sources within each thematic paragraph as well as throughout the review. Recapitulate important features of a research study, but then synthesize it by rephrasing the study's significance and relating it to your own work.

Keep Your Own Voice

While the literature review presents others' ideas, your voice [the writer's] should remain front and center. For example, weave references to other sources into what you are writing but maintain your own voice by starting and ending the paragraph with your own ideas and wording.

Use Caution When Paraphrasing

When paraphrasing a source that is not your own, be sure to represent the author's information or opinions accurately and in your own words. Even when paraphrasing an author's work, you still must provide a citation to that work.

V. Common Mistakes to Avoid

These are the most common mistakes made in reviewing social science research literature.

- Sources in your literature review do not clearly relate to the research problem;
- You do not take sufficient time to define and identify the most relevent sources to use in the literature review related to the research problem;
- Relies exclusively on secondary analytical sources rather than including relevant primary research studies or data;
- Uncritically accepts another researcher's findings and interpretations as valid, rather than examining critically all aspects of the research design and analysis;

- Does not describe the search procedures that were used in identifying the literature to review;
- Reports isolated statistical results rather than synthesizing them in chi-squared or meta-analytic methods; and,
- Only includes research that validates assumptions and does not consider contrary findings and alternative interpretations found in the literature.

1

Organizing Your Social Sciences Research Paper: Citation Tracking

Definition

Citation tracking refers to a method of measuring the impact of research studies and/or for identifying leading scholars in a particular discipline based upon a systematic analysis of who has cited a particular study, how often a specific research study has been cited by others, and by exploring what disciplines are represented by those subsequent citations.

Importance of...

Citation tracking can facilitate the review and evaluation of pertinent literature for the following reasons:

1. **It can be an effective way of using a highly cited "landmark" or influential article** to find more recent, related articles that cite the original work. It also can be an effective way of identifying important scholars in a particular field who have subsequently cited the work.

2. **It can be a useful means for evaluating a study's "impact"** within a particular discipline based upon the number of times a research study has been cited by others. A highly cited study may indicate that the research findings are unique, groundbreaking, or controversial in some way.

3. It can be an effective means of **determining the interdisciplinary value of a particular study** because you can identify the amount of subsequent citations to an article from publications in other disciplines or areas of study. Studies that have been cited in a variety

of disciplines is also a strong indication of the research study's overall impact thoughout the social sciences [and perhaps beyond].

When tracking citations, keep in mind the following points:

- **Authors do not always use the same name** throughout their careers so be sure you work from a complete and accurate list of an author's publications.
- **In the case of the <u>Web of Science</u> citation database**, it uses APA style for citing authors [last name and first initial only], so a J Smith could be John, Jeff, Jane, Julie, Jason, etc. Be sure to truncate the initial [adding an asterick *] to see a more complete list of authors, then locate a record on a topic you know the author writes about and click on that author to exclude articles written by other J Smith's. Fortunately, the database indexes more than the first author of a paper so if a second or third author has an uncommon name, you could search the unusal name instead of using an author's common name.
- **Citation services are primarily based on selected journal literature**. If the author is cited in books, foreign language periodicals, or non-scholarly publications, the usefulness of your citation analysis is limited. In addition, citation databases such as Web of Science rarely cover articles published in scholarly open-access journals [journals published freely on the web], although this is slowly changing. In this case, be sure to check the "cited by" references in **Google Scholar** as it often includes citations founds in other publications besides scholarly journals.
- **Pay attention to how recent the citations are when reviewing a particular study**. An article published in 1990 may have 130 total citations but if the most recent citation is from 2008, then this is an indication that the study's impact has faded or there is a lack of progress in the field [unlikely]. The absence of recent citations does not necessarily mean a study no longer has value, but it's a strong indication that more recent research has overtaken prior studies or that external factors have influenced scholars to focus on other areas of inquiry.

Resources for Tracking Citations
Databases/Search Engines
- **<u>Communication Source</u>** -- use the "Cited References" search to find out how many times a specific article or author has been cited in the database.

- **CSA Illumina Databases (PsycINFO, COMM Abstracts, Linguistics & Language Behavior, Sociological Abstracts** -- click on "advanced search" and choose the 'references' field from the drop-down menu.
- **Google Scholar** -- search results that have been "cited by" reference followed by a linked number [i.e., cited by 53] indicate subsequent citations to the record. Note that rResults can be inconsistent.
- **HeinOnline** -- includes a citation analysis tool which allows you to view the most cited law review articles. Search results include a "Cited by" link to a list of articles that cite that article or document.
- **JSTOR** -- select "article locator" and search by author name and/or parts of the title. Click on the article title to see the number of times cited in the database (on the right). Most current publications not included.
- **Proquest Research Library** -- click on "advanced search" and do a "Citation and Document Text Search." Find the author's name in footnotes by typing the author's last name.
- **Web of Knowledge** -- select "Cited Reference Search" to find articles that cite the work(s) of an author. The database uses APA style of last name and first initial (e.g., Odell J*). Be sure to truncate the initial by adding an asterick after the letter (e.g., R*) to see a complete list of authors. The database does index more than the first author of an article.

Journal Publishers
- **Cambridge University Press** -- there is no citation searching on this site per se, but you can enter name of full name of the author in "full text" text box to get results.
- **Elsevier ScienceDirect** -- click the "Search tab. Enter the name of the author and choose "References" from the drop-down menu.
- **Sage Premier** -- click on "advanced search" and select the "References" field from the drop-down box.
- **SpringerLink Journals** -- there is no citation searching on this site per se, but you can enter name of full name of the author in "full text" text box to get results.
- **Wiley InterScience** -- enter the name of the author and choose "References" from the drop-down menu.

2

Organizing Your Social Sciences Research Paper: Content Alert Services

Definition

In general, "alert services" refer to features included with scholarly databases or made available by journal publishers that allow you to be notified by email or text message when something of interest to you has been added to a database or published in a journal. Alert services can be set up to notify you about newly published resources on a specific topic or when new articles are published in a journal.

USC Libraries subscribe to a number of databases that make electronic alert services available to users. Three different types of alert services are:

1. **Table of contents alerts** -- updates of the table of contents of the most current issues of the journals you specify when signing up.
2. **Daily/weekly email alerts** -- alerts that notify subscribers of articles matching submitted topics. Alert frequencies vary depending on the publisher's database updates.
3. **Saved search alerts** -- emailed notifications of recent articles matching previously submitted searches.

Importance of...

While conducting a literature review, content alert services can be especially useful because:

1. They can alert you to new articles in journals of particular interest or that you know are most likely to publish research on the topic you are investigating.
2. Databases that index journals from a variety of different fields of study offer you multidisciplinary coverage of articles related to your topic of interest.
3. They can alert you to new "pre-published" research [essentially final drafts of articles] before they are distributed to libraries and subscribers.

NOTE: In order to sign up for an alert service, an email address is required along with a username and password that you create. Be sure you read the privacy policy carefully before signing up so that you avoid receiving unwanted spam and solicitations from publishers.

Journal Contents Alert Services

Multidisciplinary alert services that notify you when a new issue of a journal is published.

- **CiteULike** -- currently has details of over 13,000 journals. You can search or browse for journal titles, and then scan recent articles in these journals. If you know aboutt RSS feeds, you can get a CiteULike feed for each journal table of contents. Access to the full text will depend on institutional or personal subscriptions. Registration is free.
- **My Favorite Journals** -- this service allows you can select journals of interest from over 10,000 titles, and these are then added to 'My Favorite Journals', then you can select any of these favorites to view the latest Table of Contents. Access to the full text will depend on institutional or personal subscriptions. Registration is free.
- **ticTOCs** -- covers over 12,500 journal table of contents from more than 430 publishers. You can search for journal titles, view the latest table of contents for each journal, link to the full text of around 390,000 articles (where institutional or personal subscription allows), export table of content feeds to popular feedreaders, and select and save journal titles in order to view future table of contents (you need to register to ensure your 'MyTOCs' are permanently saved). Registration is free.

Procedures for setting up alert services from indexes and databases available from the USC Libraries.

- **CQ Researcher** -- log in or create a user profile. Select "Create New Alert" to customize your e-mail alerts. Use the "Start/Stop" action to start or stop receiving e-mail alerts you have saved in your account. Link:
- http://library.cqpress.com/xsite/profile.php?source=cqresearcher
- **CSA Illumina Database** -- click on the "Alerts" link located on the right hand side of the search page to login and create alerts. CSA social science databases subscribed to by USC include: <u>Avery Index to Architectural Periodicals</u>, <u>EconLit</u>, <u>ERIC</u>, <u>Index Islamicus</u>, <u>Linguistics and Language Behavior Abstracts</u>, <u>Pollution Abstracts</u>, <u>PsycINFO</u>, <u>Social Services Abstracts</u>, <u>Sociological Abstracts</u>, <u>Worldwide Political Science Abstracts</u>.
- **EBSCO databases** -- conduct a search in one of the Ebsco databases. Select Search History/Alerts, then go to: Save Searches. Log in to your account (or register) to Create or Edit Saved Search Alerts. EBSCO databases in the social sciences include: <u>AgeLine</u>, <u>America: History and Life</u>, <u>ATLA Religion Database</u>, <u>BusinessSource Complete</u>, <u>Communication and Mass Media Complete</u>, <u>Criminal Justice Abstracts</u>, <u>Environment Index</u>, <u>Historical Abstracts</u>, <u>LGBT Life</u>, <u>Public Administration Abstracts</u>, <u>Social Work Abstracts</u>, <u>Urban Studies Abstracts</u>, <u>Women's Studies International</u>.

- **Project MUSE** -- allows you to set up alerts by journal name or by subject area or both. You will need to set up an alerts account with a username and password and an email address. You can make selections for journal titles individually or with a mix of subject collections.
- **Web of Knowledge** -- register with an email and password. For detailed instructions on how to setup alerts for journal content and citations, click on "Tutorial" link on the opening web page and follow the steps to setup alerts.

3

Organizing Your Social Sciences Research Paper: Evaluating Sources

Importance of Evaluating Sources

Evaluating the authority, usefulness, and reliability of resources is a crucial step in developing a literature review that effectively covers pertinent research as well as demonstrating to the reader that you know what you're talking about. The process of evaluating scholarly materials also enhances your general skills and ability to:

1. Seek out alternate points of view and differing perspectives,
2. Identify possible bias in the work of others,
3. Distinguish between fact, fiction, and opinion,
4. Develop and strengthen your ability to distinguish between relevant and irrelevant content,
5. Draw cogent, well thought out conclusions, and
6. Synthesize information, extracting meaning through a deliberate process of interpretation and analysis.

Strategies for Critically Evaluating Sources

The act of thinking critically about the validity and reliability of a research resource generally involves asking yourself a series of questions about the quality of both the item and the content of that item.

Evaluating the Source

Inquiring about the Author

What are the author's credentials, such as, institutional affiliation [where he or she works], educational background, past writings, or experience? Is the book or article written on a topic in the author's area of expertise? Has your instructor mentioned this author? Have you seen the author's name cited in other sources or bibliographies? Is the author associated with a reputable institution or organization? What are the basic values or goals of that organization or institution?

Inquiring about the Date of Publication
When was the source published? Is the source current or out-of-date for your topic?

Inquiring about the Edition or Revision
Is this a first edition of this publication or not? Further editions usually indicate a source has been revised and updated to reflect changes in knowledge, to include prior omissions, and to better harmonize the contents with the intended needs of its readers. If you are using a web source, do the pages indicate last revision dates?

Inquiring about the Publisher
Note the publisher. If the source is published by a university press, it is likely to be scholarly. Although the fact that a publisher is reputable does not necessarily guarantee quality, it does show that the publisher has a high regard for the source being published [their reputation as an academic publisher relies on it].

Inquiring about the Title of Journal
Is this a scholarly or a popular journal? This distinction is important because it indicates different levels of complexity in conveying ideas and the intended readership.

Evaluating the Content

Intended Audience
What type of audience is the author addressing? Is the publication aimed at a specialized or a general audience? Is this source too elementary, too technical, too advanced, or just right for your needs?

Objectivity
Is the information covered considered to be fact, opinion, or propaganda? It is not always easy to separate fact from opinion. Facts can usually be verified; opinions, though they may be based on factual information, evolve from the interpretation of facts. Does the information appear to be valid and well-researched, or is it questionable and unsupported by evidence? Note errors or omissions. Are the ideas and arguments advanced more or less in line with other works you have read on the same topic?

Coverage
Does the work update or clarify prior knowledge, substantiate other materials you have read, or add new information? Does it extensively or only marginally cover your topic? Does it provide a balanced perspective? If the

item in question does not meet this criteria, you should review enough sources to obtain a variety of viewpoints.

Writing Style

Is the publication organized logically? Are the main points clearly presented? Do you find the text easy to read, or is it stilted or choppy? Is the author's argument repetitive?

Evaluative Reviews

In the case of books, locate critical reviews of the work in a database such as **Book Review Index**. Is the review positive? Is the book under review considered a valuable contribution to the field? Do reviewers agree on the value or attributes of the book or are there strong differences of opinion? Does the reviewer mention other books that might be better? If so, locate these sources for more information on your topic.

Strategies for Critically Evaluating Web Content

Web Content Requires Additional Methods of Evaluation

The principles that guide your evaluation of books, journal articles, reports, and other print materials also applies to web resources. However, the interactive and multimedia dynamics of online content increases the level of assessment you must apply to ensure that you are viewing a valid source of information.

Additional things to look for when considering using a web-based resource include:

- **Source of the content is stated** -- determine whether content original or borrowed, quoted, or imported from elsewhere. Note that content imported from another source via RSS feed can be difficult to identify, as this material can blend in with other content on the page without being appropriately labeled.
- **Don't be fooled by an attractive, professional-looking presentation** -- just because a site looks professional doesn't mean that it is. However, poorly organized web page designs or poorly written content is easy to recognize and can be a signal that you should carefully scrutinze the material.
- **Site is currently being maintained** -- check for posting or last revised dates.
- **Links are relevant and appropriate, and are in working order** -- a site with a lot of broken links is an indication of neglect and out-of-date content.
- **The site includes contact information** -- if a site is produced anonymously, you cannot verify the legitimacy of its creator.
- **Domain location in the site address (URL) is relevant to the focus of the material** [e.g., .edu for educational or research materials; .org for

profit or non-profit organizations; .gov for government sites]. Note that the domain is not necessarily a primary indicator of site content. For example, some authors post their content on blog or wiki platforms hosted by companies with .com addresses. Note as well that the tilde (~) usually indicates a personal page.

Detecting Author Bias

Bias, whether done intentionally or not, occurs when a statement reflects a partiality, preference, or prejudice for or against an object, person, place, or idea. Listed below are issues to look for when determining if the source is biased in some way.

1. **Distortion or Stretching the Facts** -- the act of making issues, problems, or arguments appear more extreme by using misinformation or exaggerated and/or imprecise language to describe research outcomes [e.g., "Everyone agreed the policy was a complete disaster." Who's everyone? And, how does one specifically define something as a disaster? Is there sufficient evidence to support such a broad statement?].

2. **Flawed Research Design** -- bias can enter the narrative as a result of a poorly designed study; this may include a claim or generalization about the findings based upon too small a sample, manipulating statistics, or failing to report contrary conclusions from other studies or failing to recognize negative results [results that do not support your hypothesis].

3. **Lack of Citations** -- refers to broad, declarative statements or information presented as fact that does not include proper citation to a source or to sources that support the researcher's position, or that such statements are not explicitly framed as the author's opinion.

4. **Misquoting a Source** -- this is when an author rewords, paraphrases, or manipulates a statement, the information about a source is incomplete, or a quote is presented in such a way that it misleads or conveys a false impression.

5. **Persuasive or Inflammatory Language** -- using words and phrases intended to elicit a positive or negative response from the reader or that leads the reader to arrive at a specific conclusion [e.g., referring to one side of an armed conflict as "terrorists" and the other side as "peace-loving"].

6. **Selective Facts** -- taking information out of context or selectively data-picking only information that supports the argument while omitting the rest.

NOTE: The act of determining bias in scholarly research is also an act of constant self-reflection. Everyone has biases. Therefore, it is important that you minimize the influence of your own biases by approaching the assessment of another person's research introspectively and with a degree of self-awareness.

4

Organizing Your Social Sciences Research Paper: Primary Sources

Definition

Primary sources were either created during the time period being studied or were created at a later date by a participant in the events being studied, such as, a childhood memoir. They are original documents [i.e., they are not about another document or account] and reflect the individual viewpoint of a participant or observer. Primary sources represent direct, uninterpreted records of the subject of your research study.

Value of Primary Sources

Primary sources enable you to get as close as possible to understanding the lived experiences of others and discovering what actually happened during an event. However, what constitutes a primary or secondary source depends on the context in which it is being used. For example, David McCullough's biography of John Adams could be a secondary source for a paper about John Adams, but a primary source for a paper about how various historians have interpreted the life of John Adams. **When in doubt, ask a librarian for assistance!**

Reviewing primary source material can be of value in improving your overall research paper because they:

1. Are original materials,
2. Were created from the time period involved,
3. Have not been filtered through interpretation or evaluation by others, and
4. Represent original thinking or experiences, reporting of a discovery, or the sharing of new information.

Examples of primary documents you could review as part of your overall study include:

- Artifacts [e.g. furniture or clothing, all from the time under study]
- Audio recordings [e.g. radio programs]
- Diaries

- Internet communications on email, listservs, blogs, Twitter, Facebook, and other social media platforms
- Interviews [e.g., oral histories, telephone, e-mail]
- Newspaper articles written at the time
- Original Documents [i.e. birth certificate, will, marriage license, trial transcript]
- Patents
- Personal correspondence [e.g., letters]
- Photographs
- Proceedings of meetings, conferences and symposia
- Records of organizations, government agencies [e.g. annual report, treaty, constitution, government document]
- Speeches
- Survey Research [e.g., market surveys, public opinion polls]
- Transcripts of radio and television programs
- Video recordings
- Works of art, architecture, literature, and music [e.g., paintings, sculptures, musical scores, buildings, novels, poems]

5

Organizing Your Social Sciences Research Paper: Secondary Sources

Definition

In the social sciences, a secondary source is usually a scholar book, journal article, or digital or print document that was created by someone who did not directly experience or participate in the events or conditions under investigation. Secondary sources are not evidence per se, but rather, provide an interpretation, analysis, or commentary derived from the content of primary source materials.

Value of Secondary Sources

To do research, you must cite research. Primary sources do not represent research per se, but only the artifacts from which most research is derived. Therefore, the majority of sources in a literature review are secondary sources that present research findings, analysis, and the evaluation of other researcher's works.

Reviewing secondary source material can be of value in improving your overall research paper because secondary sources facilitate the communication of what is known about a topic. This literature also helps you understand the level of uncertainty about what is currently known and what additional information is needed from further research. It is important to note, however, that secondary sources are not the subject of your analysis. Instead, they represent various opinions, interpretations, and arguments about the research problem you are investigating--opinions, interpretations, and arguments with which you may either agree or disagree with as part of your own analysis of the literature.

Examples of secondary sources you could review as part of your overall study include:
* Bibliographies [also considered tertiary]
* Biographical works
* Books, other than fiction and autobiography
* Commentaries, criticisms
* Dictionaries, Encyclopedias [also considered tertiary]
* Histories
* Journal articles [depending on the disciple can be primary]
* Magazine and newspaper articles [this distinction varies by discipline]
* Textbooks [also considered tertiary]
* Web site also considered primary]

6

Organizing Your Social Sciences Research Paper: Tiertiary Sources

Definition
A tertiary source consolidates and organizes primary and secondary sources together into one source in order to facilitate quick access to information. Tertiary sources are good starting points for research projects because they often extract the essential meaning or most important aspects of large amounts of information into a convenient format.

Value of Tertiary Sources
The distinctions between primary, secondary, and tertiary sources are frequently ambiguous depending upon the context in which an item is used. Some writers don't make the distinction between tertiary and secondary

because both types of materials do not represent original works [primary sources]. However, for the purposes of reviewing the literature, it is important to understand how tiertiary sources can contribute to your overall search for relevant information about the research problem.

Reviewing tertiary source material can be of value in improving your overall research paper because they:

- **Often compile factual information in one place.** Searching for the data in mutliple sources takes time [e.g., searching for names of heads of state in an almanac],
- **Lead the reader to additional sources.** For example, rather than citing in your literature review a long list of additional sources on a topic, you can simply cite to a comprehensive bibliography compiled by another researcher,
- **Distill large quantities of closely related information or data** [e.g., a statistical compendium], and
- **Often contain references and bibliographies** that can point you to key primary and secondary sources.

Examples of tiertiary sources you could review as part of your overall study include:

* Abstracts
* Almanacs
* Bibliographies [also considered secondary]
* Chronologies
* Dictionaries and encyclopedias [also considered secondary]
* Directories
* Fact books
* Handbooks
* Indexes, databases, search engines, and bibliographies used to locate primary and secondary sources
* Manuals
* Statistical compendiums
* Textbooks and course readers [may also be secondary]

Tertiary sources also include any type of user-contributed online resource such as Wikipedia.

Subject	Primary Source	Secondary Source	Tertiary Source
Business	NASDAQ stock quotes	Trade journal article on NASDAQ stock trends	*ABI/Inform* database
Communications	Transcript of television news program	Newspaper article about person interviewed on the news	Guide to television news programs
Economics	Bureau of the Census population datasets	Working paper on demographics in California and small business growth	*Statistical Abstract of California*
Education	Focus group interview of teachers	Journal article about teaching methods	Handbook of effective teaching methods
Environmental Studies	Fieldwork data measuring glacial melting	Book on the impact of climate change	World atlas
Geography	Archival maps of Los Angeles	Website of digitized maps	Finding aid of maps held at the Los Angeles Public Library
International Relations	Diplomatic cables between the United States and Japan	Journal article examining foreign relations between the U.S. and Japan	*Columbia International Affairs Online* database
Law	Testimony before Congress	Television news report on Congressional hearing	Congressional committee website
Political Science	*Public Papers of the Presidents of the United States*	Biography of a president	Encyclopedia about American presidents
Psychology	Clinical notes	Journal article about the psychological condition	*Mental Measurements Yearbook*
Social Work	Fieldwork	Research report on	Directory of prison

	observation of prison conditions	prison conditions	facilities
Sociology	Survey of adolescent addiction to alcohol	Journal article about alcoholism among young adults	Textbook on addictions

Comparison for Sources in Selected Social Science Disciplines

7

Organizing Your Social Sciences Research Paper: What Is Scholarly vs. Popular?

Scholarly Journals versus Popular Publications

Feature	SCHOLARLY JOURNAL	POPULAR MAGAZINE	BUSINESS TRADE PUBLICATION	NEWSPAPER
Author	Scholar or researcher in field with stated credentials and affiliations	Staff writer, journalist, often a generalist	Staff writer, journalist often with expertise in field	Staff writer, journalist, columnist
Sources and Documentation	All references cited; extensive bibliographies and/or footnotes	No formal list of references; original sources may be obscure	May refer to reports; no formal list of references	May refer to reports; no formal list of references
Editoral Process	Peer-reviewed by subject experts	Reviewed by a single editor	Reviewed by a single editor	Reviewed by a single editor
Purpose	To present research findings and expand knowledge in a discipline or field	To inform about current or popular events, issues or popular culture; to entertain	To identify trends in a specific field or commerce; report on an industry and its related products	To inform about current events and issues internationally, domestically, and locally

Structure of Articles	Long (10+ pages) articles with sections such as: Abstract, literature review, methodology, results, conclusion	Mix of short with in-depth articles on a variety of subjects	Industry specific articles of varying length	Brief articles, unless feature
Frequency of Publication	Annually, semi-annually, quarterly, or monthly	Monthly or weekly	Monthly or weekly	Weekly or daily
Titles	May contain the words "Journal of", "Review" or "Annals"; may contain the name of a discipline or field; may be lengthy	Straightforward; may address a general theme or subject	Usually short and catchy; may contain the name of a trade or industry	Usually reflects a geographic location
Print Appearance	Book-like; primarily black and white; mostly dense text with few graphics; no ads	Very glossy and colorful; high impact visuals and design; some feature columns; many full page advertisements	Glossy with high impact graphics; regularly scheduled featured columns; pictorials of industry events; industry-related advertisements	Newsprint; lengthy and brief articles; regularly scheduled featured columns
Language	Complex and academic; includes field-specific jargon	Simple and non-technical	Mix of jargon and technical	Mix of simple and sophisticated
Illustrations	Complex tables or graphs to display reseach data	Photos and colorful graphics for entertainment and visual impact	Colorful graphics and photos for emphasis	Photos and graphics for emphasis

Advertisements	Rare or none at all	Very frequent	Frequent, targeting a specific trade or industry	Frequent
Intended Audience	Scholars, academics, researchers, advanced students	General public	Industry members, professionals and stakeholders	General public, some with slant (for instance, *Wall Street Journal* for business people)

Below is a chart developed by the USC Libraries instruction team that can help you distinguish between a scholarly [a.k.a., peer-reviewed or academic] journal and a popular, **general** interest publication.

Organizing Your Social Sciences Research Paper: 6.The Methodology

Definition

The methods section describes the rationale for the application of specific procedures or techniques used to identify, select, and analyze information applied to understanding the research problem, thereby, allowing the reader to critically evaluate a study's overall validity and reliability. The methodology section of a research paper answers two main questions: How was the data collected or generated? And, how was it analyzed? The writing should be direct and precise and always written in the past tense.

Kallet, Richard H. "How to Write the Methods Section of a Research Paper." *Respiratory Care* 49 (October 2004): 1229-1232.

Importance of a Good Methodology Section

You must explain how you obtained and analyzed your results for the following reasons:

- Readers need to know how the data was obtained because the method you chose affects the findings and, by extension, how you likely interpreted them.
- Methodology is crucial for any branch of scholarship because an unreliable method produces unreliable results and, as a consequence, undermines the value of your interpretations of the findings.
- In most cases, there are a variety of different methods you can choose to investigate a research problem. The methodology section of your paper should clearly articulate the reasons why you chose a particular procedure or technique.
- The reader wants to know that the data was collected or generated in a way that is consistent with accepted practice in the field of study. For example, if you are using a multiple choice questionnaire,

readers need to know that it offered your respondents a reasonable range of answers to choose from.

- The method must be appropriate to fulfilling the overall aims of the study. For example, you need to ensure that you have a large enough sample size to be able to generalize and make recommendations based upon the findings.
- The methodology should discuss the problems that were anticipated and the steps you took to prevent them from occurring. For any problems that do arise, you must describe the ways in which they were minimized or why these problems do not impact in any meaningful way your interpretation of the findings.
- In the social and bahavioral sciences, it is important to always provide sufficient information to allow other researchers to adopt or replicate your methodology. This information is particularly important when a new method has been developed or an innovative use of an exisiting method is utilized.

Structure and Writing Style
I. Groups of Research Methods
There are two main groups of research methods in the social sciences:

1. The **empirical-analytical group** approaches the study of social sciences in a similar manner that researchers study the natural sciences. This type of research focuses on objective knowledge, research questions that can be answered yes or no, and operational definitions of variables to be measured. The empirical-analytical group employs deductive reasoning that uses existing theory as a foundation for formulating hypotheses that need to be tested. This approach is focused on explanation.

2. The **interpretative group of methods is focused on understanding phenomenon in a comprehensive, holistic way**. Interpretive methods focus on analytically disclosing the meaning-making practices of human subjects [the why, how, or by what means people do what they do], while showing how those practices arrange so that it can be used to generate observable outcomes. Interpretive methods allow you to recognize your connection to the phenomena under study but, because the interpretative group focuses more on subjective knowledge, it requires careful interpretation of variables.

II. Content
An effectively written methodology section should:

- **Introduce the overall methodological approach for investigating your research problem**. Is your study qualitative or quantitative or a combination of both (mixed method)? Are you going to take a special approach, such as action research, or a more neutral stance?
- **Indicate how the approach fits the overall research design**. Your methods should have a clear connection with your research problem. In other words, make sure that your methods will actually address the problem. One of the most common deficiencies found in research papers is that the proposed methodology is not suitable to achieving the stated objective of your paper.
- **Describe the specific methods of data collection you are going to use**, such as, surveys, interviews, questionnaires, observation, archival research. If you are analzying existing data, such as a data set or archival documents, describe how it was originally created or gathered and by whom.
- **Explain how you intend to analyze your results**. Will you use statistical analysis? Will you use specific theoretical perspectives to help you analyze a text or explain observed behaviors? Describe how you plan to obtain an accurate assessment of relationships, patterns, trends, distributions, and possible contradictions found in the data.
- **Provide background and a rationale for methodologies that are unfamiliar for your readers**. Very often in the social sciences, research problems and the methods for investigating them require more explanation/rationale than widely accepted rules governing the natural and physical sciences. Be clear and concise in your explanation.
- **Provide a justification for subject selection and sampling procedure**. For instance, if you propose to conduct interviews, how do you intend to select the sample population? If you are analyzing texts, which texts have you chosen, and why? If you are using statistics, why is this set of statistics being used? If other data sources exist, explain why the data you chose is most appropriate to addressing the research problem.
- **Describe potential limitations**. Are there any practical limitations that could affect your data collection? How will you attempt to control for potential confounding variables and errors? If your methodology may lead to problems you can anticipate, state this openly and show why

pursuing this methodology outweighs the risk of these problems cropping up.

NOTE: Once you have written all of the elements of the methods section, subsequent revisions should focus on how to present those elements as clearly and as logically as possibly. The description of how you prepared to study the research problem, how you gathered the data, and the protocol for analyzing the data should be organized chronologically. For clarity, when a large amount of detail must be presented, information should be presented in sub-sections according to topic.

III. Problems to Avoid

Irrelevant Detail

The methodology section of your paper should be thorough but to the point. Do not provide any background information that doesn't directly help the reader to understand why a particular method was chosen, how the data was gathered or obtained, and how it was analyzed.

Unnecessary Explanation of Basic Procedures

Remember that you are not writing a how-to guide about a particular method. You should make the assumption that readers possess a basic understanding of how to investigate the research problem on their own and, therefore, you do not have to go into great detail about specific methodological procedures. The focus should be on how you *applied a method*, not on the mechanics of *doing a method.*

NOTE: An exception to this rule is if you select an unconventional approach to doing the method; if this is the case, be sure to explain why this approach was chosen and how it enhances the overall research process.

Problem Blindness

It is almost a given that you will encounter problems when collecting or generating your data. Do not ignore these problems or pretend they did not occur. Often, documenting how you overcame obstacles can form an interesting part of the methodology. It demonstrates to the reader that you can provide a cogent rationale for the decisions you made to minimize the impact of any problems that arose.

Literature Review

Just as the literature review section of your paper provides an overview of sources you have examined while researching a particular topic, the methodology section should cite any sources that informed your choice and application of a particular method [i.e., the choice of a survey should include any citations to the works you used to help construct the survey].

It's More than Sources of Information!

A description of a research study's method should not be confused with a description of the sources of information. Such a list of sources is useful in itself, especially if it is accompanied by an explanation about the selection and use of the sources. The description of the project's methodology complements a list of sources in that it sets forth the organization and interpretation of information emanating from those sources.

1

Organizing Your Social Sciences Research Paper: Qualitative Methods

Definition

The word qualitative implies an emphasis on the qualities of entities and on processes and meanings that are not experimentally examined or measured [if measured at all] in terms of quantity, amount, intensity, or frequency. Qualitative researchers stress the socially constructed nature of reality, the intimate relationship between the researcher and what is studied, and the situational constraints that shape inquiry. Such researchers emphasize the value-laden nature of inquiry. They seek answers to questions that stress how social experience is created and given meaning. In contrast, quantitative studies emphasize the measurement and analysis of causal relationships between variables, not processes. Qualitative forms of inquiry are considered by many social and behavioral scientists to be as much a perspective on how to approach investigating a research problem as it is a method.

Characteristics of Qualitative Research

Below are the three key elements that define a qualitative research study and the applied forms each take in the investigation of a research problem.

The Design

- **Naturalistic** -- refers to studying real-world situations as they unfold naturally; nonmanipulative and noncontrolling; the researcher is open to whatever emerges [i.e., there is a lack of predetermined constraints on findings].
- **Emergent** -- acceptance of adapting inquiry as understanding deepens and/or situations change; the researcher avoids rigid designs that eliminate responding to opportunities to pursue new paths of discovery as they emerge.

- **Purposeful** -- cases for study [e.g., people, organizations, communities, cultures, events, critical incidences] are selected because they are "information rich" and illuminative. That is, they offer useful manifestations of the phenomenon of interest; sampling is aimed at insight about the phenomenon, not empirical generalization derived from a sample and applied to a population.

The Collection of Data

- **Data** -- observations yield a detailed, "thick description" [in-depth understanding]; interviews capture direct quotations about people's personal perspectives and lived experiences; often derived from carefully conducted case studies and review of material culture.
- **Personal experience and engagement** -- researcher has direct contact with and gets close to the people, situation, and phenomenon under investigation; the researcher's personal experiences and insights are an important part of the inquiry and critical to understanding the phenomenon.
- **Empathic neutrality** -- an empathic stance in working with study responents seeks vicarious understanding without judgment [neutrality] by showing openness, sensitivity, respect, awareness, and responsiveness; in observation, it means being fully present [mindfulness].
- **Dynamic systems** -- there is attention to process; assumes change is ongoing, whether the focus is on an individual, an organization, a community, or an entire culture, therefore, the researcher is mindful of and attentive to system and situationational dynamics.

The Analysis

- **Unique case orientation** -- assumes that each case is special and unique; the first level of analysis is being true to, respecting, and capturing the details of the individual cases being studied; cross-case analysis follows from and depends upon the quality of individual case studies.
- **Inductive analysis** -- immersion in the details and specifics of the data to discover important patterns, themes, and inter-relationships; begins by exploring, then confirming findings, guided by analytical principles rather than rules.
- **Holistic perspective** -- the whole phenomenon under study is understood as a complex system that is more than the sum of its parts; the focus is on complex interdependencies and system dynamics that cannot be reduced in any meaningful way to linear, cause and effect relationships and/or a few discrete variables.

- **Context sensitive** -- places findings in a social, historical, and temporal context; researcher is careful about [even dubious of] the possibility or meaningfulness of generalizations across time and space; emphasizes careful comparative case analyses and extrapolating patterns for possible transferability and adaptation in new settings.
- **Voice, perspective, and reflexivity** -- the qualitative methodologist owns and is reflective about her or his own voice and perspective; a credible voice conveys authenticity and trustworthiness; complete objectivity being impossible and pure subjectivity undermining credibility, the researcher's focus reflects a balance between understanding and depicting the world authentically in all its complexity and of being self-analytical, politically aware, and reflexive in consciousness.

Basic Research Design for Qualitative Studies

Unlike positivist or experimental research that utilizes a linear and one-directional sequence of design steps, there is considerable variation in how a qualitative research study is organized. In general, qualitative researchers attempt to describe and interpret human behavior based primarily on the words of selected individuals [a.k.a., "informants" or "respondents"] and/or through the interpretation of their material culture or occupied space. There is a reflexive process underpinning every stage of a qualitative study to ensure that researcher biases, presuppositions, and interpretations are clearly evident, thus ensuring that the reader is better able to interpret the overall validity of the research. According to Maxwell (2009), there are five, not necessarily ordered or sequential, components in qualitative research designs. How they are presented depends upon the research philosophy and theoretical framework of the study, the methods chosen, and the general assumptions underpinning the study.

Goals

Describe the central research problem being addressed but avoid describing any anticipated outcomes. Questions to ask yourself are: Why is your study worth doing? What issues do you want to clarify, and what practices and policies do you want it to influence? Why do you want to conduct this study, and why should the reader care about the results?

Conceptual Framework

Questions to ask yourself are: What do you think is going on with the issues, settings, or people you plan to study? What theories, beliefs, and prior research findings will guide or inform your research, and what literature, preliminary studies, and personal experiences will you draw upon for understanding the people or issues you are studying? Note to not only report the results of other studies in your review of the literature, but note the methods used as well. If appropriate, describe why earlier studies using quantitative methods were inadequate in addressing the research problem.

Research Questions

Usually there is a research problem that frames your qualitative study and that influences your decision about what methods to use, but qualitative designs generally lack an accompanying hypothesis or set of assumptions because the findings are emergent and unpredictable. In this context, more specific research questions are generally the result of an interactive design process rather than the starting point for that process. Questions to ask yourself are: What do you specifically want to learn or understand by conducting this study? What do you not know about the things you are studying that you want to learn? What questions will your research attempt to answer, and how are these questions related to one another?

Methods

Structured approaches to applying a method or methods to your study help to ensure that there is comparability of data across sources and researchers and, thus, they can be useful in answering questions that deal with differences between phenomena and the explanation for these differences [variance questions]. An unstructured approach allows the researcher to focus on the particular phenomena studied. This facilitates an understanding of the processes that led to specific outcomes, trading generalizability and comparability for internal validity and contextual and evaluative understanding. Questions to ask yourself are: What will you actually do in conducting this study? What approaches and techniques will you use to collect and analyze your data, and how do these constitute an integrated strategy?

Validity

In contrast to quantitative studies where the goal is to design, in advance, "controls" such as formal comparisons, sampling strategies, or statistical manipulations to address anticipated and unanticipated threats to validity, qualitative researchers must attempt to rule out most threats to validity after the research has begun by relying on evidence collected during the research process itself in order to effectively argue that any alternative explanations for a phenomenon are implausible. Questions to ask yourself are: How might your results and conclusions be wrong? What are the plausible alternative interpretations and validity threats to these, and how will you deal with these? How can the data that you have, or that you could potentially collect, support or challenge your ideas about what's going on? Why should we believe your results?

Conclusion
Although Maxwell does not mention a conclusion as one of the components of a qualitative research design, you should formally conclude your study. Briefly reiterate the goals of your study and the ways in which your research addressed them. Discuss the benefits of your study and how stakeholders can use your results. Also, note the limitations of your study and, if appropriate, place them in the context of areas in need of further research.

Strengths of Using Qualitative Methods
The advantage of using qualitative methods is that they generate rich, detailed data that leave the participants' perspectives intact and provide multiple contexts for understanding the phenomenon under study. In this way, qualitative research can be used to vividly demonstrate phenomena or to conduct cross-case comparisons and analysis of individuals or groups.
Among the specific strengths of using qualitative methods to study social science research problems is the ability to:
- Obtain a more realistic view of the lived world that cannot be understood or experienced in numerical data and statistical analysis;
- Provide the researcher with the perspective of the participants of the study through immersion in a culture or situation and as a result of direct interaction with them;
- Allow the researcher to describe existing phenomena and current situations;
- Develop flexible ways to perform data collection, subsequent analysis, and interpretation of collected information;
- Yield results that can be helpful in pioneering new ways of understanding;
- Respond to changes that occur while conducting the study]e.g., extended fieldwork or observation] and offer the flexibility to shift the focus of the research as a result;
- Provide a holistic view of the phenomena under investigation;
- Respond to local situations, conditions, and needs of participants;
- Interact with the research subjects in their own language and on their own terms; and,

- Create a descriptive capability based on primary and unstructured data.

Limitations of Using Qualitative Methods

It is very much true that most of the limitations you find in using qualitative research techniques also reflect their inherent strengths. For example, small sample sizes help you investigate research problems in a comprehensive and in-depth manner. However, small sample sizes undermine opportunities to draw useful generalizations from, or to make broad policy recommendations based upon, the findings. Additionally, as the primary instrument of investigation, qualitative researchers are often imbedded in the cultures and experiences of others. However, cultural imbeddedness increases the opportunity for bias to enter into the way data is gathered, interpreted, and reported.

Some specific limitations associated with using qualitative methods to study research problems in the social sciences include the following:

- Drifting away from the original objectives of the study in response to the changing nature of the context under which the research is conducted;
- Arriving at different conclusions based on the same information depending on the personal characteristics of the researcher;
- Replicatication of a study is very difficult;
- Research using human subjects increases the chance of ethical dilemmas that undermine the overall validity of the study;
- An inability to investigate causality between different research phenomena;
- Difficulty in explaining differences in the quality and quantity of information obtained from different respondents and arriving at different, non-consistent conclusions;
- Data gathering and analysis is often time consuming and/or expensive;
- Requires a high level of experience from the researcher to obtain the targeted information from the respondent;
- May lack consistency and reliability because the researcher can employ different probing techniques and the respondent can choose to tell some particular stories and ignore others; and,
- Generation of a signficant amount of data that cannot be randomized into managable parts for analysis.

2

Organizing Your Social Sciences Research Paper: Quantitative Methods

Definition

Quantitative methods emphasize objective measurements and the statistical, mathematical, or numerical analysis of data collected through polls, questionnaires, and surveys, or by manipulating pre-existing statistical data using computational techniques. Quantitative research focuses on gathering numerical data and generalizing it across groups of people or to explain a particular phenomenon.

Characteristics of Quantitative Research

Your goal in conducting quantitative research study is to determine the relationship between one thing [an independent variable] and another [a dependent or outcome variable] within a population. Quantitative research designs are either **descriptive** [subjects usually measured once] or **experimental** [subjects measured before and after a treatment]. A descriptive study establishes only associations between variables; an experimental study establishes causality.

Quantitative research deals in numbers, logic, and an objective stance. Quantitative research focuses on numeric and unchanging data and detailed, convergent reasoning rather than divergent reasoning [i.e., the generation of a variety of ideas about a research problem in a spontaneous, free-flowing manner].

Its main characteristics are:

- The data is usually gathered using structured research instruments.
- The results are based on larger sample sizes that are representative of the population.
- The research study can usually be replicated or repeated, given its high reliability.
- Researcher has a clearly defined research question to which objective answers are sought.
- All aspects of the study are carefully designed before data is collected.
- Data are in the form of numbers and statistics, often arranged in tables, charts, figures, or other non-textual forms.

- Project can be used to generalize concepts more widely, predict future results, or investigate causal relationships.
- Researcher uses tools, such as questionnaires or computer software, to collect numerical data.

The overarching aim of a quantitative research study is to classify features, count them, and construct statistical models in an attempt to explain what is observed.

Things to keep in mind when reporting the results of a study using quantiative methods:

1. **Explain the data collected** and their statistical treatment as well as all relevant results in relation to the research problem you are investigating. Interpretation of results is not appropriate in this section.

2. **Report unanticipated events** that occurred during your data collection. Explain how the actual analysis differs from the planned analysis. Explain your handling of missing data and why any missing data does not undermine the validity of your analysis.

3. **Explain the techniques** you used to "clean" your data set.

4. **Choose a minimally sufficient statistical procedure**; provide a rationale for its use and a reference for it. Specify any computer programs used.

5. **Describe the assumptions** for each procedure and the steps you took to ensure that they were not violated.

6. **When using inferential statistics**, provide the descriptive statistics, confidence intervals, and sample sizes for each variable as well as the value of the test statistic, its direction, the degrees of freedom, and the significance level [report the actual p value].

7. **Avoid inferring causality**, particularly in nonrandomized designs or without further experimentation.

8. **Use tables to provide exact values**; use figures to convey global effects. Keep figures small in size; include graphic representations of confidence intervals whenever possible.

9. **Always tell the reader what to look for in tables and figures**.

NOTE: When using pre-existing statistical data gathered and made available by anyone other than yourself [e.g., government agency], you still must report on the methods that were used to gather the data and describe any missing data that exists and, if there is any, provide a clear explanation why the missing datat does not undermine the validity of your final analysis.

Basic Research Design for Quantitative Studies

Before designing a quantitative research study, you must decide whether it will be descriptive or experimental because this will dictate how you gather, analyze, and interpret the results. A descriptive study is governed by the following rules: subjects are generally measured once; the intention is to only establish associations between variables; and, the study may include a sample population of hundreds or thousands of subjects to ensure that a valid estimate of a generalized relationship between variables has been obtained. An experimental design includes subjects measured before and after a particular treatment, the sample population may be very small and purposefully chosen, and it is intended to establish causality between variables.

Introduction

The introduction to a quantitative study is usually written in the present tense and from the third person point of view. It covers the following information:

- **Identifies the research problem** -- as with any academic study, you must state clearly and concisely the research problem being investigated.
- **Reviews the literature** -- review scholarship on the topic, synthesizing key themes and, if necessary, noting studies that have used similar methods of inquiry and analysis. Note where key gaps exist and how your study helps to fill these gaps or clarifies existing knowledge.
- **Describes the theoretical framework** -- provide an outline of the theory or hypothesis underpinning your study. If necessary, define unfamiliar or complex terms, concepts, or ideas and provide the appropriate background information to place the research problem in proper context [e.g., historical, cultural, economic, etc.].

Methodology

The methods section of a quantitative study should describe how each objective of your study will be achieved. Be sure to provide enough detail to enable the reader can make an informed assessment of the methods being used to obtain results associated with the research problem. The methods section should be presented in the past tense.

- **Study population and sampling** -- where did the data come from; how robust is it; note where gaps exist or what was excluded. Note the procedures used for their selection;
- **Data collection** – describe the tools and methods used to collect information and identify the variables being measured; describe the methods used to obtain the data; and, note if the data was pre-existing [i.e., government data] or you gathered it yourself. If you

gathered it yourself, describe what type of instrument you used and why. Note that no data set is perfect--describe any limitations in methods of gathering data.

- **Data analysis** -- describe the procedures for processing and analyzing the data. If appropriate, describe the specific instruments of analysis used to study each research objective, including mathematical techniques and the type of computer software used to manipulate the data.

Results

The finding of your study should be written objectively and in a succinct and precise format. In quantitative studies, it is common to use graphs, tables, charts, and other non-textual elements to help the reader understand the data. Make sure that non-textual elements do not stand in isolation from the text but are being used to supplement the overall description of the results and to help clarify key points being made. Further information about how to effectively present data using charts and graphs can be found **here**.

- **Statistical analysis** -- how did you analyze the data? What were the key findings from the data? The findings should be present in a logical, sequential order. Describe but do not interpret these trends or negative results; save that for the discussion section. The results should be presented in the past tense.

Discussion

Discussions should be analytic, logical, and comprehensive. The discussion should meld together your findings in relation to those identified in the literature review, and placed within the context of the theoretical framework underpinning the study. The discussion should be presented in the present tense.

- **Interpretation of results** -- reiterate the research problem being investigated and compare and contrast the findings with the research questions underlying the study. Did they affirm predicted outcomes or did the data refute it?
- **Description of trends, comparison of groups, or relationships among variables** -- describe any trends that emerged from your analysis and explain all unanticipated and statistical insignificant findings.
- **Discussion of implications** – what is the meaning of your results? Highlight key findings based on the overall results and note findings that you believe are important. How have the results helped fill gaps in understanding the research problem?

- **Limitations** -- describe any limitations or unavoidable bias in your study and, if necessary, note why these limitations did not inhibit effective interpretation of the results.

Conclusion

End your study by to summarizing the topic and provide a final comment and assessment of the study.

- **Summary of findings** – synthesize the answers to your research questions. Do not report any statistical data here; just provide a narrative summary of the key findings and describe what was learned that you did not know before conducting the study.
- **Recommendations** – if appropriate to the aim of the assignment, tie key findings with policy recommendations or actions to be taken in practice.
- **Future research** – note the need for future research linked to your study's limitations or to any remaining gaps in the literature that were not addressed in your study.

Strengths of Using Quantitative Methods

Quantitative researchers try to recognize and isolate specific variables contained within the study framework, seek correlation, relationships and causality, and attempt to control the environment in which the data is collected to avoid the risk of variables, other than the one being studied, accounting for the relationships identified.

Among the specific strengths of using quantitative methods to study social science research problems:

- Allows for a broader study, involving a greater number of subjects, and enhancing the generalization of the results;
- Allows for greater objectivity and accuracy of results. Generally, quantitative methods are designed to provide summaries of data that support generalizations about the phenomenon under study. In order to accomplish this, quantitative research usually involves few variables and many cases, and employs prescribed procedures to ensure validity and reliability;
- Applying well-establshed standards means that the research can be replicated, and then analyzed and compared with similar studies;
- You can summarize vast sources of information and make comparisons across categories and over time; and,
- Personal bias can be avoided by keeping a 'distance' from participating subjects and using accepted computational techniques.

Limitations of Using Quantiative Methods

Quantitative methods presume to have an objective approach to studying research problems, where data is controlled and measured, to address the accumulation of facts, and to determine the causes of behavior. As a consequence, the results of quantitative research may be statistically significant but are often humanly insignificant.

Some specific limitations associated with using quantitative methods to study research problems in the social sciences include:

- Quantitative data is more efficient and able to test hypotheses, but may miss contextual detail;
- Uses a static and rigid approach and so employs an inflexible process of discovery;
- The development of standard questions by researchers can lead to "structural bias" and false representation, where the data actually reflects the view of the researcher instead of the participating subject;
- Results provide less detail on behavior, attitudes, and motivation;
- Researcher may collect a much narrower and sometimes superficial dataset;
- Results are limited as they provide numerical descriptions rather than detailed narrative and generally provide less elaborate accounts of human perception;
- The research is often carried out in an unnatural, artificial environment so that a level of control can be applied to the exercise. This level of control might not normally be in place in the real world thus yielding "laboratory results" as opposed to "real world results"; and,
- Preset answers will not necessarily reflect how people really feel about a subject and, in some cases, might just be the closest match to the preconceived hypothesis.

Organizing Your Social Sciences Research Paper: 7. The Results

Definition

The results section of the research paper is where you report the findings of your study based upon the methodology [or methodologies] you applied to gather information. The results section should simply state the findings of the research arranged in a logical sequence without bias or interpretation. The results section should always be written in the past tense. A section describing results [a.k.a., "findings"] is particularly necessary if your paper includes data generated from your own research.

Importance of a Good Results Section

When formulating the results section, it's important to remember that the results of a study do not prove anything. Findings can only confirm or reject the hypothesis underpinning your study. However, the act of articulating the results helps you to understand the problem from within, to break it into pieces, and to view the research problem from various perspectives.

The page length of this section is set by the amount and types of data to be reported. Be concise, using non-textual elements appropriately, such as figures and tables, to present results more effectively. In deciding what data to describe in your results section, you must clearly distinguish information that would normally be included in a research paper from any raw data or other content that could be included as an appendix. In general, unsummerized raw data should not be included in the main text of your paper unless requested to do so by your professor.

Avoid providing data that is not critical to answering the research question. The background information you described in the introduction section should provide the reader with any additional context or explanation needed to understand the results. A good strategy is to always re-read the background section of your paper after you have written up your results to ensure that the reader has enough context to understand the results [and, later, how you interpreted the results in the discussion section of your paper].

Structure and Writing Style
I. Organization and Approach

For most research paper formats, there are two possible ways of presenting and organizing the results. Both approaches are appropriate in how you report finding in the social sciences, but use only one or the other.

1. **Present a synopsis of the results followed by an explanation of key findings**. For example, you may have noticed an unusual correlation between two variables during the analysis of your findings. It is correct to point this out in the results section. However, speculating as to why this correlation exists, and offering a hypothesis about what may be happening, belongs in the discussion section of your paper.

2. **Present a result and then explain it, before presenting the next result then explaining it, and so on**. This is more common in longer papers because it helps the reader to better understand each finding. In this model, it is helpful to provide a brief conclusion that ties each of the findings together and provides a narrative bridge to the discussion section of the your paper.

NOTE: The discussion section that follows with an interpretation and description of the significance of your results should utilize the same approach you used in presenting and organizing the results [i.e., a thorough explanation of the results or a sequential description and explanation of each finding].

II. Content

In general, the content of your results section should include the following elements:

1. An introductory context for understanding the results by restating the research problem underpinning your study.

2. A summary of your key findings arranged in a logical sequence that generally follows your methodology section.

3. Inclusion of non-textual elements, such as, figures, charts, photos, maps, tables, etc. to further illustrate key findings, if appropriate.

4. A systematic description of your results, highlighting for the reader observations that are most relevant to the topic under investigation [remember that not all results that emerge from the methodology used to gather the data may be relevant].

5. Use of the past tense when referring to your results.
6. The page length of your results section is guided by the amount and types of data to be reported. However, focus only on findings that are important and related to addressing the research problem.

III. Problems to Avoid
When writing the results section, avoid doing the following:
1. **Discussing or interpreting your results**. Save all this for the next section of your paper, although where appropriate, you should compare or contrast specific results to those found in other studies [e.g., "Similar to Smith [1990], one of the findings of this study is the strong correlation between motivation and academic achievement...."].
2. **Reporting background information or attempting to explain your findings.** This should have been done in your Introduction section, but don't panic! Often the results of a study point to the need for additional background information or to explain the topic further, so don't think you did something wrong. Revise your introduction as needed.
3. **Ignoring negative results**. If some of your results fail to support your hypothesis, do not ignore them. Document them, then state in your discussion section why you believe a negative result emerged from your study. Note that negative results, and how you handle them, offer you the opportunity to write a more engaging discussion section, therefore, don't be afraid to highlight them.
4. **Including raw data or intermediate calculations**. Ask your professor if you need to include any raw data generated by your study, such as transcripts from interviews or data files. If raw data is to be included, place it in an appendix or set of appendices that are referred to in the text.
5. **Be as factual and concise as possible in reporting your findings**. Do not use phrases that are vague or non-specific, such as, "appeared to be greater or lesser than..." or "demonstrates promising trends that...."
6. **Presenting the same data or repeating the same information more than once**. If it is important to highlight a particular finding, you will have an opportunity to do that in the discussion section.
7. **Confusing figures with tables**. Be sure to properly label any non-textual elements in your paper. Don't call a chart an illustration or a figure a table. If you are not sure, **go here**.

1

Organizing Your Social Sciences Research Paper: Using Non-Textual Elements

Definitions of Common Non-Textual Elements

Chart -- see "graph."

Diagram -- a drawing that illustrates or visually explains a thing or idea by outlining its component parts and the relationships among them. Also a line drawing, made to accompany and illustrate a geometrical theorem, mathematical demonstration, etc.

Figure -- a form bounded by three or more lines; one or more digits or numerical symbols representing a number.

Flowchart -- a pictorial summary [graphical algorithm] of the decisions and flows [movement of information] that make up a procedure or process from beginning to end. Also called flow diagram, flow process chart, or network diagram.

Graph -- a two-dimensional drawing showing a relationship [usually between two set of numbers] by means of a line, curve, a series of bars, or other symbols. Typically, an independent variable is represented on the horizontal line (X-axis) and an dependent variable on the vertical line (Y-axis). The perpendicular axis intersect at a point called origin, and are calibrated in the units of the quantities represented. Though a graph usually has four quadrants representing the positive and negative values of the variables, usually only the north-east quadrant is shown when the negative values do not exist or are of no interest. Often used interchangeably with the term "chart."

Histogram -- step-column chart that displays a summary of the variations in (frequency distribution of) quantities [called Classes] that fall within certain lower and upper limits in a set of data. Classes are measured on the horizontal ('X') axis, and the number of times they occur [or the percentages of their occurrences] are measured on the vertical ('Y') axis. To construct a histogram, rectangles or blocks are drawn on the x-axis [without any spaces between them] whose areas are proportional to the classes they represent. Histograms [and histographs] are used commonly where the subject item is discrete (such as the number of students in a school) instead of being continuous [such as the variations in their heights]. Also called frequency diagram, a histogram is usually preferred over a histograph where the number of classes is less than eight.

Illustration -- a visual representation [e.g., picture or diagram] that is used to make a subject in a paper more pleasing or easier to understand.

Map -- a visual representation of an area. It is considered to be a symbolic depiction highlighting relationships between elements of that space such as objects, regions, and themes. Examples of types include climate, economic, resource, physical, political, road, and topographic maps.

Pictograph -- visual presentation of data using icons, pictures, symbols, etc., in place of or in addition to common graph elements [bars, lines, points]. Pictographs use relative sizes or repetitions of the same icon, picture, or symbol to show comparison. Also called a pictogram, pictorial chart, pictorial graph, or picture graph.

Symbol -- Mark, sign, or word that indicates, signifies, or is understood as representing an idea, object, or relationship.

Table -- an orderly arrangement of quantitative data in columns and rows. Also called a "matrix."

Importance of Using Non-Textual Elements
There are a variety of reasons for including non-textual elements in your paper. Among them are:

1. **A picture is worth a thousand words**. Embedding a chart, illustration, table, graph, map, photograph, or other non-textual element into your research paper can bring added clarity to a study because it provides a clean, concise way to report findings that would otherwise take several long [and boring] paragraphs to describe.

2. **Non-textual elements are useful tools for summarizing information**, especially when you have a great deal of data to present. Non-textual elements help the reader grasp a large amount of data quickly and in an orderly fashion.

3. **Non-textual elements help you highlight important pieces of information without breaking up the narrative flow of your paper.** Illustrations, photographs, maps, and the like can be used as a quick reference to information that helps to highlight key issues found in the text. For example, a street map showing the distribution of health care facilities can be included in a larger study documenting the struggles of poor families to find adequate health care.

4. **Non-textual elements are visually engaging.** Using a chart or photograph, for example, can help enhance the overall presentation of your research and provide a way to stimulate a reader's interest in the study.

Structure and Writing Style

Use non-textual elements, such as figures, tables, graphs, maps, photographs, etc., to support your key findings. Readers should be able to understand non-textual elements on their own without having to refer to the text to understand the data being presented. Reference to a non-textual element in the text of your paper should focus on describing its significance in relation to the research problem or the topic being discussed.

Non-textual elements must have neat, legible labels, be simple, and have detailed captions that are written in complete sentences and that fully explain the item without forcing the reader to refer to the text. Conversely, the reader should not have to refer back and forth from the text to the elements to understand the paper.

General rules about using non-textual elements in your research paper

- Each non-textual element must have a short, descriptive title, numbered consecutively and complete with a heading [e.g., Table 1. National Sales Activity from 2009-2014].
- Decide on a suitable font and caption format and use it consistently throughout your paper.
- Either place figures, tables, charts, etc. within the text of the result being described, or refer to them in an appendix--do one or the other but never both.
- You should explicitly reference the number of the figures, tables, graphs, etc. in the text [i.e., "Table 6 shows..."]. Avoid expressions like, "in the chart on the following page" or "in the table below."
- If you choose to place non-textual elements within the paper, they should be positioned as close as possible to where it is first mentioned in the text.
- If you place non-textual elements in an appendix, make sure they are clearly distinguished from any raw data.
- Each non-textual element must be commented on and its relevance and significance explained in relation to the research problem.
- All non-textual elements should have a consistent look about them. This can be achieved by the following do's and don'ts
  - do use a box or frame to surround the element.
  - do not use a different text font to that used in the body of the work [e.g., Ariel vs. New Times Roman].
  - do use small caps when formatting headings.
  - do not use fancy fonts.
- If the non-textual element within the text is not adapted from another source but totally your own creation, take credit for your work and say so! Otherwise, you must cite where you found the data. You

must also cite the source even if you reorganize or rearrange the data.

- You may refer to non-textual elements by using parentheses with or without the verb "see" (i.e., "see Table 1"). However, it is important to be consistent with whichever choice you make.

References to non-textual elements are generally put in parentheses, e.g. "(see Figure 1)" or "(Chart 2)" because this information is generally supplementary to the results themselves; most of the text should focus on highlighting key findings.

NOTE: Do not overuse non-textual elements! Include them sparingly and only in cases where they are an effective means for enhancing and/or supplementing information already described in your paper. Using too many non-textual elements disrupts the narrative flow of your paper, making it more difficult for the reader to synthesize and interpret your overall research. If you have to use a lot of non-textual elements, consider organizing them in an appendix.

ANOTHER NOTE: Excel and other computer programs are capable of creating very elaborate, colorful, and dramatic looking non-textual elements. However, be careful not to let aesthetics and artistry overwhelm the message you are trying to convey to the reader. Use these features only to help enhance the reader's understanding of the information being presented.

Organizing Your Social Sciences Research Paper:8. The Discussion

Definition

The purpose of the discussion is to interpret and describe the significance of your findings in light of what was already known about the research problem being investigated, and to explain any new understanding or fresh insights about the problem after you've taken the findings into consideration. The discussion will always connect to the introduction by way of the research questions or hypotheses you posed and the literature you reviewed, but it does not simply repeat or rearrange the introduction; the discussion should always explain how your study has moved the reader's understanding of the research problem forward from where you left them at the end of the introduction.

Importance of a Good Discussion

This section is often considered the most important part of your research paper because this is where you:

1. Most effectively demonstrates your ability as a researcher to think critically about an issue, to develop creative solutions to problems based upon a logical synthesis of the findings, and to formulate a deeper, more profound understanding of the research problem under investigation.

2. Present the underlying meaning of your research, note possible implications in other areas of study, and explore possible improvements that can be made in order to further develop the concerns of your research.

3. Highlight the importance of your study and how it may be able to contribute to and/or fill existing gaps in the field. If appropriate, the discussion section is also where you state how the findings from your study revealed new gaps in the literature that had not been previously exposed or adequately described.

4. Engage the reader in thinking critically about issues based upon an evidence-based interpretation of findings; it is not governed strictly by objective reporting of information.

Structure and Writing Style
I. General Rules
These are the general rules you should adopt when composing your discussion of the results:

- Do not be verbose or repetitive
- Be concise and make your points clearly
- Avoid using jargon
- Follow a logical stream of thought
- Use the present verb tense, especially for established facts; however, refer to specific works or prior studies in the past tense
- If needed, use subheadings to help organize your discussion or to group your interpretations into themes

II. The Content
The content of the discussion section of your paper most often includes:

1. **Explanation of results**: comment on whether or not the results were expected and present explanations for each set of results; go into greater depth when explaining findings that were unexpected or especially profound. If appropriate, note any unusual or unanticipated patterns or trends that emerged from your results and explain their meaning.
2. **References to previous research**: compare your results with the findings from other studies, or use the studies to support a claim. This can include re-visiting key sources already cited in your literature review section, or, save them to cite later in the discussion section if they are more important to compare with your results than being part of the general research you used to provide context and background information.
3. **Deduction**: a claim for how the results can be applied more generally. For example, describing lessons learned, proposing recommendations that can help improve a situation, or recommending best practices.
4. **Hypothesis**: a more general claim or possible conclusion arising from the results [which may be proved or disproved in subsequent research].

III. Organization and Structure
Keep the following sequential points in mind as you organize and write the discussion section of your paper:

1. Think of your discussion as an inverted pyramid. Organize the discussion from the general to the specific, linking your findings to the literature, then to theory, then to practice [if appropriate].

2. Use the same key terms, narrative style, and verb tense [present] that you used when when describing the research problem in your introduction.

3. Begin by briefly re-stating the research problem you were investigating and answer all of the research questions underpinning the problem that you posed in the introduction.

4. Describe the patterns, principles, and relationships shown by each major findings and place them in proper perspective. The sequence of this information is important; first state the answer, then the relevant results, then cite the work of others. If appropriate, refer the reader to a figure or table to help enhance the interpretation of the data. The order of interpreting each major finding should be in the same order as they were described in your results section.

5. A good discussion section includes analysis of any unexpected findings. This part of the discussion should begin with a description of any unanticipated findings, followed by a brief interpretation as to why you believe it appeared and, if necessary, its possible significance in relation to the overall study. If more than one unexpected finding emerged during the study, describe each them in the order they appeared as you gathered or analyzed the data.

6. Before concluding the discussion, identify potential limitations and weaknesses. Comment on their relative importance in relation to your overall interpretation of the results and, if necessary, note how they may affect the validity of your findings. Avoid using an apologetic tone; however, be honest and self-critical [e.g., in retrospective, you wish you had included a particular question on a survey instrument].

7. The discussion section should end with a concise summary of the principal implications of the findings regardless of statistical significance. Give a brief explaination about why you believe the findings and conclusions of your study are important and how they support broader knowledge or understanding of the research problem. This can be followed by any recommendations for further research. However, do not offer recommendations which could have been easily addressed within the study. This would demonstrate to the reader that you have inadequately examined and interpreted the data.

IV. Overall Objectives

The objectives of your discussion section should include the following:

I. Reiterate the Research Problem/State the Major Findings

Briefly reiterate for your readers the research problem or problems you are investigating and the methods you used to investigate them, then move quickly to describe the major findings of the study. You should write a direct, declarative, and succinct proclamation of the study results.

II. Explain the Meaning of the Findings and Why They are Important

No one has thought as long and hard about your study as you have. Systematically explain the meaning of your findings and why you believe they are important. After reading the discussion section, you want the reader to think critically about the results ["why hadn't I thought of that?"]. You don't want to force the reader to go through the paper multiple times to figure out what it all means. Begin this part of the section by repeating what you consider to be your most important or surprising finding first, then systematically review each finding.

III. Relate the Findings to Similar Studies

No study in the social sciences is so novel or possesses such a restricted focus that it has absolutely no relation to previously published research. The discussion section should relate your results to those found in other studies, particularly if questions raised from prior studies served as the motivation for your research. This is important because comparing and contrasting the findings of other studies helps to support the overall importance of your results and it highlights how and in what ways your study differs from other research about the topic.

IV. Consider Alternative Explanations of the Findings

It is important to remember that the purpose of research is to *discover* and not to *prove*. When writing the discussion section, you should carefully consider all possible explanations for the study results, rather than just those that fit your hypothesis or prior assumptions and biases.

V. Acknowledge the Study's Limitations

It is far better for you to identify and acknowledge your study's limitations than to have them pointed out by your professor! Note any unanswered questions or issues your study did not address. Describe the generalizability of your results to other situations, if it is applicable to the method chosen, then describe in detail problems you encountered in the method(s) you used to gather information.

VI. Make Suggestions for Further Research

Although your study may offer important insights about the research problem, there are likely to be other questions related to the problem that remain unanswered. Moreover, previously hidden unanswered questions may have become more obvious as a result of conducting your study. You should make suggestions for further research in the discussion section [or, you can choose to note them in the conclusion if you prefer, but not both!].

NOTE: Besides the literature review section, the preponderance of references to sources in your research paper is usually found in the discussion section. A few historical references may be helpful for perspective but most of the references should be relatively recent and included to aid in the interpretation of your results and/or linked to similar studies. If a study that you cited disagrees with your findings, don't ignore it--clearly explain why your research findings differ from theirs.

V. Problems to Avoid

- **Do not waste entire sentences restating your results.** Should you need to remind the reader of the finding to be discussed, use "bridge sentences" that relate the result to the interpretation. An example would be: "In the case of available housing to single women with children in rural areas of Texas, the findings suggest that..." [then move to the interpretation of this finding].

- **Recommendations for further research can be included in either the discussion or conclusion of your paper** but do not repeat your recommendations in the both sections.

- **Do not introduce new results in the discussion.** Be wary of mistaking the reiteration of a specific finding for an interpretation.

- **Use of the first person is acceptable, but** too much use of the first person may actually distract the reader from the main points.

2

Organizing Your Social Sciences Research Paper: Limitations of the Study

Definition

The limitations of the study are those characteristics of design or methodology that impacted or influenced the interpretation of the findings from your research. They are the constraints on generalizability, applications to practice, and/or utility of findings that are the result of the ways in which you initially chose to design the study and/or the method used to establish internal and external validity.

Importance of...

Always acknowledge a study's limitations. It is far better for you to identify and acknowledge your study's limitations than to have them pointed out by your professor and be graded down because you appear to have ignored them.

Keep in mind that acknowledgement of a study's limitations is an opportunity to make suggestions for further research. If you do connect your study's limitations to suggestions for further research, be sure to explain the ways in which these unanswered questions may become more focused because of your study.

Acknowledgement of a study's limitations also provides you with an opportunity to demonstrate that you have thought critically about the research problem, understood the relevant literature published about it, and correctly assessed the methods chosen for studying the problem. A key objective of the research process is not only discovering new knowledge but to also confront assumptions and explore what we don't know.

Claiming limitiations is a subjective process because you must evaluate the impact of those limitations. Don't just list key weaknesses and the magnitude of a study's limitations. To do so diminishes the validity of your research because it leaves the reader wondering whether, or in what ways, limitation(s) in your study may have impacted the results and conclusions. Limitations require a critical, overall appraisal and interpretation of their impact. You should answer the question: do these problems with errors, methods, validity, etc. eventually matter and, if so, to what extent?

Descriptions of Possible Limitations

All studies have limitations. However, it is important that you restrict your discussion to limitations related to the research problem under investigation. For example, if a meta-analysis of existing literature is not a stated purpose of your research, it should not be discussed as a limitation. **Do not apologize for not addressing issues that you did not promise to investigate in the introduction of your paper.**

Here are examples of limitations related to methodology and the research process you may need to describe and to discuss how they possibly impacted your results. Descriptions of limitations should be stated in the past tense because they were discovered after you completed your research.

Possible Methodological Limitations

- **Sample size** -- the number of the units of analysis you use in your study is dictated by the type of research problem you are investigating. Note that, if your sample size is too small, it will be difficult to find significant relationships from the data, as statistical tests normally require a larger sample size to ensure a representative distribution of the population and to be considered representative of groups of people to whom results will be generalized or transferred. Note that sample size is less relevant in qualitative research.

- **Lack of available and/or reliable data** -- a lack of data or of reliable data will likely require you to limit the scope of your analysis, the size of your sample, or it can be a significant obstacle in finding a trend and a meaningful relationship. You need to not only describe these limitations but to offer reasons why you believe data is missing or is unreliable. However, don't just throw up your hands in frustration; use this as an opportunity to describe the need for future research.

- **Lack of prior research studies on the topic** -- citing prior research studies forms the basis of your literature review and helps lay a foundation for understanding the research problem you are investigating. Depending on the currency or scope of your research topic, there may be little, if any, prior research on your topic. **Before assuming this to be true, consult with a librarian!** In cases when a librarian has confirmed that there is a lack of prior research, you may be required to develop an entirely new research typology [for example, using an exploratory rather than an explanatory research design]. Note again that this limitiation can serve as an important opportunity to describe the need for further research.

- **Measure used to collect the data** -- sometimes it is the case that, after completing your interpretation of the findings, you discover that the way in which you gathered data inhibited your ability to conduct a thorough analysis of the results. For example, you regret not including a specific question in a survey that, in retrospect, could have helped address a particular issue that emerged later in the study. Acknowledge the deficiency by stating a need for future researchers to revise the specific method for gathering data.

- **Self-reported data** -- whether you are relying on pre-existing data or you are conducting a qualitative research study and gathering the data yourself, self-reported data is limited by the fact that it rarely can be independently verified. In other words, you have to take what people say, whether in interviews, focus groups, or on questionnaries, at face value. However, self-reported data can contain several potential sources of bias that you should be alert to and note as limitations. These biases become apparent if they are incongruent with data from other sources. These are: (1) **selective memory** [remembering or not remembering experiences or events that occurred at some point in the past]; (2) **telescoping** [recalling events that occurred at one time as if they occurred at another time]; (3) **attribution** [the act of attributing positive events and outcomes to one's own agency but attributing negative events and outcomes to external forces]; and, (4) **exaggeration** [the act of representing outcomes or embelishing events as more significant than is actually suggested from other data].

Possible Limitations of the Researcher

- **Access** -- if your study depends on having access to people, organizations, or documents and, for whatever reason, access is denied or limited in some way, the reasons for this need to be described.

- **Longitudinal effects** -- unlike your professor, who can literally devote years [even a lifetime] to studying a single topic, the time available to investigate a research problem and to measure change or stability over time is pretty much constrained by the due date of your assignment. Be sure to choose a problem that does not require an excessive amount of time to complete the literature review, apply the methodology, and gather and interpret the results. If you're unsure whether you can complete your research within the confines of the assignment's due date, talk to your professor.

- **Cultural and other type of bias** -- we all have biases, whether we are conscience of them or not. Bias is when a person, place, or thing is viewed or shown in a consistently inaccurate way. Bias is usually negative, though one can have a positive bias as well, especially if that bias reflects your reliance on research that only support for your hypothesis. When proof-reading your paper, be especially critical in reviewing how you have stated a problem, selected the data to be studied, what may have been omitted, the manner in which you have ordered events, people, or places, how you have chosen to represent a person, place, or thing, to name a phenomenon, or to use possible words with a positive or negative connotation. **NOTE:** If you detect bias in prior research, it must be acknowledged and you should explain what measures were taken to avoid perpetuating that bias.

- **Fluency in a language** -- if your research focuses on measuring the perceived value of after-school tutoring among Mexican-American ESL [English as a Second Language] students, for example, and you are not fluent in Spanish, you are limited in being able to read and interpret Spanish language research studies on the topic. This deficiency should be acknowledged.

Structure and Writing Style

Information about the limitiations of your study are generally placed either at the beginning of the discussion section of your paper so the reader knows and understands the limitations before reading the rest of your analysis of the findings, or, the limitiations are outlined at the conclusion of the discussion section as an aknowledgement of the need for further study. Statements about a study's limitations should not be buried in the body [middle] of the discussion section unless a limitation is specific to something covered in that part of the paper. If this is the case, though, the limitation should be reiterated at the conclusion of the section.

If you determine that your study is seriously flawed due to important limitations, such as, an inability to acquire critical data, consider reframing it as a pilot study intended to lay the groundwork for a more complete research study in the future. Be sure, though, to specifically explain the ways that these flaws can be successfully overcome in a new study.

But, do not use this as an excuse for not developing a thorough research paper! Review the tab in this guide for developing a research topic. If serious limitations exist, it generally indicates a likelihood that your research problem is too narrowly defined or that the issue or event under study is too recent and, thus, very little research has been written about it. If serious limitations do emerge, consult with your professor about possible ways to overcome them or how to reframe your study.

When discussing the limitations of your research, be sure to:
- Describe each limitation in detailed but concise terms;
- Explain why each limitation exists;
- Provide the reasons why each limitation could not be overcome using the method(s) chosen to acquire or gather the data [cite to other studies that had similar problems when possible];
- Assess the impact of each limitation in relation to the overall findings and conclusions of your study; and,
- If appropriate, describe how these limitations could point to the need for further research.

Remember that the method you chose may be the source of a significant limitation that has emerged during your interpretation of the results [for example, you didn't interview a group of people that you later wish you had]. If this is the case, don't panic. Acknowledge it, and explain how applying a different or more robust methodology might address the research problem more effectively in a future study. A underlying goal of scholarly research is not only to show what works, but to demonstrate what doesn't work or what needs further clarification.

Organizing Your Social Sciences Research Paper: 9. The Conclusion

Definition
The conclusion is intended to help the reader understand why your research should matter to them after they have finished reading the paper. A conclusion is not merely a summary of the main topics covered or a re-statement of your research problem but a synthesis of key points and, if applicable, where you recommend new areas for future research. For most essays, one well-developed paragraph is sufficient for a conclusion, although in some cases, a two or three paragraph conclusion may be required.

Importance of a Good Conclusion
A well-written conclusion provides you with important opportunities to demonstrate to the reader your overall understanding of the research problem. These include:

1. **Presenting the last word on the issues you raised in your paper**. Just as the introduction gives a first impression to your reader, the conclusion offers a chance to leave a lasting impression. Do this, for example, by highlighting key points in your analysis or results or by noting important or unexpected implications applied to practice.
2. **Summarizing your thoughts and conveying the larger significance of your study**. The conclusion is an opportunity to succinctly answer the "So What?" question by placing the study within the context of past research about the topic you've investigated.
3. **Demonstrating the importance of your ideas**. Don't be shy. The conclusion offers you the opportunity to elaborate on the impact of your findings.
4. **Introducing possible new or expanded ways of thinking about the research problem**. This does not refer to introducing new information [which should be avoided], but to offer new insight and

creative approaches for framing/contextualizing the research problem based on the results of your study.

Structure and Writing Style
I. General Rules
When writing the conclusion to your paper, follow these general rules:
- State your conclusions in clear, simple language. State how your findings differ or support those of others and why.
- Do not simply reiterate your results or the discussion. Provide a synthesis of arguments presented in the paper to show how these converge to address the research problem or study objectives.
- Indicate opportunities for future research, as long as you haven't already done so in the discussion section of your paper. Highlighting areas for further research provides the reader with evidence that you have an in-depth awareness of the research problem you studied.

The function of your paper's conclusion is to restate the main argument. It reminds the reader of the strengths of your main argument(s) and reiterates the most important evidence supporting those argument(s). Make sure, however, that your conclusion is not simply a repetitive summary of the findings. This reduces the impact of the argument(s) you have developed in your essay. Do clearly state the context, background, and necessity of pursuing the research problem you investigated in relation to an issue, controversy, or a gap found in the literature.

Consider the following points to help ensure your conclusion is appropriate:
1. If the argument or purpose of your paper is complex, you may need to summarize the argument for your reader.
2. If, prior to your conclusion, you have not yet explained the significance of your findings or if you are proceeding inductively, use the end of your paper to describe your main points and explain their significance.
3. Move from a detailed to a general level of consideration that returns the topic to the context provided by the introduction or within a new context that emerges from the data.

The conclusion also provides a place for you to persuasively and succinctly restate your research problem, given that the reader has now been presented with all the information about the topic. Depending on the discipline you are writing in, the concluding paragraph may contain your reflections on the evidence presented, or on the essay's central research problem. However, the nature of being introspective about the research you have done will depend on the topic and whether your professor wants you to express your observations in this way.

NOTE: Do not delve into idle speculation. Being introspective means looking within yourself as an author to try and understand an issue more deeply, not to guess at possible outcomes.

II. Developing a Compelling Conclusion
Strategies to help you move beyond merely summarizing the key points of your research paper may include any of the following.

1. If your essay deals with a contemporary problem, warn readers of the possible consequences of not attending to the problem.
2. Recommend a specific course or courses of action that, if adopted, could address a specific problem in practice or in the development of new knowledge.
3. Cite a relevant quotation or expert opinion to lend authority to the conclusion you have reached [a good place to look is research from your literature review].
4. Restate a key statistic, fact, or visual image to drive home the ultimate point of your paper.
5. If your discipline encourages personal reflection, illustrate your concluding point with a relevant narrative drawn from your own life experiences.
6. Return to an anecdote, an example, or a quotation that you presented in your introduction, but add further insight derived from the findings of your study; use your interpretation of results to reframe it in new ways.
7. Provide a "take-home" message in the form of a strong, succinct statement that you want the reader to remember about your study.

III. Problems to Avoid
Failure to be concise
The conclusion section should be concise and to the point. Conclusions that are too lengthy often have unnecessary information. The conclusion section is not the place for details about your methodology or results. Although you should give a summary of what was learned from your research, this summary should be relatively brief, since the emphasis in the conclusion is on the implications, evaluations, insights, and other forms of analysis that you make.

Failure to comment on larger, more significant issues
In the introduction, your task was to move from general [the field of study] to specific [your research problem]. However, in the conclusion, your task is to move from a specific discussion [your research problem] back to a general discussion [i.e., how your research contributes new understanding or fills an important gap in the literature]. In short, the conclusion is where you should place your research within a larger context.

Failure to reveal problems and negative results
Negative aspects of the research process should never be ignored. Problems, drawbacks, and challenges encountered during your study should be summarized as a way of qualifying your overall conclusions. If you encountered negative results [findings that are validated outside the research context in which they were generated], you must report them in the results section and discuss their implications in the discussion section of your paper. In the conclusion, use yhour summary of the negative results as an opportunity to explain how they provide information on which future research can be based.

Failure to provide a clear summary of what was learned
In order to be able to discuss how your research fits back into your field of study [and possibly the world at large], you need to summarize briefly and directly how it contributes to new knowledge or a new understanding about the research problem. Often this element of your conclusion is only a few sentences long.

Failure to match the objectives of your research
Often research objectives in the social sciences change while the research is being carried out. This is not a problem unless you forget to go back and refine the original objectives in your introduction. As these changes emerge they must be documented so that they accurately reflect what you were trying to accomplish in your research [not what you thought you might accomplish when you began].

Resist the urge to apologize
If you've immersed yourself in studying the research problem, you presumably should know a good deal about it, perhaps even more than your professor! Nevertheless, by the time you have finished writing, you may be having some doubts about what you have produced. Repress those doubts! Don't undermine your authority by saying something like, "This is

just one approach to examining this problem; there may be other, much better approaches that...."

1

Organizing Your Social Sciences Research Paper: Appendices

Definition

An appendix contains supplementary material that is not an essential part of the text itself but which may be helpful in providing a more comprehensive understanding of the research problem and/or it is information which is too cumbersome to be included in the body of the paper. A separate appendix should be used for each distinct topic or set of data and always have a title descriptive of its contents.

Importance of...

Your research paper must be complete without the appendices, and it must contain all information including tables, diagrams, and results necessary to address the research problem. The key point to remember when you are writing an appendix is that the information is non-essential; if it were removed, the study would still be understandable to the reader.

It is appropriate to include appendices...

- When the incorporation of material in the body of the work would make it poorly structured
- When the information is too long and detailed to be easily summarized in the body of the paper, and
- To ensure inclusion of helpful, supporting, or essential material that would otherwise clutter or break up the narrative flow of the paper, or it would be distracting to the reader.

Structure and Writing Style

I. General Points to Consider

When considering whether to include content in an appendix, keep in mind the following points:

1. **It is usually good practice to include your raw data** in an appendix, laying it out in a clear format so the reader can re-check your results. Another option if you have a large amount of raw data

is to consider placing it online and note this as the appendix to your research paper.

2. **Any tables and figures included in the appendix should be numbered as a separate sequence from the main paper**. Remember that appendices contain non-essential information that, if removed, would not diminish a reader's understanding of the overall research problem being investigated. This is why non-textual elements should not carry over the sequential numbering of elements in the paper.

3. **If you have more than three appendices, consider listing them on a separate page at the beginning of your paper**. This will help the reader know before reading the paper what information is included in the appendices [always list the appendix or appendices in a table of contents].

4. **The appendix can be a good place to put maps, photographs, diagrams, and other non-textual elements**, if you feel that it will help the reader to understand the content of your paper, while keeping in mind the point that the paper should be understandable without them.

5. **An appendix should be streamlined and not loaded with a lot information**. If you have a very long and complex appendix, it is a good idea to break it down into separate appendices, allowing the reader to find relevant information quickly.

II. Contents
Appendices may include some of the following, all of which should be referred to or summarized in the text of your paper:

- Supporting evidence [e.g. raw data]
- Contributory facts or specialized data [raw data appear in the appendix, but with summarized data appearing in the body of the text].
- Sample calculations
- Technical figures, graphs, tables, statistics
- Detailed description of research instruments
- Maps, charts, photographs, drawings
- Letters, emails, and other copies of correspondance
- Questionnaire/survey instruments, with the results appearing in the text
- Interview protocols and complete transcripts of interviews
- Complete field notes from observations
- Specification or data sheets

NOTE: Do not include vague or irrelevant information in an appendix; this additional information will not help the reader's overall understanding and interpretation of your research and may only succeed in distracting the reader from understanding your research study.

III. Format

Here are some general guideline on how to format appendices, but consult the writing style guide [e.g., APA] your professor wants you to use, if needed:

- Appendices may precede or follow your list of references.
- Each appendix begins on a new page.
- The order they are presented is dictated by the order they are mentioned in the text of your research paper.
- The heading should be "Appendix," followed by a letter or number [e.g., "Appendix A" or "Appendix 1"], centered and written in bold type.
- Appendices must be listed in the table of contents [if used].
- The page number(s) of the appendix/appendices will continue on with the numbering from the last page of the text.

Organizing Your Social Sciences Research Paper:
10. Proofreading Your Paper

Definition

Proofreading is the act of searching for errors before you hand in the your final research paper. Errors can be both grammatical and typographical in nature, but also include identifying problems with the narrative flow of your paper [i.e., the logical sequence of thoughts and ideas], issues with concise writing, and finding any word processing errors [e.g., different font types, indented paragraphs, line spacing, uneven margins, etc.].

Strategies for Proofreading your Paper

Before You Proofread

- **Be sure you've revised the larger aspects of the text**. Don't make corrections at the sentence and word level [the act of editing] if you still need to work on the overall focus, development, and organization of the paper or you need to re-arrange or change specific sections [the act of revising].
- **Set your text aside for a while between writing and proofreading**. Give yourself some time between the writing of your paper and proofreading it. This will help you identify mistakes more easily.
- **Eliminate unnecessary words before looking for mistakes**. Throughout your paper, you should try to avoid using inflated diction if a simpler phrase works equally well. Simple, precise language is easier to proofread than overly complex sentence constructions and vocabulary.

- **Know what to look for**. Make a mental note of the mistakes you need to watch for based on comments from your professor on previous drafts of the paper or that you have received about papers written in other classes. This will help you to identify repeated patterns of mistakes more readily.

NOTE: Do not confuse the act of revising your paper with the act of editing it. Editing is intended to tighten up language so that your paper is easier to read and understand. This should be the focus when you proofread. If your professor asks you to revise your paper, the implication is that there is something within the text that needs to be changed, improved, or re-organized in some significant way. If the reason for a revision is not specified, always ask for clarification.

Strategies to Help Identify Errors

1. **Work from a printout, not a computer screen**. Besides sparing your eyes the strain of glaring at the computer, proofreading from a printout allows you to easily skip around to where errors might have been repeated throughout the paper [e.g., misspelled name of a person].

2. **Read out loud**. This is especially helpful for spotting run-on sentences, but you'll also hear other problems that you may not have identified while reading the text out loud. This will also helps you play the role of the reader, thereby, encouraging you to understand the paper as your audience might.

3. **Use a ruler or blank sheet of paper to cover up the lines below the one you're reading**. This technique keeps you from skipping over possible mistakes. This also helps you deliberately pace yourself as you read through your paper.

4. **Circle or highlight every punctuation mark in your paper**. This forces you to pay attention to each mark you used and to question its purpose in each sentence or paragraph. This is a particularly helpful strategy if you tend to misuse or overuse a punctuation mark, such as a comma or semi-colon.

5. **Use the search function of the computer to find mistakes**. Using the search [find] feature of your word processor can help you identify common errors faster. For example, if you overuse a phrase or use the same qualifier over and over again, you can do a search for those words or phrases and in each instance make a decision about whether to remove it or use a synonym.

6. **If you tend to make many mistakes, check separately for each kind of error**, moving from the most to the least important, and

following whatever technique works best for you to identify that kind of mistake. For instance, read through once [backwards, sentence by sentence] to check for fragments; read through again [forward] to be sure subjects and verbs agree, and again [perhaps using a computer search for "this," "it," and "they"] to trace pronouns to antecedents.

7. **End with using a computer spell checker or reading backwards word by word**. Remember that a spell checker won't catch mistakes with homonyms [e.g., "they're," "their," "there"] or certain typos [like "he" when you meant to write "the"]. The spell-checker function is not a substitute for carefully reviewing the text for spelling errors.

8. **Leave yourself enough time**. Since many errors are made and overlooked by speeding through writing and proofreading, setting aside the time to carefully review your writing will help you catch errors you might otherwise miss. Always read through your writing slowly. If you read through the paper at a normal speed, you won't give your eyes sufficient time to spot errors.

9. **Ask a friend to read your paper**. Offer to proofread a friend's paper if they will review yours. Having another set of eyes look over your writing will often spot errors that you would have otherwise missed.

Individualize the Act of Proofreading

In addition to following the suggestions above, **individualizing your proofreading process to match weaknesses in your writing will help you proofread more efficiently and effectively**. For example, I still tend to make subject-verb agreement errors. Accept the fact that you likely won't be able to check for everything, so be introspective about what your typical problem areas are and look for each type of error individually. Here's how:

- **Think about what errors you typically make**. Review instructors' comments about your writing and/or set up an appointment review your paper with a staff member in the Writing Center.
- **Learn how to fix those errors**. Talk with your professor about helping you understand why you make the errors you do make so that you can learn how to avoid them.
- **Use specific strategies**. Develop strategies you are most comfortable with to find and correct your particular errors in usage, sentence structure, spelling, and punctuation.
- **Where you proofread is important!** Effective and efficient proofreading requires extended focus and concentration. If you are

easily distracted by external activity or noise, proofread in a quiet corner of the library rather than at a table in Starbucks.

- **Proofread in several short blocks of time.** Avoid trying to proofread you entire paper all at once, otherwise, it will be difficult to maintain your concentration. A good strategy is to start your proofreading each time at the beginning of your paper. It will take longer to make corrections, but you'll be amazed at how many mistakes you find in text that you have already reviewed.

In general, verb tense should be in the following format, although variations can occur within the text depending on the narrative style of your paper. Note that references to prior research mentioned anywhere in your paper should always be stated in the past tense.

1. Abstract--past tense [a summary description of what I did]
2. Introduction--present tense [I am describing the study to you now]
3. Literature Review--past tense [the studies you are reviewing have already been written]
4. Methodology--past tense [the way that you gathered and synthesized data has already happened, otherwise, how could you write your paper?]
5. Results--past tense [the findings have already been discovered]
6. Discussion--present tense [I am talking to you now about how I interpreted the findings]
7. Conclusion--present tense [I am summarizing the study for you now]

1

Organizing Your Social Sciences Research Paper: Common Grammar Mistakes

Avoid These Common Grammar Mistakes!
Cartoonist Doug Larson once observed: "If the English language made any sense, a catastrophe would be an apostrophe with fur" [The Quotations Page]. Given the rules and the multiple exceptions to every rule that characterizes the English language, there are many sites on the web that

discuss how to avoid mistakes in grammar and word usage. Here are a few that I have found particularly helpful:

- **English Grammar**
- **Guide to Grammar and Writing**
- **Lingua Franca Column**, Chronicle of Higher Education
- **Online Course Lady Writing Laboratory Blog**
- **Plain Language.gov**

Listed below are the most common mistakes made and, thus, the ones you should focus on locating and removing while proofreading your research paper.

1. **Affect / effect** -- welcome to what I consider to be the most confusing aspect in the English language. "Effect" is most often a noun and generally means "a result." However, "effect" can be used as a verb that essentially means "to bring about," or "to accomplish." The word "affect" is almost always a verb and generally means "to influence." However, affect can be used as a noun when you're talking about the mood that someone appears to have. [Ugh!]

2. **Apostrophes** -- the position of an apostrophe depends upon whether the noun is singular or plural. For singluar words, add an "s" to the end, even if the final letter is an "s." For contractions, replace missing letters with an apostrophe; but remember that it is where the letters no longer are, which is not always where the words are joined [e.g., "is not" and "isn't"]. Note that contractions are rarely used in scholarly writing.

3. **Capitalization** -- a person's title is capitalized when it precedes the name and, thus, is seen as part of the name [e.g., President Zachary Taylor]; once the title occurs, further references to the person holding the title appear in lowercase [e.g., the president]. For groups or organizations, the name is capitalized when it is the full name [e.g., the United States Department of Justice]; further references should be written in lowercase [e.g., the department]. In general, the use of capital letters should be minimized as much as possible.

4. **Colorless verbs and bland adjectives** -- passive voice, use of the to be verb, is a lost opportunity to use a more interesting and accurate verb when you can. Adjectives can also be used very specifically to add to the sentence. Try to avoid generic or bland adjectives and be specific. Use adjectives that add to the meaning of the sentence.

5. **Comma splices** -- a comma splice is the incorrect use of a comma to connect two independent clauses (an independent clause is a phrase that is grammatically and conceptually complete: that is, it can stand on its own as a sentence). To correct the comma splice, you can:

replace the comma with a period, forming two sentences; replace the comma with a semicolon; or, join the two clauses with a conjunction such as "and," "because," "but," etc.

6. **Compared with vs. compared to** -- compare *to* is to point out or imply resemblances between objects regarded as essentially of a different order; compare *with* is mainly to point out differences between objects regarded as essentially of the same order [e.g., life has been compared to a journey; Congress may be compared with the British Parliament].

7. **Confusing singular possessive and plural nouns** ─ singular possessive nouns always take an apostrophe, with few exceptions, and plural nouns never take an apostrophe. Omitting an apostrophe or adding one where it does not belong makes the sentence unclear.

8. **Coordinating conjunctions** -- words, such as "but," "and," "yet," join grammatically similar elements [i.e., two nouns, two verbs, two modifiers, two independent clauses]. Be sure that the elements they join are equal in importance and in structure.

9. **Dangling participle** -- a participial phrase at the beginning of a sentence must refer to the grammatical subject of the sentence.

10. **Dropped commas around clauses**--place commas around words, phrases, or clauses that interrupt a sentence. Do not use commas around restrictive clauses, which provide essential information about the subject of the sentence.

11. **The Existential "this"** -- always include a referent with "this," such as "this theory..." or "this approach to understanding the...." With no referent, "this" can confuse the reader.

12. **The Existential "it"** -- the "existential it" gives no reference for what "it" is. Be specific!

13. **Its / it's**--"its" is the possessive form of "it." "It's" is the contraction of "it is" or "it has." They are not interchangeable and the latter should be avoided in scholarly writing.

14. **Fewer / Less** -- if you can count it, then use the word fewer; if you cannot count it, use the word less.

15. **Interrupting clause** ─ this clause or phrase interrupts a sentence, such as, "however." Place a comma on either side of the interrupting clause.

16. **Know your non-restrictive clauses** ─ this clause or phrase modifies the subject of the sentence, but it is not essential to understanding the sentence. The word "which" is the relative pronoun usually used to introduce the nonrestrictive clause.

17. **Know your restrictive clauses** — this clause limits the meaning of the nouns it modifies. The restrictive clause introduces information that is essential to understanding the meaning of the sentence. The word "that" is the relative pronoun normally used to introduce this clause. Without this clause or phrase, the meaning of the sentence changes.

18. **Literally** -- this word means that exactly what you say is true, no metaphors or analogies. Be aware of this if you are using "literally" to describe something. The term literally should never be applied to subjective expressions [i.e., "literally the most comfortable meeting"] or to imprecise measuerments [i.e., "literally dozens of protesters"].

19. **Lonely quotes** — unlike in journalistic writing, quotes in scholarly writing cannot stand on their own as a sentence. Integrate them into a paragraph.

20. **Misuse and abuse of semicolons** — semicolons are used to separate two related independent clauses or to separate items in a list that contains commas. Do not abuse semicolons by using them often; they are best used sparingly.

21. **Overuse of unspecific determinates** -- words such as "super" [as in super strong] or "very" [as in very strong], are unspecific determinates. How many/much is "very"? How incredibly awesome is super? If you ask ten people how cold, "very cold" is, you would get ten different answers. Academic writing should be precise, so eliminate as many unspecific determinants as possible.

22. **Semicolon usage** -- a semicolon is most often used to separate two complete but closely related clauses. Consider the semicolon as marking a shorter pause than a period but a longer pause than a comma (this is easy to remember since a semicolon is the combination of a period and a comma). In the same way, semicolons are also used to separate complicated lists of three or more items.

23. **Sentence fragments** — these occur when a dependent clause is punctuated as a complete sentence. Dependent clauses must be used together with an independent clause.

24. **Singular words that sound plural** -- when using words like "each," "every," "everybody," "nobody," or "anybody" in a sentence, we're likely thinking about more than one person or thing. But all these words are grammatically singular: they refer to just one person or thing at a time. And unfortunately, if you change the verb to correct the grammar, you create a pedantic phrase like "he or she" or "his or her."

25. **Split Infinitive** -- an infinitive is the form of a verb that begins with "to." Splitting an infinitive means placing another word or words between the "to" and the infinitive verb. This is considered incorrect by purists, but nowadays it is considered a matter of style rather than poor grammar. Nevertheless, in academic writing, it's best to avoid split infinitives.

26. **Subject/pronoun disagreement** — there are two types of subject/pronoun disagreement. Shifts in number refer to the shifting between singular and plural in the same sentence. Be consistent. Shifts in person occurs when the person shifts within the sentence from first to second person, from second to third person, etc.

27. **That vs. which** -- *that* clauses (called restrictive) are essential to the meaning of the sentence; *which* clauses (called nonrestrictive) merely add additional information. In general, most nonrestrictive clauses in academic writing are incorrect or superfluous. While proofreading, go on a "which" hunt and turn most of them into restrictive clauses. Also, "that" never follows a comma but "which" does.

28. **Verb Tense Agreement** -- do not switch verbs from present to past or from past to present without a good reason.

29. **Who / whom** -- who is used as the subject of the clause it introduces; whom is used as the object of a preposition, as a direct object, or as an indirect object. A key to remembering which word to use is to simply substitute who or whom with a pronoun. If you can substitute he, she, we, or they in the clause, and it still sounds okay, then you know that who is the correct word to use. If, however, him, her, us, or them sounds more appropriate, then whom is the correct choice for the sentence.

2

Organizing Your Social Sciences Research Paper: Writing Concisely

Writing Concisely

Academic writing in the social sciences often examines abstruse topics that require in-depth analysis and explanation. As a result, a common challenge to writing college-level research papers is expressing your thoughts clearly by utilizing language that communicates essential information unambiguously. When you proofread your paper, critically review your writing style and the terminology you used throughout your paper. Pay particular attention to identifying and editing the following common categories of imprecise writing.

1. **Problems with wordiness**– the use of more words than is necessary to communicate a thought or idea.

- **Cliches**– these are phrases that have become bland and ordinary through overuse. Besides indicating lazy thinking because they are often used as a substitute for carefully thinking about what to say, cliches should not be used due to the fact that they're often embedded within a specific cultural context. For example, if you say, "The Iraqi diplomat is going out on a limb if he does not protect his country's economic interests during negotiations with the United States." Americans may know what it means to be "out on a limb" [derived from the sport of hunting–get it?], but would someone from another culture know what this refers to?

- **Intensifiers**– these include modifying words such as very, literally, radically, definitely, significantly, greatly, extremely, moderately, basically, exceptionally, obviously, really, uncommonly, etc. Intensifiers create the illusion of accentuating words but, in academic writing, intensifiers actually have the opposite effect because they do not covey anything measurable. And editing intensifiers does not imply exchanging the term "extremely large" with the word "huge"; if something is unusual or it needs highlighting, quantify its uniqueness and place it in a comparative context [e.g., instead of saying, "...an extremely large increase in hospital visitations," state as, "...a 45% increase in hospital visitations since 2010"]. If there is no data to quantify the phenomena, then describe its importance using precise language.

- **Nominalizations**– this refers to a verb, adjective, or adverb that has been converted into a noun or noun phrase. Although this practice is not grammatically incorrect, overuse of nominalizations can clutter your writing. Examples include: "take action," "draw conclusions," and "make assumptions." These phrases can be reduced to: "act," "conclude," and "assume." Other nominalizations take the form of adding derivational suffixes to a verb, such as, --ance (deliver to deliverance) or -ize (modern to modernize). Editing the action of the sentence back into a verb will undo the nominalization, making the sentence more succinct and easier to read.

- **Stock phrases**– this refers to phrases that compromise clarity in your writing by adding unnecessary complexity to the sentence; stock phrases are similar to cliches in that they are overused terms. Examples include: "has the ability to," "due to the fact that," "regardless of the fact," or "at this point in time." Stock phrases often can and should be reduced to one word. Therefore, the above phrases can be reduced to "can," "because," although," and "now."
- **Verbal phrases**– these are also phrases that contribute little or no meaning to the overall sentence. They are similar to stock phrases but can be reduced to a single action verb. Examples include: "to come to a conclusion," "to take into consideration," or "to make a determination." The above phrases can be reduced to "conclude," "consider," or "determine."

2. **Problems with redundancy**– refers to the use of words that possess the same or almost the same meaning.

- **Implied modifiers**– this refers to the meaning of a word or phrase possessing the same or very similar meaning of the modifier. These types of modifying words can be subtle and difficult to locate but eliminating them will help clarify your writing. There are two ways to edit these modifiers. For example, if you say, "The next decision of the Supreme Court is difficult to anticipate in advance." Think about the implied meaning of "anticipate in advance"; if something is happening in advance, it is inherently anticipatory. Restate the sentence using only one of those words. However, implied modifiers can also suggest an incomplete thought about the subject of the sentence. Consider the sentence, "The maritime negotiations between Japan and China remain a difficult challenge." Any type of challenge is inherently difficult. However, by inserting an explanation ["because"] within the sentence, you expand the thought more completely. Therefore, you can either say, "The maritime negotiations between Japan and China remain a challenge because it is difficult to...," or you can say, "The maritime negotiations between Japan and China remain difficult because the main challenge is...."
- **Paired synonyms**– words paired together that have the same basic meaning may sound appealing when read aloud but they are unnecessary. Examples include: each and every, peace and quiet, first and foremost, alter or change, true and accurate, true and correct, always and forever. Choose only one word from the pairing that reflects the meaning you are trying to convey or use a thesaurus to find a word that more accurately reflects your thoughts. Other

word pairings are over-used catch phrases, such as, "first and foremost," "end result," "various differences," "sudden crisis," or "completely eliminate." They are redundant and re-state the obvious; choose only one word or eliminate them altogether.

3. **Problems with unclear sentence constructions**--short, declarative sentences are easier to comprehend than lengthy narratives.

- **Active voice**– some professors, particularly in the areas of business, technical, or scientific writing, may prefer that you write papers using a passive voice because they want you to convey objectivity by using an authoritative tone that focuses on the main idea or recommended action rather than the conscious intent underlying the idea or action. However, the passive voice frequently requires more words than is necessary to covey a thought or idea. Unless instructed not to do so, always write using an active voice. Here is an example: Passive–"It is believed by the state legislature that a person's picture on their drivers license must be updated every five years" [21 words]. In the active voice, the sentence would read: "The state legislature believes that a drivers license picture must updated every five years" [14 words]. Notice here as well the phrase, "a person's drivers license"; who else would own a drivers license but a person? The word "person's" is redundant and can also be deleted.

- **Combining sentences**– it is most often true that writing shorter, declarative sentences helps the reader better understand the content of each thought or idea. However, it is also the case that two or more sentences may be combined to convey the information more effectively using fewer words. Review your paper and look for paragraphs that appear wordy. This may indicate opportunities to condense sentences. Here is an example: "The BP oil spill occurred in 2010. This oil spill in the Gulf of Mexico prompted greater attention to regulating offshore drilling. Among these regulations was a rule governing procedures for capping wells." These three sentences can be combined to read: "The 2010 BP oil spill in the Gulf of Mexico prompted greater attention to regulatory procedures for capping offshore drilling wells." All of the essential information remains, but it is stated more concisely.

Organizing Your Social Sciences Research Paper: 11. Citing Sources

Definition

A citation is a reference to a published or unpublished source that you consulted and obtained information from while writing your research paper. The way in which you document your sources depends on the writing style manual your professor wants you to use for the class [e.g., APA, MLA, Chicago, Turabian, etc.]. Note that some disciplines have their own citation method [e.g., law].

Importance of a Citing your Sources

Citations show your readers where you obtained your material, provides a means of critiquing your study, and offers the opportunity to obtain additional information about the research problem under investigation. The act of citing sources is also a defense against allegations of plagiarism.

Properly citing the works of others is important because:

1. **Proper citation allows readers to locate the materials you used**. Citations to other sources helps readers expand their knowledge on a topic. In most social sciences disciplines, one of the most effective strategies for locating authoritative, relevant sources about a topic is to follow footnotes or references from known sources ["citation tracking"].

2. **Citing other people's words and ideas indicates that you have conducted thorough review of the literature on your topic** and, therefore, you are operating from an informed perspective. This increases your credibility as the author of the work.

3. **Other researcher's ideas can be used to reinforce your arguments**, or, if you disagree with them, can act as positions from which to argue an alternative viewpoint. In many cases, another researcher's arguments can act as the primary context from which

you can emphasize a different viewpoint or to clarify the importance of what you are proposing.

4. **Just as other researcher's ideas can bolster your arguments and act as evidence for your ideas, they can also detract from your credibility if they are found to be mistaken or fabricated**. Properly citing information not unique to you prevents your reputation from being tarnished if the facts or ideas of others are proven to be inaccurate or off-base.

5. **Outside academe, ideas are considered intellectual property and there can serious repercussions if you fail to cite where you got an idea from**. In the professional world, failure to cite other people's intellectual property ruins careers and reputations and can result in legal action. Given this, it is important to get into the habit of citing sources.

In any academic writing, you are required to identify for your reader which ideas, facts, theories, concepts, etc., are yours and which are derived from the research and thoughts of others. Whether you summarize, paraphrase, or use direct quotes, if it's not your original idea, the source needs to be acknowledged. **The only exception to this rule is** information that is considered to be common knowledge [e.g., George Washington was the first president of the United States]. If in doubt regarding whether something is common knowledge, take the safe route and cite it, or ask your professor for clarification.

Structure and Writing Style
Referencing your sources means systematically showing what information or ideas you are quoting or paraphrasing from another author's work, and where they come from. You must cite research in order to do research, but at the same time, you must indicate what are your original thoughts and ideas and what are the thoughts and ideas of others.

Procedures used to reference the sources you have relied uopn vary among different fields of study. However, **always speak with your professor about what writing style for citing sources should be used for the class** because it is important to fully understand the citation style to be used in your paper, and to apply it consistently.

GENERAL GUIDELINES
1. Should I avoid referencing other people's work?
No! Referencing other people's work is never an indication that your work is poor or lacks originality if placed in the proper context. In fact, the opposite is true. If you write your paper with no references to previous research, you

are indicating to the reader that you are not familiar with the research that has already been done, thereby, undermining your credibility as an author and the validity of your study. Including references in academic writing not only defends you against allegations of plagiarism, but is a way of demonstrating your knowledge of pertinent literature about the research problem.

2. What should I do if I find that my idea has already been published by another researcher?

Acknowledge the other researcher's work by writing in the text of your paper something like this: [see also Smith, 2002]. Do not ignore another author's work because doing so will lead your readers to believe that you have either taken the idea or information without properly referencing it [this is plagiarism] and/or that you have failed to conduct a thorough review of the literature in your field.

3. What should I do if I want to use an adapted version of someone else's work?

You still must cite the original work. For example, maybe you are using a table of statistics from a journal article published in 1996 by author Smith, but you have altered or added new data to it. Reference the revised chart as: [adapted from Smith, 1996]. You can also use other terms in order to specify the exact relationship between the source and the version you have presented, such as, "based on Smith [1996]...," "summarized from Smith [1996]...," and so forth. Citing the original source helps the reader locate the original information and evaluate how you adapted it.

4. What should I do if several authors have published very similar information or ideas?

You can indicate that the idea or information can be found in the work of more than one author by stating something similar to the following example: "Though in fact many authors have applied this theory to understanding economic relations among nations [for example, Smith, 1989; Jones, 19991; Johnson, 1994], little work has been done on applying it to understand the actions of non-governmental organizations." If you only reference one author or only the most recent study, then your readers may assume that only one author has published on this topic, or, conclude that you have not reviewed the literature thoroughly. Referencing multiple authors gives your readers a clear idea of the breadth of analysis you conducted in preparing to study the research problem.

5. What if I find exactly what I want to say in the writing of another researcher?

It depends on what it is; if someone else has thoroughly investigated precisely the same research problem as you, then you likely will have to change your topic, or at the very least, find something new to say about what you're researching. However, if it is someone else's particularly succinct expression, but it fits perfectly with what you are trying to say, then you can quote directly, citing the page reference as well as the author and year of publication. Don't see this as a setback, though. Finding someone else who has stated or made the same point you thought of on your own is an opportunity to reinforce and add legitimacy to your own interpretation of the research problem.

Citation Research Guides

The following USC Libraries research guide can help you properly cite sources in your research paper:

- **Citation Guide** -- **a guide to various citation styles, including tips for citation analysis and writing, with links to guides on how to cite resources using APA, MLA, or Chicago guidelines.**

Listed below are particularly well-done and comprehensive websites that provide specific examples of how to cite sources under different style guidelines.

- **Northwest Missouri State University, Owens Library**
- **Purdue University Online Writing Lab**
- **University of Wisconsin Writing Center**

This guide provides good information on the act of citation analysis, whereby you count the number of times a published work is cited by other works in order to measure the impact of a publication or author.

- **Measuring Your Impact: Impact Factor, Citation Analysis, and other Metrics: Citation Analysis** [Sandy De Groote, University of Illinois, Chicago]

Automatic Citation Generators

Type in your information and have a citation compiled for you. Note that these are **not** foolproof systems so it is important that you verify that your citation is correct and check your spelling, capitalization, etc. However, they can be useful in creating basic types of citations, particularly for online sources.

- **BibMe** -- APA, MLA, Chicago, and Turabian styles
- **DocsCite** -- for citing government publications in APA or MLA formats
- **EasyBib** -- APA, MLA, and Chicago styles
- **KnightCite** -- APA, MLA, and Chicago styles
- **Scholar Space** -- APA, MLA, and Chicago styles including citing uncommon sources
- **Son of Citation Machine** -- APA, MLA, Chicago, and Turabian styles

1

Organizing Your Social Sciences Research Paper: Avoiding Plagiarism

Definition

According to USC's Office of Student Judicial Affairs and Community Standards, plagiarism is:

1. The submission of material authored by another person but represented as the student's own work, whether that material is paraphrased or copied in verbatim or near-verbatim form.
2. The submission of material subjected to editorial revision by another person that results in substantive changes in content or major alteration of writing style.
3. Improper acknowledgement of sources in essays or papers.

Avoiding Allegations of Plagiarism

Credit must be given when using one of the following in your own research paper:

- Another person's idea, opinion, or theory;
- Any facts, statistics, graphs, drawings, or other non-textual elements used or that you adapted from another source;
- Any pieces of information that are not common knowledge;
- Quotations of another person's actual spoken or written words; or
- Paraphrase of another person's spoken or written words.

To introduce students to the process of citing other people's work, the USC Social Work Librarians have created a useful online tutorial on avoiding plagiarism. It describes what constitutes plagiarism and offers helpful advice on how to properly cite sources. In addition, because plagiarism is such a problem on campus, whether it is done intentionally or unintentionally, the Office of Student Judicial Affairs and Community Standards has also published, "Trojan Integrity: A Guide for Avoiding Plagiarism." This guide provides a comprehensive explanation for how to defend against allegations of violating the university's policy on academic integrity.

If you have any doubts about whether to cite a particular source concerning an argument or statement made in your paper, protect yourself by citing a source or sources that support your position. Note that not citing a source not only raises concerns about the integrity of your paper, but it also tells the reader that you have not conducted an effective or thorough review of the literature in support of the research problem under investigation.

2

Organizing Your Social Sciences Research Paper: Footnotes or Endnotes?

Definition
Endnote
Note citing a particular source or making a brief explanatory comment placed at the end of a research paper.
Footnote
Note citing a particular source or making a brief explanatory comment placed at the bottom of a page corresponding to the item cited.

Structure and Writing Style
Advantages of Using Endnotes
- Endnotes are less distracting to the reader and allows the narrative to flow better.
- Endnotes don't clutter up the page.
- As a separate section of a research paper, endnotes allow the reader to read and contemplate all the notes at once.

Disadvantages of Using Endnotes
- If you want to look at the text of a particular endnote, you have to flip to the end of the research paper to find the information.
- Depending on how they are created [i.e., continuous numbering or numbers that start over for each chapter], you may have to remember the chapter number as well as the endnote number in order to find the correct one.
- Endnotes may carry a negative connotation much like the proverbial "fine print" or hidden disclaimers in advertising. A reader may believe you are trying to hide something by burying it in a hard-to-find endnote.

Advantages of Using Footnotes
- Readers interested in identifying the source or note can quickly glance down the page to find what they are looking for.
- It allows the reader to immediately link the footnote to the subject of the text without having to take the time to find the note at the back of the paper.
- Footnotes are automatically included when printing off specific pages.

Disadvantages of Using Footnotes
- Footnotes can clutter up the page and, thus, negatively impact the overall look of the page. If there are multiple columns, charts, or tables below only a small segment of text that includes a footnote, then you must decide where the footnotes should appear.
- If the footnotes are lengthy, there's a risk they could dominate the page, although this issue is considered acceptable in legal scholarship.

Things to keep in mind when considering using either endnotes or footnotes in your research paper:

1. **Footnotes are numbered consecutively throughout a research paper, except for those notes accompanying special material** (e.g., figures, tables, charts, etc.). Numbering of footnotes are "superscript"--arabic numbers typed slightly above the line without periods, parentheses or slashes. They can follow all punctuation marks except dashes. In general, to avoid interrupting the continuity of the text, footnote numbers are placed at the end of the sentence, clause or phrase containing the quoted or paraphrased material.

2. **Depending on the writing style used in your class, endnotes may take the place of a list of resources cited** in your paper or they may represent non-bibliographic items, such as comments or observations, followed by a separate list of references to the sources you cited and arranged alphabetically by the author's last name.

3. **In general, the use of footnotes in most academic writing is now considered a bit outdated** and has been replaced by endnotes, which are much easier to place in your paper, even with the advent of word processing programs. However, some disciplines, such as law and history, still predominently utilize footnotes. Consult with your professor about which form to use and always remember that, whichever style of citation you choose, apply it consistently throughout your paper.

NOTE: Always think critically about the information you place in a footnote or endnote. Ask yourself, is this supplementary or tangential information that would otherwise disrupt the flow of the text or is this essential information that I should integrate into the main text? If you are not sure, it's better to work it into the text. Too many notes implies a disorganized paper.

3

Organizing Your Social Sciences Research Paper: Further Readings

Definition

Further readings provide references to sources that the author has deemed useful to a reader seeking additional information about the research problem but that is not essential to understanding the overall paper. The list of further readings contains sources that have not been cited in the research paper.

Structure and Writing Style

Depending on the writing style you are asked to use [e.g., APA], a list of further readings should be located at the end of your paper after the endnotes or references but before any appendices. The list should begin under the heading "Further Readings." Items are generally arranged alphabetically by the author's last name but can be categorized under sub-headings by material type [e.g., books, articles, websites, etc.] or content type [e.g., theory, methods,etc.].

If you choose to include a list of further readings, keep in mind the following:

1. **The references to further readings are not critcal to understanding the central research problem**. In other words, if further readings were not included, the citations in the paper would be sufficent for the reader to evaluate the credibility of your literature review and analysis of the existing research on the topic.
2. **Although further readings represent additional or suggested sources, they still must be viewed as relevant to the research problem**. Don't include further readings simply to show off your search skills. Even though they may not be central to understanding the research problem, each item must relate in some way to helping

the reader locate additional information or obtaining a broader understanding of the topic.

3. **Do not include basic survey texts or reference books like encyclopedias and dictionaries**. Including these types of sources in a list of further readings implies reference to either very general or very specific information that likely should have been integrated into the text of your paper.

To identify possible titles to include in a list of further readings, review the sources you found while researching your paper but that you ended up not citing. Review these sources and, playing the role of reader, think about which of these items may provide additional insight or background information about the research problem you have investigated.

Organizing Your Social Sciences Research Paper: 12. Annotated Bibliography

Definition

An annotated bibliography is a list of citations related to a particular topic or theme that include a brief descriptive and/or evaluative summary. The annotated bibliography can be arranged chronologically by date of publication or alphabetically by author, with citations to print and/or digital materials, such as, books, newspaper articles, journal articles, dissertations, government documents, pamphlets, web sites, etc., and multimedia sources like films and audio recordings.

Importance of a Good Annotated Bibliography

In lieu of writing a formal research paper, your professor may ask you to develop an annotated bibliography. You may be assigned to write an annotated bibliography for a number of reasons, including to: 1) show that you understand the literature underpinning a research problem; 2) demonstrate that you can conduct an effective and thorough review of pertinent literature; or, 3) share sources among your classmates so that, collectively, everyone in the class obtains a comprehensive understanding of key research about a particular topic. Think of an annotated bibliography as a more deliberate, in-depth review of the literature than what is normally conducted for a research paper.

On a broader level, writing an annoted bibliography can be excellent preparation for conducting a larger research project by allowing you to evaluate what research has already been conducted and where your proposed study may fit within it. By reading and critically analyzing a variety of sources associated with a research problem, you can begin to evaluate what the issues are and to gain a better perspective on what scholars are saying about your topic. As a result, you are better prepared to develop your own point of view and contributions to the literature.

In summary, a good annotated bibliography...

- Encourages you to think critically about the content of the works you are using, their place within the broader field of study, and their relation to your own research, assumptions, and ideas;
- Provides evidence that you have read and understood your sources;
- Establishes validity for the research you have done and of you as a researcher;
- Gives you an opportunity to consider and include key digital, multimedia, or archival materials among your review of the literature;
- Situates your study and underlying research problem in a continuing professional conversation;
- Provides an opportunity for others to determine whether a source will be helpful for their research; and,
- Could help researchers determine whether they are interested in a topic by providing background information and an idea of the kind of scholarly investigations that have been conducted in a particular area of study.

Structure and Writing Style
I. Types

1. **Descriptive**: This annotation describes the source without summarizing the actual argument, hypothesis, or message in the content. Like an abstract, it describes what the source addresses, what issues are being investigated, and any special features, such as appendices or bibliographies, that are used to supplement the main text. What it does not include is any evaluation or criticism of the content. This type of annotation seeks to answer the question: Does this source cover or address the topic I am researching?

2. **Informative/Summative**: This type of annotation summarizes what the content, message, or argument of the source is. It generally contains the hypothesis, methodology, and conclusion or findings, but like the descriptive type, you are not offering your own evaluative comments about such content. This type of annotation seeks to answer these types of questions: What are the author's main arguments? What conclusions did the author draw?

3. **Evaluative/Critical/Analytical**: This annotation includes your evaluative statements about the content of a source. It is the most

common type of annotation your professor will ask you to write. Your critique may focus on describing a study's strengths and weaknesses or it may describe the applicability of the conclusions to the research problem you are studying. This type of annotation seeks to answer these types of questions: Is the reasoning sound? Is the methodology sound? Does this source address all the relevant issues? How does this source compare to other sources on this topic?

NOTE: Strategies about how to critcally evaluate a source can be found **here**.

II. Choosing Sources for Your Bibliography

There are two good strategies you should use to begin identifying possible sources for your bibliography--one that looks back into the literature and one that looks forward.

1. The first strategy is to identify several recent scholarly books or journal articles on the topic of your annotated bibliography and review the sources cited by the author(s). Often, the items cited by an auther will effectively lead you to related sources about the topic.

2. The second strategy is to identify one or more important books, book chapters, journal articles, or other documents on your topic and paste the title of the item in <u>Google Scholar</u> [e.g., from *Negotiation Journal*, entering the article, "Civic Fusion: Moving from Certainty through Not Knowing to Curiosity"], placing quotation marks around the title so Google Scholar searches as a phrase rather than a combination of individual words. Below the citation may be a "Cited by" reference followed by a linked number. This link will direct you to a list of other study's that have cited that particular item after it was published.

Your method for selecting which sources to annotate depends on the purpose of the assignment and the research problem you are investigating. For example, if the research problem is to compare the social factors that led to protests in Egypt with the social factors that led to protests against the government of the Phillipines in the 1980's, you will have to consider including non-U.S., historical, and, if possible, foreign language sources in your bibliography.

NOTE: Appropriate sources to include can be **anything** that has value in understanding the research problem. Be creative in thinking about possible sources, including non-textual items, such as, films, maps, photographs, and audio recordings, or archival documents and primary source materials, such as, diaries, government documents, collections of personal correspondence, meeting minutes, and official memorandums. Consult with a librarian if you're not sure how to locate these types of materials for your bibliography.

III. Strategies to Define the Scope of your Bibliography

It is important that the sources cited and described in your bibliography are well-defined and sufficiently narrow in coverage to ensure that you're not overwhelmed by the number of potential items to consider including. Many of the general strategies used to narrow a topic for a research paper are the same that you can use to define the scope of your bibliography. These are:

- **Aspect** -- choose one lens through which to view the research problem, or look at just one facet of your topic [e.g., rather than a bibliography of sources about the role of food in religious rituals, create a bibliography on the role of food in Hindu ceremonies].
- **Time** -- the shorter the time period to be covered, the more narrow the focus [e.g., rather than political scandals of the 20th century, cite literature on political scandals during the 1930s and the 1990s].
- **Geography** -- the smaller the region of analysis, the fewer items there are to consider including in your bibliography [e.g., rather than cite sources about trade relations in West Africa, include only sources that examine trade relations between Niger and Cameroon].
- **Type** -- focus your bibliography on a specific type or class of people, places, or things [e.g., rather than health care provision in Japan, cite research on health care provided to elderly men in Japan].
- **Source** -- your bibliography includes specific types of materials [e.g., only books, only scholarly journal articles, only films, etc.]. However, be sure to describe why only one type of source is appropriate.
- **Combination** -- use two or more of the above strategies to focus your bibliography very narrowly or to broaden coverage of a very specific research problem [e.g., cite literature only about political scandals during the 1930s and the 1990s and that have only taken place in Great Britain].

IV. Assessing the Relevance and Value of Sources

All the items you include in your bibliography should reflect the source's contribution to understanding the research problem or the overall issue being addressed. In order to determine how you will use the source or define its contribution, you will need to assess the quality of the central argument within the source. Specific elements to assess include an item's overall value in relation to other sources on the topic, its limitations, its effectiveness in defining the research problem, the methodology used, the quality of the evidence, and the author's conclusions and/or recommendations.

With this in mind, determining whether a source should be included in your bibliography depends on how you think about and answer the following questions related to its content:

- Are you interested in the way the author frames the research questions or in the way the author goes about answering it [the method]?
- Does the research findings make new connections or promote new ways of understanding a problem?
- Are you interested in the way the author uses a theoretical framework or a key concept?
- Does the source refer to and analyze a particular body of evidence that you want to cite?
- How are the author's conclusions relevant to your overall investigation of the topic?

V. Format and Content

The format of an annotated bibliography can differ depending on its purpose and the nature of the assignment. Contents may be listed alphabetically by author or arranged chronologically by publication date. If the bibliography includes a lot of sources, items may also be subdivided thematically or by type. If you are unsure, ask your professor for specific guidelines in terms of length, focus, and the type of annotation you are to write.

Introduction

Your bibliography should include a brief introductory paragraph that explains the method used to identify possible sources [including what sources, such as databases, you searched], the rationale for selecting the sources, and a statement, if appropriate, regarding what sources were deliberately excluded and the reasons why.

Citation

This first part of your entry contains the bibliographic information written in a standard documentation style, such as, MLA, Chicago, or APA. Ask your professor what style is most appropriate and be consistent!

Annotation

The second part should summarize, in paragraph form, the content of the source. What you say about the source is dictated by the type of annotation you are asked to write. In most cases, however, your annotation should provide critical commentary that examines the source and its relationship to the topic. Things to think critically about when writing the annotation include: Does the source offer a good introduction on the issue? Does the source effectively address the issue? Would novices find the work accessible or is it intended for an audience already familiar with the topic? What limitations does the source have [reading level, timeliness, reliability, etc.]? Are any special features, such as, appendices or non-textual elements effectively presented? What is your overall reaction to the source? If it's a website or online resource, is it up-to-date, well-organized, and easy to read, use, and navigate?

Length

Annotations can vary significantly in length, from a couple of sentences to a couple of pages. However, they are normally about 300 words. The length will depend on the purpose. If you're just writing summaries of your sources, the annotations may not be very long. However, if you are writing an extensive analysis of each source, you'll need to devote more space.

Organizing Your Social Sciences Research Paper: 13. Giving an Oral Presentation

Preparing for Your Oral Presentation
In some classes, writing the research paper is only part of what is required. Your professor may also require you to give an oral presentation about your study. Here are some things to think about before you are scheduled to give your presentation.

1. What should I say?
If your professor hasn't explicitly stated what your presentation should focus on, think about what you want to achieve and what you consider to be the most important things that members of the audience should know about your study. Think about the following: Do I want to inform my audience, inspire them to think about my research, or convince them of a particular point of view?

2. Oral communication is different from written communication
Your audience only has one chance to hear your talk; they can't "re-read" your words if they get confused. Focus on being clear, particularly if the audience can't ask questions during the talk. There are two well-known ways to communicate your points effectively. The first is the K.I.S.S. method (keep it simple stupid). Focus your presentation on getting one to three key points across. Second, repeat key insights: tell them what you're going to tell them (Forecast), tell them, and then tell them what you just told them (Summarize).

3. Think about your audience
Yes, you want to demonstrate to your professor that you have conducted a good study. But professors often ask students to give an oral presentation to practice the art of communicating and to learn to speak clearly and audibly about yourself and your research. Questions to think about include: What background knowledge do they have about my topic? Does the audience

have any particular interests? How am I going to involve them in my presentation?

Organizing the Content

First of all, think about what you want to achieve and think about how are you going to involve your audience in the presentation.
Then...

1. **Brainstorm** your topic and write a rough outline. Don't get carried away—remember you have a limited amount of time for your presentation.
2. **Organize** your material and draft what you want to say [see below].
3. **Summarize** your draft into key points to write on overhead slides and/or notecards.
4. **Prepare** your visual aids.
5. **Rehearse** your presentation and practice getting the presentation completed within the time given. Ask a friend to listen and time you.

GENERAL OUTLINE

I. Introduction [may be written last]

- **Capture your listeners' attention**. Begin with a question, an amusing story, a startling comment, or anything that will engage your audience and make them think.
- **State your purpose**. For example, "I'm going to talk about..."; "This morning I want to explain...."
- **Present an outline of your talk**. For example, "I will concentrate on the following points: First of all...Then...This will lead to...And finally..."

II. The Body

- **Present your main points one by one in a logical order**.
- **Pause at the end of each point**. Give people time to take notes, or time to think about what you are saying.
- **Make it clear when you move to another point**. For example, "The next point is that..."; "Of course, we must not forget that..."; "However, it's important to realize that...."
- **Use clear examples to illustrate your points and/or key findings**.
- **If appropriate, consider using visual aids to make your presentation more interesting** [e.g., a map, chart, picture, etc.].

III. The Conclusion

- **Leave your audience with a clear summary of everything that you have covered.**

- **Don't let the talk just fizzle out**. Make it obvious that you have reached the end of the presentation.
- **Summarize the main points again**. For example, use phrases like: "So, in conclusion..."; "To recap the main issues...," "In summary, it is important to realize...."
- **Restate the purpose of your talk, and say that you have achieved your aim**: "My intention was ..., and it should now be clear that...."
- **Thank the audience, and invite questions**: "Thank you. Are there any questions?"

NOTE: When asking your audience if anyone has any questions, give people time to contemplate what you have said and to formulate a question. It may seem like an awkward pause to wait ten seconds or so for someone to raise their hand, but it's frustrating to have a question come to mind but be cutoff because the presenter rushed to end the talk.

Delivering Your Presentation
Pay attention to language!

- **Keep it simple**. The aim is to communicate, not to show off your vocabulary. Using complex words or phrases increases the chance of stumbling over a word or losing your train of thought.
- **Emphasize the key points**. Make sure people realize which are the key points of your study. Repeat them using different phrasing to help your audience remember them.
- **Check the pronunciation of difficult, unusual, or foreign words beforehand**. Keep it simple, but if you have to use unfamiliar words, write them out phonetically in your notes. This is particularly important when pronouncing proper names.

Use your voice to communicate clearly

- **Speak loudly enough for everyone in the room to hear you**. This may feel uncomfortably loud at first, but if people can't hear you, they won't try to listen.
- **Speak slowly and clearly**. Don't rush! Speaking fast makes it harder for people to understand you.
- **Practice to avoid saying um, ah, you know, like.** These words occur most often during transitions from one idea to another and are distracting to an audience. The better you know your presentation, the better you can control these verbal tics.

- **Vary your voice quality**. If you always use the same volume and pitch [for example, all loud, or all soft, or in a monotone] your audience will stop listening.
- **Speakers with accents need to slow down** [so do most others]. Non-native speakers often speak English faster than we slow-mouthed native speakers, usually because most non-English languages flow more quickly than English. Slowing down helps the audience to comprehend your talk.
- **When you begin a new point, use a higher pitch and volume**. Use the tone of voice to help emphasize the transition to a new point.
- **Slow down for key points**. These are also moments in your presentation to consider using body language, such as hand gestures, to help emphasize key points.
- **Use pauses**. Don't be afraid of short periods of silence. They give you a chance to gather your thoughts, and your audience a chance to think about what you've said.

Use your body language to communicate too!

- **Stand straight and comfortably**. Do not slouch or shuffle about. If you appear bored or uninterested in what your talking about, the audience will be as well. This is not the time to wear a wool sweater or high heels for the first time.
- **Hold your head up**. Look around and make eye contact with people in the audience. Do not just look at your professor the whole time! Do not stare at a point on the carpet or the wall. If you don't include the audience, they won't listen to you.
- When you are talking to your friends, you naturally **use your hands, your facial expression, and your body to add to your communication**. Do it in your presentation as well. It will make things far more interesting for the audience.
- **Don't turn your back on the audience and don't fidget!** Neither moving around nor standing still is wrong. Practice either to make yourself comfortable.
- **Keep your hands out of your pocket**. This is a natural habit when speaking. One hand in your pocket gives the impression of being relaxed, but both hands in pockets looks too casual and should be avoided.

Interact with the audience

- **Be aware of how your audience is reacting to your presentation**. Are they interested or bored? If they look confused, stop and ask them [e.g., "Is anything I've covered so far unclear?"]. Stop and explain a point again if needed.

- **Check after highlighting key points to ask if the audience is still with you.** "Does that make sense?"; "Is that clear?"
- **Do not apologize for anything.** If you believe something will be hard to read or understand, don't use it. If you apologize for feeling awkward or nervous, you'll only succeed in drawing attention to the fact you are feeling awkward or nervous. Your audience will begin looking for it rather than focusing on what you are saying.
- **Be open to questions.** If someone raises their hand, or asks a question in the middle of your talk, answer it. If it disrupts your train of thought momentarily, that's ok because your audience will understand. Questions show that the audience is listening with interest and, therefore, should not be regarded as an attack on you, but as a collaborative search for deeper understanding. However, don't engage in an extended conversation with an audience member or the rest of the audience will begin to feel left out. If an audience member persists, kindly tell them that the issue can be addressed after you've completed the rest of your presentation and note to them that their issue may be addressed by things you say in the rest of your presentation [it may not be, but at least saying so allows you to move on].
- **Be ready to get the discussion going after your presentation.** Professors often want a brief discussion to take place after a presentation. Just in case nobody has anything to say or no one asks any questions, be prepared to ask your audience some provocative questions or bring up key issues for discussion.

1

Organizing Your Social Sciences Research Paper: Dealing with Nervousness

Dealing with Nervousness

Being nervous before and during a presentation is natural and should be considered a good thing--a little adrenalin often helps you perform better because it sharpens your senses and self-awareness. However, if it is not

182 :: How to write a research proposal, paper or thesis

held in check, nervousness can also undermine your confidence and be a distraction to you and your audience. As a consequence, the audience focuses on you being nervous rather than the content of your presentation.

Keep the following strategies in mind to help control your nervousness:

1. **Be well-prepared**. Practice giving your talk more than once. Practice in front of a mirror so you are aware of any unintentional body language [e.g., swaying back and forth; not looking up to engage your audience, etc.] and practice in front of someone whom you trust will give you an honest assessment of your delivery.

2. **Be organized**. If you are well organized, your task will be easier. If your overheads slides are out of order, or your notes are disorganized, you will likely get flustered and lose focus, and so will your audience.

3. **Remember: The way you perform is the way your audience will feel**! Giving an oral presentation is a performance--view yourself as an actor. If you act the part of someone enjoying themselves and feeling confident, you will not only communicate these positive feelings to the audience, you will also feel much better as you proceed with your presentation.

4. **Practice, practice, practice.** Even the most accomplished public speakers can feel nervous before and during a talk. The skill comes in not communicating your nervousness and in not letting it take over from the presentation. Over time and with repeated practice, you will feel less nervous and better able to control your nervousness.

Here are some things to consider doing to help ensure that nervousness does not become a problem during your presentation:

1. **Smile!** Your audience will react warmly to you if you smile and at least look relaxed.

2. **Treat your audience like friends.** Think of your presentation as a welcomed opportunity to share the research topic with the audience.

3. **Breathe deeply**. It will help calm you down and help to control the slight shaking that you might get in your hands and voice.

4. **Bring a water bottle**. Constantly sipping water can be a distraction to your audience but, on the other hand, if you feel yourself getting a dry mouth while speaking and you begin to show it, you'll be glad you have some water on hand. Taking a sip of water also gives you a chance gather your thoughts.

5. **Slow down!** When people are nervous, they tend to get confused easily. So your mind may start to race, and you may feel panicky.

Make use of pauses; force yourself to stop at the end of a sentence, take a breath, and think before you continue.

2

Organizing Your Social Sciences Research Paper: Using Visual Aids

Using Visual Aids

Tips for Using Presentation Software Effectively

1. **State no more than three or four main points on a slide** [slides that have too many words on them are a big turn-off]. Remember that the slides are intended to supplement and enhance what you are saying, not to replace it.
2. **Give your audience time to take notes**. Pausing also gives you the opportunity to collect your thoughts before moving on to the next point.
3. **Don't read from the slides!** Audiences really hate this. Summarize or explain what's on a slide. Only read quotes or statements when you want to emphasize something.
4. **Make sure your audience can see the screen**. Think about where are you standing. Do not stand in front of the screen. If there is no angle where everyone can see, then move around before moving to the next slide [for example, point to something for emphasis].
5. **Don't overcrowd your slides with too much detail**. Using color, pictures, and graphs can make your slides more interesting, but be aware of the fact that certain color combinations can be very hard to read from a distance.
6. Remember that PowerPoint or Prezi may look great, but **if the technology goes wrong, it's a good idea to print out a handout**, or have some traditional overheads as a backup just in case. If the audience is too large to do this, ensure that your notes are sufficiently detailed so that you can talk in detail about your topic.
7. I know you may be tempted to spend more time on producing graphics than on the actual talk but remember: **if your talk is poor, no amount of fancy graphics will save it!**

Text Guidelines for Presentation Slides

- Use the same colors and fonts throughout; select graphic images in the same style
- Keep the background consistent and subtle
- Be sure text contrasts well with the background
- Generally use no more than six words per a line
- Generally use no more than six lines per a slide
- Avoid long sentences unless it is a important quotation
- Larger font indicates more important information
- Font size generally ranges from 18 to 48 point
- Fancy or cursive fonts can be hard to read
- Words in all capital letters are hard to read
- Avoid abbreviations and acronyms
- Limit punctuation marks

Handouts

Handouts are a great idea if your audience isn't too big [you don't want to spend a lot of time distributing handouts]. Think about whether you want to distribute them before or after your presentation. It is always good idea to include your references and contact information on a handout so that people can review them later or contact you if needed. You could also include some follow-up questions for discussion in your handouts.

Using the Whiteboard

If possible, put your contact information on the whiteboard before your talk begins, otherwise, you will have to turn your back on the audience and break your eye contact with them, which is never a good idea. Writing on a board is also time-consuming. Use alternative visual aids wherever possible. If you really must use a whiteboard, come prepared with the right pens [black or dark blue] and write in large, neat handwriting, so that people can read it.

Know the Space

Know the room from the front before you have to give your presentation. The front of a classroom feels different from the seats you are normally used to. Also, check the lighting so you avoid fiddling with the lights before your presentation.

Organizing Your Social Sciences Research Paper: 14. Grading Someone Else's Paper

Definition

The act of grading someone else's paper [a.k.a., student peer grading, peer assessment; peer evaluation; self-regulated learning] is a cooperative learning technique that refers to activities conducted either inside or outside of the classroom whereby students review, evaluate, and, in some cases, actually recommend grades on the quality of their peer's work. Peer grading is usually guided by a rubric developed by the instructor. A rubric is a performance-based assessment that uses specific criteria as a basis for evaluation. An effective rubric makes grading more clear, consistent, and equitable.

The Benefits of Peer Grading

Professors assign students to grade the work of their classmates based on findings in educational research that suggests the act of grading someone else's paper increases learning outcomes for students. Professors use peer grading as a way for students to practice recognizing quality research, with the hope that this will carry over to their own work, and as an aid to improving group performance or determining individual effort on team projects. Grading someone else's paper can also enhance learning outcomes by empowering students to take ownership over the selection of criteria used to evaluate the work of peers [the rubric]. Finally, professors may assign peer grading is a way to engage students in the act of seeing themselves as members of a community of researchers.

Other potential benefits include:

1. Increasing the amount of feedback students receive about their work;

2. Encouraging students to be actively involved with, and to take responsibility for, their own learning;

3. Providing an opportunity for reinforcing essential skills that can be used in professional life, such as, being able to effectively assess the work of others and to become comfortable with having one's own work evaluated by others;

4. Fostering a more in-depth and comprehensive process for understanding and analyzing a research problem through repetition and reinforcement of key criteria essential to learning a task;

5. Providing motivation for improvement in course assignments and a more comprehensive perspective on learning; and,

6. Using the process of grading as a model for the internal self-assessment of your own learning [at a higher cognitive level, this is known as reflexivity, or, the process of understanding one's own contribution to the construction of meaning throughout the research process].

How to Approach Peer Grading Assignments
I. Best Practices

Best practices in peer assessment vary depending on the type of assignment or group project being evaluated, the quality of the rubric guiding what you are to evaluate, and the course you are taking. The process can be intimidating but know that everyone probably feels the same way you do when first informed you will be grading the work of others--cautious and uncomfortable!

Given this, the following questions should be answered by your professor before beginning:

- Exactly who [which students] will be evaluated and by whom?
- What does the evaluation include? What parts are not to be evaluated?
- At what point during a group project or the assignment will the evaluation be done?
- What learning outcomes are expected from this exercise?
- How will their peers' evaluation affect everyone's grades?

II. Things to Consider
When informed that you will be assessing the work of others, consider the following:

1. **Carefully read the rubric given to you by the professor**. If he/she hasn't distributed a rubric to everyone, be sure to clarify what

guidelines or rules you are to follow and specifically what parts of the assignment or group project are to be evaluated. If you are asked to help develop a rubric, ask to see examples. They can vary considerably and it is helpful to have a sense of what your professor is looking for.

2. **Consider how your assessment should be reported**. Is it simply a rating [i.e., rate 1-5 the quality of work], are points given for each item graded [i.e., 0-20 points], are you expected to write a brief synopsis of your assessment, or is it any combination of these approaches? If you are asked to write an evaluation, be succient and avoid subjective modifiers. Cite specific examples whenever possible.

3. **Clarify how you will receive feedback from your professor regarding how effectively you assessed the work of your peers**. Take advantage of receiving this feedback to also discuss how the rubric could be improved or whether the process of completing the assignment or group project was enhanced using peer grading methods.

Organizing Your Social Sciences Research Paper: 15. How to Manage Group Projects

The Benefits of Group Work

As stressful as group work is in college, it can actually be beneficial in the long run because it closely parallels the group dynamics of participating on a committee, task force, or on a collaborative team project found in many workplaces. Whatever form the group assignment takes in your course, the opportunity to work with others, rather than on your own, can provide distinct benefits. These include:

1. **Increased productivity and performance** -- groups that work well together can achieve much more than individuals working on their own. A broader range of skills can be applied to practical activities and the process of sharing and discussing ideas can play a pivotal role in deepening your understanding of the research problem. This process also enhances opportunities for applying strategies of critical inquiry and creative or radical problem-solving to an issue.

2. **Skills development** -- being part of a team will help you develop your interpersonal skills. This can include expressing your ideas clearly, listening carefully to others, participating effectively in group deliberations, and clearly articulating to group members the results of your research. Group work also help develop collaborative skills, such as, team-based leadership and effectively motivating others. These skills will be useful throughout your academic career and all are highly sought after by employers.

3. **Knowing more about yourself** -- collaborating with others will help identify your own strengths and weaknesses. For example, you may be a better leader than listener, or, you might be good at coming up with the 'big idea' but not so good at developing a specific plan of

action. Enhanced self-awareness about the challenges you may have in working with others will enhance learning experiences. Here again, this sense about yourself will be invaluable when you enter the workforce.

Stages of Group Work
I. Getting Started
To ensure that your group gets off to a good start, it may be beneficial to:
1. Take time for all members to introduce themselves, including name, background, and stating specific strengths in contributing to the overall goals of the assignment.
2. Nominate or vote to have someone act as the group leader or facilitator or scheduler. If the burdon might be too great, comsider deciding to rotate this responsibility among all group members.
3. Exchange current contact information, such as, email addresses, social media information, and cell phone numbers.
4. Consider creating an online workspace account to facilitate discussions, editing documents, sharing files, exchanging ideas, and to manage a group calendar. There are many free online platforms available for this type of work.

II. Discussing Goals and Tasks
After you and the other members of the group agree about how to approach the assignment, take time to make sure everyone understands what it is they will need to achieve. Consider the following:
1. What are the goals of the assignment? Develop a shared understanding of the assignment's expected learning outcomes to ensure that everyone knows what their role is supped to be within the group.
2. Note when the assignment is due [or when each part is due] so that everyone is on the same schedule and any potential conflicts with other class assignment due dates can be addressed ahead of time by members of the group.
3. Discuss how you are going to specifically meet the requirements of the assignment. For example, if the assignment is to write a sample research grant, what topic are you going to research and what organizations will you solicit funding from?
4. If your professor allows considerable flexibility in pursuing the goals of the assignment, it often helps to brainstorm a number of ideas and then assess the merits of each one separately. Ask

yourselves as a group: How much do you know about this topic already? Is the topic interesting to everyone? If it is not interesting to some, they may not be motivated to work as hard as they might on a topic they found interesting. Can you do a good job on this topic in the available time? With the available people? With the available resources? How easy or hard would it be to obtain good information on the topic? [**NOTE:** Consult with a librarian before assuming finding information will be too difficult!].

III. Planning and Preparation

This is the stage when your group should plan exactly what needs to be done, how it needs to be done, and who should do what. Pay attention to the following:

1. Work together to break the project up into separate tasks and decide on the tasks or sub-tasks each member is responsible for. Make sure that work is equally distributed among the group.
2. Assign due-dates for each task, keeping in mind you must have time at the end to pull everything together.
3. Develop mechanisms for keeping in touch, meeting periodically, and the preferred methods for sharing information. Discuss and identify any potential stumbling blocks that may arise that could hinder your work.

NOTE: Try to achieve steps 1, 2, and 3 in a group meeting that is scheduled as soon as possible after you have received the assignment and your group is formed. The sooner these preliminary tasks are completed, the sooner each group member can focus on their particular responsibilities.

IV. Implementation

While each member carries out their individual tasks, it is important to preserve your group's focus and sense of purpose. Effective communication is vital, particularly when your group activity extends over an extended period of time. Here are some tips to promote good communication.

1. Keep in touch with each other frequently, reporting progress regularly. When the group meets for the first time, think about about setting up a specific day and time of the week for people to report on their progress.
2. If someone is having trouble completing his or her area of responsibility, work with that person to figure out how to solve the problem. Be supportive and helpful, but don't offer to do other people's work.

3. At the same time, make it clear that the group is depending on everyone doing their part; all group members should agree that it is detrimental to everyone in the group for one person to show up at the last minute without his or her work done.

V. Finishing Up

Be sure to leave enough time to put all the pieces together before the group assignment is due and to make sure nothing has been forgotten [e.g., someone forgot to correct a chart or a page is missing]. If you have a presentation at the end, go through the same process--decide who is going to do what and give everyone enough time to prepare and practice ahead of time [preferably together]. At this point, it is vital to ensure that you pay particular attention to detail, tie up any loose ends, and review the research project together as a whole rather than just looking over individual contributions.

VI. Writing Up Your Project

Writing the group report can be challenging; it is critical that you leave enough time for this final stage. If your group decided to divide responsibility for drafting sections, you will need to nominate [if not done already] a member to pull the final piece together so that the narritive flows well and isn't disjointed. Make it their assignment rather than assigning that person to also write a section of the report. It is best to choose whomever in your group is the best writer because careful copy editing at this stage is essential to ensure that the final document is well organized and logically structured. Focus on the following:

1. Have all the writers in your group use the same writing style [e.g., verb tense, diction or word choice, tone, voice, etc.]?
2. Are there smooth transitions between individual sections?
3. Are the citations to sources, abbreviations, and non-textual elements [charts, graphs, tables, etc.] consistent?

Organizing Your Social Sciences Research Paper: 16. Writing a Book Review

Definition

A book review is a thorough decription, critical analysis, and/or evaluation of the quality, meaning, and significance of a book. Reviews generally range from 500-1000 words, but may be longer or shorter depending on the length and complexity of the book being reviewed, the overall purpose of the review, and whether the review is a comparative analysis examining two or more books that focus on the same topic. Professors assign book reviews as practice in carefully analyzing complex scholarly texts and to assess your ability to effectively synthesize research to reach an informed perspective about a research problem or issue.

There are two general approaches to reviewing a book:

1. **Descriptive review:** presents the content and structure of a book as objectively as possible, describing essential information about a book's purpose and authority. This is done by stating the perceived aims and purposes of the study, often incorporating passages quoted from the text that highlight key elements of the work. Additionally, there may be some indication of the reading level and anticipated audience.

2. **Critical review:** describes and evaluates the book in relation to accepted literary and historical standards and supports this evaluation with evidence from the text and, in most cases, in contrast to and in comparison with the research of others. It should include a statement about what the author has tried to do, evaluates how well [in your opinion] the author has succeeded, and presents evidence to support this assessment. For course assignments, most professors want you to write a critical review.

How to Approach Writing Your Review

NOTE: Since most course assignments require that you write a critical rather than descriptive review, the following information about preparing to write and the paper's structure and style will focus on critical book reviews.

I. Common Features

While book reviews vary in tone, subject, and style, they share some common features. These include:

1. **A review gives the reader a concise summary of the content**. This includes a relevant description of the research topic and scope of analysis as well as an overview of the book's overall perspective, argument, and/or purpose.

2. **A review offers a critical assessment of the content**, often in relation to other studies on the same topic. This involves documenting your reactions to the work under review--what strikes you as noteworthy or important, whether or not the arguments made by the author(s) were effective or persuasive, and how the work enhanced your understanding of the research problem under investigation.

3. In addition to analyzing a book's strengths and weaknesses, a scholarly review **often recommends whether or not readers would value the work for its authenticity and overall quality**. This measure of quality includes both the author's ideas and arguments as well as practical issues, such as, readability and language, organization and layout, indexing, and the use of non-textual elements.

To maintain your focus, always keep in mind that most assignments ask you **to discuss a book's treatment of its topic, not the topic itself**. Your key sentences should say, "This book shows...," "The study demonstrates...," or "The author argues...," rather than "This happened..." or "This is the case...."

II. Developing an Assessment Strategy

There is no definitive methodological approach to writing a book review in the social sciences, although it is necessary that you think critically about the research problem under investigation before you begin to write. Therefore, writing a book review is a two-step process: 1) developing an argument about the value of the work under consideration and 2) clearly articulating that argument as you write an organized and well-supported paper.

A useful strategy in preparing to write a review is to list a set of questions that should be answered as you read the book [remember to note the page numbers so you can refer back to the text!]. The specific questions to ask yourself will depend upon the type of book you are reviewing. For example, a book that is presenting original research about a topic may require a different set of quesions to ask yourself than a work where the author is offering a personal critique of an existing policy or issue. **Here are some sample questions intended to promote critical thinking about the book as you read.**

1. What is the central thesis—or main argument—of the book? If the author wanted you to get one main idea from the book, what would it be? How does it compare or contrast to the world that you know or have experienced? What has the book accomplished?

2. What exactly is the subject or topic of the book? Does the author cover the subject adequately? Does the author cover all aspects of the subject in a balanced fashion? Can you detect any biases? What type of approach has the author adopted to explore the research problem [e.g., topical, analytical, chronological, descriptive]?

3. How does the author support his or her argument? What evidence does the author use to prove his or her point? Is the evidence based on an appropriate application of the method chosen to gather information? Do you find that evidence convincing? Why or why not? Does any of the author's information [or conclusions] conflict with other books you've read, courses you've taken, or just previous assumptions you had about the research problem?

4. How does the author structure his or her argument? Does it follow a logical order of analysis? What are the parts that make up the whole? Does the argument make sense to you? Does it persuade you? Why or why not?

5. How has this book helped you understand the research problem? Would you recommend the book to others? Why or why not?

Beyond the content of the book, you may also consider some information about the author and the general content. Question to ask may include:

- Who is the author? The nationality, political persuasion, education, intellectual interests, personal history, and historical context may provide crucial details about how a work takes shape. Does it matter, for example, that the author is affiliated with a particular organization? What difference would it make if the author participated in the events he or she wrote about? What other topics has the author written about? Does this work build on prior research or does it represent a new or unique area of research?

- What is the book's genre? Out of what discipline does it emerge? Docs it conform to or depart from the conventions of its genre? These questions can provide a historical or other contextual standard upon which to base your evaluations. If you are reviewing the first book ever written on the subject, it will be important for your readers to know this. Keep in mind, though, that declarative statements about being the "first," the "best," or the "only" book of its kind can be a risky unless you're absolutely certain because your professor [presumably] has a much better understanding of the overall research literature.

Structure and Writing Style
I. Bibliographic Information
Provide the essential information about the book using the writing style asked for by your professor [e.g., APA, MLA, Chicago, etc.]. Depending on how your professor wants you to organize your review, the bibliographic information represents the heading of your review. In general, it would look like this:

The Whites of Their Eyes: The Tea Party's Revolution and the Battle over American History. By Jill Lepore. (Princeton, NJ: Princeton University Press, 2010. xii, 207pp.).
Reviewed by [your name].

II. Scope/Purpose/Content
Begin your review by telling the reader not only the overarching concern of the book in its entirety [the subject area] but also what the author's particular point of view is on that subject [the thesis statement]. If you cannot find an adequate statement in the author's own words or if you find that the thesis statement is not well-developed, then you will have to compose your own introductory thesis statement that does cover all the material. This statement should be no more than one paragraph and must be succinctly stated, accurate, and unbiased.

If you find it difficult to discern the overall aims and objectives of the book [and, be sure to point this out in your review if you believe it this to be a deficiency], you may arrive at an understanding of the purpose by assessing the following:

- Scan the table of contents because it can help you understand how the book is organized and will aid in determining the author's main ideas and how they are developed [e.g., chronologically, topically, etc.].
- Why did the author write on this subject rather than on some other subject?
- From what point of view is the work written?
- Was the author trying to give information, to explain something technical, or to convince the reader of a belief's validity by dramatizing it in action?
- What is the general field or genre, and how does the book fit into it? If necessary, review related literature from other books and journal articles to familiarize yourself with the field.

- Who is the intended audience?
- What is the author's style? Is it formal or informal? You can evaluate the quality of the writing style by noting some of the following standards: coherence, clarity, originality, forcefulness, accurate use of technical words, conciseness, fullness of development, and fluidity.
- How did the book affect you? Were any prior assumptions you had on the subject that were changed, abandoned, or reinforced after reading the book? How is the book related to your own personal beliefs or assumptions? What personal experiences have you had that relate to the subject?
- How well has the book achieved the goal(s) set forth in the preface, introduction, and/or foreword?
- Would you recommend this book to others? Why or why not?

III. Note the Method

Illustrate your remarks with specific references and quotations that help to illustrate the literary method used to state the research problem, describe the research design, and analyze the findings. In general, authors tend to use the following literary methods, exclusively or in combination.

- **Description**: The author depicts scenes and events by giving specific details that appeal to the five senses, or to the reader's imagination. The description presents background and setting. Its primary purpose is to help the reader realize, through as many sensuous details as possible, the way persons, places, and things are within the phenomenon being described.
- **Narration**: The author tells the story of a series of events, usually thematically or in chronological order. In general, the emphasis in scholarly books is on narration of the events. Narration tells what has happened and, in some cases, using this method to forecast what could happen in the future. Its primary purpose is to draw the reader into a story and create a contextual framework for understanding the research problem.
- **Exposition**: The author uses explanation and analysis to present a subject or to clarify an idea. Exposition presents the facts about a subject or an issue clearly and as impartially as possible. Its primary purpose is to describe and explain, to document for the historical record an event or phenomenon.
- **Argument**: The author uses techniques of persuasion to establish understanding of a particular truth, often in the form of a research question, or to convince the reader of its falsity. The overall aim is to persuade the reader to believe something and perhaps to act on that

belief. Argument takes sides on an issue and aims to convince the reader that the author's position is valid, logical, and/or reasonable.

IV. Critically Evaluate the Contents

Critical comments should form the bulk of your book review. State whether or not you feel the author's treatment of the subject matter is appropriate for the intended audience. Ask yourself:

- Has the purpose of the book been achieved?
- What contribution does the book make to the field?
- Is the treatment of the subject matter objective?
- Are there facts and evidence that have been omitted?
- What kinds of data, if any, are used to support the author's thesis statement?
- Can the same data be interpreted to explain alternate outcomes?
- Is the writing style clear and effective?
- Does the book raise important or provocative issues or topics for discussion
- Does the book bring attention to the need for further research?
- What has been left out?

Support your evaluation with evidence from the text and, when possible, state the book's quality in relation to other scholarly sources. If relevant, note of the book's format, such as, layout, binding, typography, etc. Are there tables, charts, maps, illustrations, text boxes, photographs, or other non-textual elements? Do they aid in understanding the research problem? Describing this is particularly important in books that contain a lot of non-textual elements.

NOTE: It is important to carefully distinguish your views from those of the author so as not to confuse your reader. Be clear when you are describing an author's point of view versus your own.

V. Examine the Front Matter and Back Matter

Front matter refers to anything before the first chapter of the book. Back matter refers to any information included after the final chapter of the book. Front matter is most often numbered separately from the rest of the text in lower case Roman numerals [i.e. *i-xi*]. Critical commentary about front or back matter is generally only necessary if you believe there is something that diminishes the overall quality of the work [e.g., the indexing is poor] or there is something that is particularly helpful in understanding the book's contents [e.g., foreword places the book in an important context]. The following front matter may be included in a book and may be considered for evaluation when reviewing its overall quality:

- **Table of contents** -- is it clear? Is it detailed or general? Does it reflect the true contents of the book?
- **Author biography** -- also found as back matter, the biography of author(s) can be useful in determining the authority of the writer and whether the book builds on prior research or represents new research. In scholarly reviews, noting the author's affiliation can be a factor in helping the reader determine the overall validity of the work [i.e., are they associated with a research center devoted to studying the research problem under investigation].
- **Foreword** -- the purpose of a foreword is to introduce the reader to the author as well as the book itself, and to help establish credibility for both. A foreword may not contribute any additional information about the book's subject matter, but it serves as a means of validating the book's existence. Later editions of a book sometimes have a new foreword prepended [appearing before an older foreword, if there was one], which may be included to explain in how the latest edition differs from previous ones.
- **Preface** -- generally describes the genesis, purpose, limitations, and scope of the book and may include acknowledgments of indebtedness to people who have helped the author complete the study. Is the preface helpful in understanding the study? Does it provide an effective framework for understanding what's to follow?
- **Chronology** -- also may be found as back matter, a chronology is generally included to highlight key events related to the subject of the book. Do the entries contribute to the overall work? Is it detailed or very general?
- **List of non-textual elements** -- a book that contains a lot of charts, photographs, maps, etc. will often list these items after the table of contents in order that they appear in the text. Is it useful?

The following back matter may be included in a book and may be considered for evaluation when reviewing the overall quality of the book:

- **Afterword** -- this is a short, reflective piece written by the author that takes the form of a concluding section, final commentary, or closing statement. It is worth mentioning in a review if it contributes information about the purpose of the book, gives a call to action, or asks the reader to consider key points made in the book.
- **Appendix** -- is the supplementary material in the appendix or appendices well organized? Do they relate to the contents or appear superfluous? Does it contain any essential information that would have been more appropriately integrated into the text?

- **Index** -- is the index thorough and accurate? Are elements used, such as, bold or italic fonts to help identify specific places in the book?
- **Glossary of Terms** -- are the definitions clearly written? Is the glossary comprehensive or are key terms missing? Are any terms or concepts mentioned in the text not included?
- **Footnotes/Endnotes** -- examine any footnotes or endnotes as you read from chapter to chapter. Do they provide important additional information? Do they clarify or extend points made in the body of the text?
- **Bibliography/References/Further Readings** -- review any bibliography, list of references to sources, and/or further readings the author may have included. What kinds of sources appear [e.g., primary or secondary, recent or old, scholarly or popular, etc.]? How does the author make use of them? Be sure to note important omissions of sources that you believe should have been utilized.

VI. Summarize and Comment

State your general conclusions briefly and succinctly. Pay particular attention to the author's concluding chapter and/or afterword. Is the summary convincing? List the principal topics, and briefly summarize the author's ideas about these topics, main points, and conclusions. If appropriate and to help clarify your overall evaluation, use specific references and quotations to support your statements. If your thesis has been well argued, the conclusion should follow naturally. It can include a final assessment or simply restate your thesis. Do not introduce new information in the conclusion. If you've compared the book to any other works or used other sources in writing the review, be sure to cite them at the end of your book review.

1

Organizing Your Social Sciences Research Paper: Multiple Book Review Essay

Definition

A multiple book review essay involves assessing the quality of two or more books that cover the same overall subject area [e.g., analysis of European debt crisis] or that are related to each other in a particular way [e.g., applying grounded theory methods to study student access to education]. The review is written in the form of a short scholarly paper [essay] rather than as a descriptive book review. The purpose is to compare and contrast the works under review, to identify key themes and critical issues, and to evaluate each writer's contributions to understanding the overarching topics common to each book. Professors assign reviews of multiple books to help students gain experience critically evaluating the ways in which different researchers examine and interpret issues related to a specific research problem.

How to Approach Writing Your Review
Developing an Assessment Strategy
An important first step in approaching how to write a review of two or more books is to identify and think critically about the research problem that ties each of the books together. The challenge is to develop an argument about each book you are reviewing and then clearly compare, contrast, and ultimately synthesize your analysis into an well organized and well supported essay.

Think of a multiple book review essay as a type of compare and contrast paper similar to what you may have written for a general issue-oriented composition class. As you read through each book, write down questions concerning what you want to know about each book and answer them as you read [remember to note the page numbers from the book you got the information from so you can refer back it later!]. Which questions to ask yourself will depend upon the type of books you are reviewing and how the books are related to each other.

Here are a series of questions to focus your thinking:
1. What is the thesis—or main argument—of each book? If the author wanted you to get one idea from the book, what would it be? How does it compare or contrast to the world you know? What has the book accomplished?
2. What exactly is the subject or topic of each book? Does the author cover the subject adequately? Does the author cover all aspects of the subject in a balanced fashion? Can you detect any biases? What is the approach to the subject [topical, analytical, chronological, descriptive]?
3. How does the author of each book support his or her argument? What evidence does each author use to prove his or her point? Do you find that evidence convincing? Why or why not? Does any of the author's information [or conclusions] conflict with other books

you've read, courses you've taken, or just previous assumptions you had about the research problem under study?

4. How does the author structure his or her argument? What are the parts that make up the whole? Does the argument make sense to you? Does it persuade you? Why or why not?

5. How has each book helped you understand the subject? Would you recommend the books to others? Why or why not?

Beyond the content of the book, you may also consider some information about the author and the circumstances of the text's production:

- Who is the author? Nationality, political persuasion, education, intellectual interests, personal history, and historical context may provide crucial details about how a work takes shape. Does it matter, for example, that the author is affiliated with a particular organization? What difference would it make if the author participated in the events he or she writes about? What other topics has the author written about? Does this work build on prior research or does it seem to represent a new area of research?

- What is each book's genre? Out of what discipline do they emerge? Do they conform to or depart from the conventions of its genre? These questions can provide a historical or other contextual standard upon which to base your evaluations. If you are reviewing the first book ever written on the subject, it will be important for your readers to know this. Keep in mind, though, that declarative statements about being the "first," the "best," or the "only" book of its kind can be a risky unless you're absolutely certain because your professor [presumably] has a much better understanding of the overall research literature.

Structure and Writing Style
I. Bibliographic Information

Provide the essential information about each book using the writing style asked for by your professor [e.g., APA, MLA, Chicago, etc.]. Depending on how your professor wants you to organize your review, the bibliographic information represents the heading of your review. In general, they would be arranged alphabetically by title and look like this:

Racing the Storm: Racial Implications and Lessons Learned from Hurricane Katrina. Hillary Potter, ed. (Lanham, MD: Lexington Books, 2007. 320 pp)

The Sociology of Katrina: Perspectives on a Modern Catastrophe. David L. Brunsma, David Overfelt, and J. Steven Picou, eds. (Lanham, MD: Rowman and Littlefield, 2007. 288 pp.)

Through the Eye of Katrina: Social Justice in the United States. Kristin A. Bates and Richelle S. Swan, eds. (Durham, NC: Carolina Academic Press, 2007. 440 pp.)
Reviewed by [your name]

II. Thesis Statement

The thesis statement of an essay that compares and contrasts multiple works should contain an idea or claim that unites a discussion of the texts under review. It should include the argument that will be advanced in support of the claims that are being made. To begin, ask yourself: "What is the overarching subject or issue that ties together all of the books?" Why is it important?" In most scholarly works, the author(s) will state the purpose of their book in the preface or in an introductory chapter. Look for common themes as well as points of divergence among the books.

If you cannot find an adequate statement in the author's own words or if you find that the thesis statement is not well-developed, then you will have to compose your own introductory thesis statement that does cover all the material. The comparative thesis statement will vary in length depending on the number and complexity of books under review. Regardless of length, it must be succinct, accurate, unbiased, and clear.

If you find it difficult to discern the overall aims and objectives of each book [and, be sure to point this out in your review if you believe it to be a deficiency], you may arrive at an understanding of the purpose by asking yourself a the following questions:

- Scan the table of contents because it can help you understand how the book is organized and will aid in determining the author's main ideas and how they are developed [e.g., chronologically, topically, etc.].
- Why did the authors write on this subject rather than on some other subject?
- From what point of view is each work written?
- Were the authors trying to give information, to explain something technical, or to convince the reader of a belief's validity by dramatizing it in action?
- What is the general field or genre, and how does each book fit into it? If necessary, review related literature from other books and journal articles to familiarize yourself with the field.
- Who is the intended audience for each book? Is it the same or are the books intended for difference sets of readers?
- What is each author's style? Is it formal or informal? You can evaluate the quality of the writing style by noting some of the

following standards: coherence, clarity, originality, forcefulness, accurate use of technical words, conciseness, fullness of development, and fluidity.

- How did the books affect you? Were any prior assumptions you had on the subject that were changed, abandoned, or reinforced after reading the books? How are the books related to your own personal beliefs or assumptions? What personal experiences have you had that relate to the subject?
- How well has each book achieved the goal(s) set forth in the preface, introduction, and/or foreword?
- Would you recommend this book to others? Why or why not?

A useful strategy to help organize your thoughts is to create a table with a column for each book and rows for each of the questions. Enter your answer to each book in the chart. When completed, you'll have an easy guide to how each author has addressed the questions.

NOTE: **Be sure that your thesis statement includes the rationale behind why your choice of what points to compare and contrast were deliberate and meaningful and not random!**

III. Methods of Organization

Organization is critical to writing an essay that compares and contrasts multiple works because you will most likely be discussing a variety of evidence and you must be certain that the logic and narrative flow of your paper can be understood by the reader. Here are some general guidelines to consider:

1. If your professor asks you to choose the books to review, identify works that are closely related in some way so they can be easily compared or contrasted.
2. Compare according to a single organizing idea [e.g., analysis of how each author assessed the effectiveness of post-Katrina recovery].
3. Choose a method of development [see below] that works well with your organizing idea.
4. Use specific and relevant examples to support your analysis.
5. Use transitional words or phrases to help the reader understand the similarities and differences in your subject.
6. Conclude your paper by restating your thesis, summarizing the main points, and giving the reader the final "so what" of the major similarities and/or differences that you discussed. Why are they important?

There are two general methods of organizing your book review essay. If you believe one work extends another, you'll probably use the block method;

if you find that two or more works are essentially engaged in a debate or examine a topic from different perspectives, the point-by-point method will help draw attention to the conflict. However, the point-by-point method can come off as a rhetorical ping-pong match. You can avoid this effect by grouping more than one point together, thereby cutting down on the number of times you alternate from one work to another.

No matter which method you choose, you do not need to give equal time to similarities and differences. In fact, your paper will be more interesting if you state your main argument(s) as quickly as possible. For example, a book review essay evaluating three research studies that examine different interpretations of conflict resolution among nations in the Middle East might have as few as two or three sentences in the introduction regarding similarities and only a paragraph or two to set up the contrast between the author's positions. The rest of the essay, whether organized by block method or point-by-point, will be your analysis of the key differences among the books.

The Block Method

Present all the information about A, and then present parallel information about B. This pattern tends to work better for shorter book review essays, and those with few sub-topics. The method looks like this:

I. Introduction
    A. Briefly introduce the significance of the overall subject matter
    B. Thesis Statement
       --First supporting point
       --Second supporting point
       --Third supporting point

II. First book
    A. Summary of book
       --Relationship of work to first point
       --Relationship of work to second point
       --Relationship of work to third point

III. Second book
    A. Summary of book
       --Relationship of work to first point
       --Relationship of work to second point
       --Relationship of work to third point

IV. Third book
    A. Summary of book
       --Relationship of work to first point

--Relationship of work to second point
--Relationship of work to third point

V. Conclusion
   A. Restate thesis
   B. Briefly summarize how you proved your argument

The Point-by-Point Method
Present one point about A, and then go to the parallel point about B. Move to the next point, and do the same thing. This pattern tends to work better for long book review essays and those with many sub-topics. The method looks like this:

I. Introduction
   A. Briefly introduce significance of overall subject matter
   B. Thesis statement

II. Brief explanation of first book

III. Brief explanation of second book

IV. First comparative point
   A. Relation of point to first book
   B. Relation of point to second book

V. Second comparative point
   A. Relation of point to first book
   B. Relation of point to second book

VI. Third comparative point
   A. Relation of point to first book
   B. Relation of point to second book

VII. Conclusion
   A. Restate thesis
   B. Briefly summarize how your proved your argument

IV. Critically Evaluate the Contents
Regardless of whether you choose the block method or the point-by-point method, critical comments should form the bulk of your book review essay. State whether or not you feel the author's treatment of the subject matter is appropriate for the intended audience. Ask yourself:

- Has the purpose of the books been achieved?
- What contribution do the books make to the field of study or discipline?
- Is the treatment of the subject matter objective?
- Are there facts and evidence that have been omitted, either in one of the books or collectively?
- What kinds of data, if any, are used to support each author's thesis statement?
- Can the same data be interpreted to alternate ends?
- Is the writing style clear and effective?
- Do the books raise important or provocative issues or topics for discussion and further research?
- What has been left out?

Support your evaluation with evidence from each text and, when possible, in relation to other sources. If relevant, make note of each book's format, such as, layout, binding, typography, etc. Are there maps, illustrations? Do they aid in understanding the research problem? This is particular important in books that contain a lot of non-textual elements, such as tables, charts, and illustrations.

NOTE: It is important to carefully distinguish your views from those of the authors, so that you don't confuse your reader.

V. Examine the Front Matter and Back Matter

Front matter refers to anything before the first chapter of the book. Back matter refers to any information included after the final chapter of the book. Front matter is most often numbered separately from the rest of the text in lower case Roman numerals [i.e. *i-xi*]. Critical commentary about front or back matter is generally only necessary if you believe there is something that diminishes the overall quality of the work [e.g., the indexing is poor] or there is something that is particularly helpful in understanding the book's contents [e.g., foreword places the book in an important context].

The following front matter may be included in a book and may be considered for evaluation when reviewing its overall quality:

- **Table of contents** -- is it clear? Is it detailed or general? Does it reflect the true contents of the book?
- **Author biography** -- also found as back matter, the biography of author(s) can be useful in determining the authority of the writer and whether the book builds on prior research or represents new research. In scholarly reviews, noting the author's affiliation can be a factor in helping the reader determine the overall validity of the

work [i.e., are they associated with a research center devoted to studying the research problem under investigation].

- **Foreword** -- the purpose of a foreword is to introduce the reader to the author as well as the book itself, and to help establish credibility for both. A foreword may not contribute any additional information about the book's subject matter, but it serves as a means of validating the book's existence. Later editions of a book sometimes have a new foreword prepended [appearing before an older foreword, if there was one], which may be included to explain in how the latest edition differs from previous ones.

- **Preface** -- generally describes the genesis, purpose, limitations, and scope of the book and may include acknowledgments of indebtedness to people who have helped the author complete the study. Is the preface helpful in understanding the study? Does it provide an effective framework for understanding what's to follow?

- **Chronology** -- also may be found as back matter, a chronology is generally included to highlight key events related to the subject of the book. Do the entries contribute to the overall work? Is it detailed or very general?

- **List of non-textual elements** -- a book that contains a lot of charts, photographs, maps, etc. will often list these items after the table of contents in order that they appear in the text. Is it useful?

The following back matter may be included in a book and may be considered for evaluation when reviewing the overall quality of the book:

- **Afterword** -- this is a short, reflective piece written by the author that takes the form of a concluding section, final commentary, or closing statement. It is worth mentioning in a review if it contributes information about the purpose of the book, gives a call to action, or asks the reader to consider key points made in the book.

- **Appendix** -- is the supplementary material in the appendix or appendices well organized? Do they relate to the contents or appear superfluous? Does it contain any essential information that would have been more appropriately integrated into the text?

- **Index** -- is the index thorough and accurate? Are elements used, such as, bold or italic fonts to help identify specific places in the book?

- **Glossary of Terms** -- are the definitions clearly written? Is the glossary comprehensive or are key terms missing? Are any terms or concepts mentioned in the text not included?

- **Footnotes/Endnotes** -- examine any footnotes or endnotes as you read from chapter to chapter. Do they provide important additional information? Do they clarify or extend points made in the body of the text?

- **Bibliography/References/Further Readings** -- review any bibliography, list of references to sources, and/or further readings the author may have included. What kinds of sources appear [e.g., primary or secondary, recent or old, scholarly or popular, etc.]? How does the author make use of them? Be sure to note important omissions of sources that you believe should have been utilized.

NOTE: Typically, multiple book review essays do not compare and contrast the quality of the back and front matter unless the books share a common deficiency [e.g., poor indexing] or the front or back matter is particularly important in supplementing the primary content of the books.

VI. Summarize and Comment

Your conclusion should synthesize the key similarities and differences among the books and their collective contributions to understanding of the research problem. Avoid re-stating your assessment word for word; your goal is to provide a sense of closure and to leave the reader with a final perspective about the overall subject under review and whether you believe each book has effectively contributed to the overall research literature on the subject. Do not introduce new information in the conclusion. If you've compared the books to any other studies or used other sources in writing the review, be sure to cite them at the end of your book review essay.

2

Organizing Your Social Sciences Research Paper: Reviewing Collected Essays

Definition

Collected essays vary in form and content [see below], but they are generally a single volume containing chapters written by a variety of contributing authors. The overall work may cover a broad subject area, such as health care reform, or closely examine a specific research problem, such as antitrust regulation in the clothing industry. Each chapter is written by an expert in the field examining a particular aspect of that topic. Most books of collected essays include a foreword or introductory chapter written by the editor that summarizes current research about the topic and places the essays within a larger scholarly context.

How to Approach Writing Your Review
Types of Collected Works

1. **Conference Proceedings** -- a collection of papers published as part of an academic conference or other gathering of professionals. The purpose is to inform a wider audience of the papers presented at the conference as well as to document the work of scholars who have participated in that conference. Many conferences are held annually and, thus, the proceedings are published each year. Some proceedings focus on a particular theme representing a cutting edge issue in the field [e.g., Chun, Soon Ae. *Proceedings of the 10th Annual International Conference on Digital Government Research: May 17-20, 2009*. New York: ACM Press, 2009].

2. **Collection of an Author's Research** -- a collection of works by a distinguished scholar. The contents of collected works can take the form of reprints of prior research or of selected reprints with a new introductory chapter by the author or an expert in the field that synthesizes and updates the overall status of research [e.g., *The Nature of Politics: Selected Essays of Bertrand de Jouvenel*. Edited and with an introduction by Dennis Hale and Marc Landy; Foreword by Wilson Carey McWilliams. New York: Schocken Books, 1987. xxxv, 254 pp.]

3. **Festschrift** -- a volume of articles or essays by colleagues and admirers that serve as a tribute or memorial to a preeminent scholar or public figure. The essays usually relate to, or reflect upon, an honoree's contributions to their field of study, but may also include original research by the authors that build upon the research of the honoree [e.g., *Social Cognition, Social Identity, and Intergroup Relations: A Festschrift in Honor of Marilynn B. Brewer*. Roderick M. Kramer, Geoffrey J. Leonardelli, Robert W. Livingston, editors. New York: Psychology Press, 2011. xi, 423 pp.].

4. **Reader** -- a collection of articles, most often reprinted from scholarly journals, representing a cross-section of research about a particular topic. Most readers are intended to be used in the classroom. Readers serve to document the breadth and range of the important research that has developed in a particular area of study and, often, as specified over a period of time [e.g., *Companion

Reader on Violence Against Women. Claire M. Renzetti, Jeffrey L. Edleson, Raquel Kennedy Bergen, editors. Thousand Oaks, CA: Sage Publications, 2012. x, 411 pp.].

5. **Reprints** -- sometimes in the form of a multi-volume set, this is a selective collection of previously published materials. Most frequently, reprints contain scholarly journal articles gathered together to form a comprehensive overview of prior research in a particular area of study [e.g., Brooks, Thom, editor. *Rawls and Law.* Burlington, VT: Ashgate, 2012].

6. **Thematic Articles** -- the most common form of collected works in the social sciences, this is a collection of new scholarly essays from multiple authors examining a particular research problem or topic. This can be in the form of a book, a reprint, or a journal [e.g., "Monitoring Social Mobility in the Twenty-First Century." Edited by David B. Grusky, Timothy M. Smeeding and C. Matthew Snipp. *The ANNALS of the American Academy of Political and Social Science* 657 (January 2015): 1-273].

Developing an Assessment Strategy

The challenge with reviewing a book of collected essays is that you must begin by thinking critically about the research problem that underpins each of the individual essays, synthesizing the arguments of multiple authors, and then clearly organizing those arguments into conceptual categories [themes] as you write your draft.

Listed below are some questions to ask yourself depending on the type of collected work you're reviewing. Note that all types of collected works require you to first identify the overarching subject area or topic under investigation.

1. **Conference Proceedings** -- what organization is sponsoring the conference? Is there a specific theme to the conference? Why is that theme important? Was the collection of papers selectively chosen or do the proceedings represent all papers presented at the conference? If not, how were the papers selected? Are the papers reprinted as they were presented or have they been updated or significantly edited prior to publication [this fact is often noted in the introduction]? Are the proceedings online and, if so, how might this facilitate access to additional materials? Is there foreword or an introductory chapter that effectively synthesizes the collection? Is it logically organized and include important front and back matter, such as, a table of contents, profiles of each contributor, and, most

importantly, an index to locate information from among all of the papers?

2. **Collection of an Author's Research** -- who is the author and why do you believe his or her work is important enough to be gathered together for publication? Is there an underlying theme or does the collection represent a "best of" collection? What may have been ommitted? Are any original works included or are the contents only reprints? Is there a bibliography of the all of the author's writings? Is there a foreword or an introductory chapter written by the author or a guest contributor that effectively synthesizes the collection? Are the contents arranged logically [e.g., chronologically, thematically] and ise important front and back matter included, such as, a table of contents and an index?

3. **Festschrift** -- who is being honored and why? Do the contributors represent a diversity of viewpoints or perspectives? Do the contributions represent essays of general tribute or do they represent original research that builds upon the honoree's prior work? Is there a list of contributors and does it include biographical profiles of each that helps determine their relationship to the honoree? Is there a foreword or an introductory chapter that effectively synthesizes the collection? Is it logically organized and include important front and back matter, such as, a table of contents and an index?

4. **Reader** -- does the collection represent a broad spectrum of publications about a research topic or only a few? Are there underrepresented areas of research in the collection? Are the sources making up the collection representative of one or only a few areas of study or do they represent an interdisciplinary perspective about the topic? Is there a list of editors/compilers and does it include biographical profiles of each? Are the contents reprinted in their entirety or is the text only excerpted? Are the reprints readily available through other means or do they represent a compilation of hard-to-find publications? Is there a foreword or an introductory chapter that effectively synthesizes the collection? Is it logically organized and include important front and back matter, such as, a table of contents and an index?

5. **Reprints** -- does the collection represent reprints from a variety of publications or only a few? Are there underrepresented areas of research in the collection? Are the sources making up the collection representative of one or only a few areas of study or do they represent an interdisciplinary perspective about the topic? Are the reprints readily available through other means or do they represent a compilation of

hard-to-find publications? Are the reprints from relatively current or older publications? Is there a foreword or an introductory chapter that effectively synthesizes the collection? Is it logically organized and include important front and back matter such as a table of contents and an index?

6. **Thematic Articles** -- how are the contents arranged? Do the contributions survey a broad area of research or do they examine multiple issues associated with a particular research problem? Is there a list of contributors and does it include biographical profiles of each? Do you the contributors come from one or a variety of institutions? Do the contributors all come from the United States or are there any international contributors? Is there foreword or an introductory chapter that effectively synthesizes the collection? Does the work include important front and back matter, such as, a table of contents and an index?

Structure and Writing Style
I. Bibliographic Information

Provide the essential information about the book using the writing style that your professor has asked you to use for the course [e.g., APA, MLA, Chicago, etc.]. Depending on how your professor wants you to organize your review, the bibliographic information represents the heading of your review. In general, it would look like this:

El Ghonemy, Mohamad Riad. *Anti-Poverty Land Reform Issues Never Die: Collected Essays on Development Economics in Practice*. (New York: Routledge, 2010. xx, 223 pp.)
Reviewed by [your name].

II. Scope/Purpose/Content

The first challenge in reviewing any type of collected essay work is to identify and summarize its overarching scope and purpose, with additional focus on describing how the book is organized and whether or not the arrangement of its individual parts facilitates and contributes to an understanding of the subject area. Most collected essays include a general statement of purpose in the foreword or an introductory chapter. In some cases, the editor will discuss the scope and purpose at the beginning of each essay.

To help develop your own introductory thesis statement that covers all of the material, start by reviewing and taking notes about the aim and intent of each essay. Once completed, identify key issues and themes. For example, in a compilation of essays on environmental law, you may find the papers examine various legal approaches to environmental protection, describe alternatives to the law, and compare domestic and international issues. By identifying the overall themes, you create a framework from which you can cogently evaluate the contents.

As with any review, your introductory statement must be succinct, accurate, unbiased, and clearly stated. However, given that you are reviewing a number of parts within a much larger work, you may need several paragraphs to provide a comprehensive overview of the book's overall scope, purpose, and content.

If you find it difficult to discern the overall aims and objectives of the collected essay work [and, be sure to point this out in your review if you believe it to be a deficiency], you may arrive at an understanding of the purpose by asking yourself a the following questions:

- Why did the contributing authors write on this subject rather than on some other subject? Why is it important?
- From what point of view is the overall work written? Do some essays take one stance while others investigate another, or do the essays just represent a mish-mash of viewpoints?
- Were each of the authors trying to give information, to explain something technical, or to convince the reader of a belief's validity by dramatizing it in action?
- What is the general field or genre, and how does the book fit into it? Review related literature from other books and journal articles to familiarize yourself with the field, if necessary.
- Who is the intended audience?
- What are each author's style? Do they clash or do they flow together? Is it formal or informal? You can evaluate the quality of the writing style by noting some of the following standards: coherence, clarity, originality, forcefulness, correct use of technical words, conciseness, fullness of development, and fluidity.
- Scan the table of contents because it can help you understand how the book is organized and will aid in determining the main ideas covered and how they are developed [e.g., chronologically, topically, thematically, etc.]
- How did the book affect you? Were any prior assumptions you had on the subject changed, abandoned, or reinforced due to this book? Did some essays stand out more than others? In what ways?
- How is the book related to your own course or personal agenda? What personal experiences have you had that relate to the subject?
- How well has the book achieved its goal(s)?
- Would you recommend the book to others? Why or why not?

III. Critically Evaluate the Contents

Critical comments should form the bulk of your book review. A good method for reviewing a collected essays work is to follow the arrangement of contents, particularly if the essays are grouped in a particular way, and to frame the analysis in the context of the key issues and themes you identified in the introduction. State whether or not you feel the overall treatment of the subject matter is appropriate for the intended audience. Ask yourself:

- Has the purpose of the book been achieved?
- Have all of the essays contributed something important to the overall purpose? If not, how have some author's failed to add something meaningful?
- What contribution does the book make to the field?
- Is the treatment of the subject matter fair and unbiased?
- Are there facts and evidence that have been omitted?
- What kinds of data, if any, are used to support the author's thesis statement?
- Can the same data be interpreted to alternate ends?
- Is the writing style clear and effective?
- Considered collectively, did the essays cover the topic or research problem thoroughly? If not, what issue or perspective about the topic do you believe has been omitted?
- Does the book raise important or provocative issues or topics for discussion and further research?

Support your evaluation with evidence from the text and, when possible, in relation to other sources. Do not evaluate each essay one at a time but group the analysis around the key issues and themes you first identified. If relevant, make note of the book's format, such as, layout, binding, typography, etc. Do some or all of the essays include tables, charts, maps, illustrations, or other non-textual elements? Do they aid in understanding the research problem?

IV. Examine the Front Matter and Back Matter

Front matter refers to anything before the first chapter of the book. Back matter refers to any information included after the final chapter of the book. Front matter is most often numbered separately from the rest of the text in lower case Roman numerals [i.e. *i-xi*]. Critical commentary about front or back matter is generally only necessary if you believe there is something that diminishes the overall quality of the work [e.g., the indexing is poor] or there is something that is particularly helpful in understanding the book's contents [e.g., foreword places the book in an important context].

The following front matter may be included in a book and may be considered for evaluation when reviewing its overall quality:

- **Table of contents** -- is it clear? Is it detailed or general? Does it reflect the true contents of the book?
- **Author biography** -- also found as back matter, the biography of author(s) can be useful in determining the authority of the writer and whether the book builds on prior research or represents new research. In scholarly reviews, noting the author's affiliation can be a factor in helping the reader determine the overall validity of the work [i.e., are they associated with a research center devoted to studying the research problem under investigation].
- **Foreword** -- the purpose of a foreword is to introduce the reader to the author as well as the book itself, and to help establish credibility for both. A foreword may not contribute any additional information about the book's subject matter, but it serves as a means of validating the book's existence. Later editions of a book sometimes have a new foreword prepended [appearing before an older foreword, if there was one], which may be included to explain in how the latest edition differs from previous ones.
- **Preface** -- generally describes the genesis, purpose, limitations, and scope of the book and may include acknowledgments of indebtedness to people who have helped the author complete the study. Is the preface helpful in understanding the study? Does it provide an effective framework for understanding what's to follow?
- **Chronology** -- also may be found as back matter, a chronology is generally included to highlight key events related to the subject of the book. Do the entries contribute to the overall work? Is it detailed or very general?
- **List of non-textual elements** -- a book that contains a lot of charts, photographs, maps, etc. will often list these items after the table of contents in order that they appear in the text. Is it useful?

The following back matter may be included in a book and may be considered for evaluation when reviewing the overall quality of the book:

- **Afterword** -- this is a short, reflective piece written by the author that takes the form of a concluding section, final commentary, or closing statement. It is worth mentioning in a review if it contributes information about the purpose of the book, gives a call to action, or asks the reader to consider key points made in the book.
- **Appendix** -- is the supplementary material in the appendix or appendices well organized? Do they relate to the contents or appear

superfluous? Does it contain any essential information that would have been more appropriately integrated into the text?

- **Index** -- is the index thorough and accurate? Are elements used, such as, bold or italic fonts to help identify specific places in the book?
- **Glossary of Terms** -- are the definitions clearly written? Is the glossary comprehensive or are key terms missing? Are any terms or concepts mentioned in the text not included?
- **Footnotes/Endnotes** -- examine any footnotes or endnotes as you read from chapter to chapter. Do they provide important additional information? Do they clarify or extend points made in the body of the text?
- **Bibliography/References/Further Readings** -- review any bibliography, list of references to sources, and/or further readings the author may have included. What kinds of sources appear [e.g., primary or secondary, recent or old, scholarly or popular, etc.]? How does the author make use of them? Be sure to note important omissions of sources that you believe should have been utilized.

V. Summarize and Comment

State your general conclusions succinctly. Pay particular attention to any capstone chapter that summarizes the work. Collected essays often have one written by the editor. List the principal topics, and briefly summarize the key themes and issues, main points, and conclusions. If appropriate and to help clarify your overall evaluation, use specific references and quotations to support your statements. If your thesis has been well argued, the conclusion should follow naturally. It can include a final assessment or simply restate your thesis. Do not introduce new information in the conclusion.

Organizing Your Social Sciences Research Paper: 17. Writing a Case Study

Definition

The term case study refers to both a method of analysis and a specific research design for examining a problem, both of which are used in most circumstances to generalize across populations. This tab focuses on the latter--how to design and organize a research paper in the social sciences that analyzes a specific case.

A case study research paper examines a person, place, event, phenomenon, or other type of subject of analysis in order to extrapolate key themes and results that help predict future trends, illuminate previously hidden issues that can be applied to practice, and/or provide a means for understanding an important research problem with greater clarity. A case study paper usually examines a single subject of analysis, but case study papers can also be designed as a comparative investigation that shows relationships between two or among more than two subjects. The methods used to study a case can rest within a quantitative, qualitative, or mixed-method investigative paradigm.

How to Approach Writing a Case Study Research Paper

General information about how to choose a topic to investigate can be found under the "Choosing a Research Problem" tab in this writing guide. Review this page because it may help you identify a subject of analysis that can be investigated using a single case study design.

However, **identifying a case to investigate involves more than choosing the research problem**. A case study encompasses a problem contextualized around the application of in-depth analysis, interpretation, and discussion, often resulting in specific recommendations for action or for improving existing conditions. As Seawright and Gerring note, practical considerations such as time and access to information can influence case selection, but these issues should not be the sole factors used in describing the methodological justification for identifying a particular case to study. Given this, selecting a case includes considering the following:

- **Does the case represent an unusual or atypical example of a research problem that requires more in-depth analysis?** Cases often represent a topic that rests on the fringes of prior investigations because the case may provide new ways of understanding the research problem. For example, if the research problem is to identify strategies to improve policies that support girl's access to secondary education in predominantly Muslim nations, you could consider using Azerbaijan as a case study rather than selecting a more obvious nation in the Middle East. Doing so may reveal important new insights into recommending how governments in other predominantly Muslim nations can formulate policies that support improved access to education for girls.

- **Does the case provide important insight or illuminate a previously hidden problem?** In-depth analysis of a case can be based on the hypothesis that the case study will reveal trends or issues that have not been exposed in prior research or will reveal new and important implications for practice. For example, anecdotal evidence may suggest drug use among homeless veterans is related to their patterns of travel throughout the day. Assuming prior studies have not looked at individual travel choices as a way to study access to illicit drug use, a case study that observes a homeless veteran could reveal how issues of personal mobility choices facilitate regular access to illicit drugs. Note that it is important to conduct a thorough literature review to ensure that your assumption about the need to reveal new insights or previously hidden problems is valid and evidence-based.

- **Does the case challenge and offer a counter-point to prevailing assumptions?** Over time, research on any given topic can fall into a trap of developing assumptions based on outdated studies that are still applied to new or changing conditions or the idea that something should simply be accepted as "common sense," even though the issue has not been thoroughly tested in practice. A case may offer you an opportunity to gather evidence that challenges prevailing assumptions about a research problem and provide a new set of recommendations applied to practice that have not been tested previously. For example, perhaps there has been a long practice among scholars to apply a particular theory in explaining the relationship between two subjects of analysis. Your case could challenge this assumption by applying an innovative theoretical framework [perhaps borrowed from another discipline] to the study a case in order to explore whether this approach offers new ways of understanding the research problem. Taking a contrarian stance is one of the most important ways that new knowledge and understanding develops from existing literature.

- **Does the case provide an opportunity to pursue action leading to the resolution of a problem?** Another way to think about choosing a case to study is to consider how the results from investigating a particular case may result in findings that reveal ways in which to resolve an existing or emerging problem. For example, studying the case of an unforeseen incident, such as a fatal accident at a railroad crossing, can reveal hidden issues that could be applied to preventative measures that contribute to reducing the chance of accidents in the future. In this example, a case study investigating the accident could lead to a better understanding of where to strategically locate additional signals at other railroad crossings in order to better warn drivers of an approaching train, particularly when visibility is hindered by heavy rain, fog, or at night.

- **Does the case offer a new direction in future research?** A case study can be used as a tool for exploratory research that points to a need for further examination of the research problem. A case can be used when there are few studies that help predict an outcome or that establish a clear understanding about how best to proceed in addressing a problem. For example, after conducting a thorough literature review [very important!], you discover that little research exists showing the ways in which women contribute to promoting water conservation in rural communities of Uganda. A case study of how women contribute to saving water in a particular village can lay the foundation for understanding the need for more thorough research that documents how women in their roles as cooks and family caregivers think about water as a valuable resource within their community throughout rural regions of east Africa. The case could also point to the need for scholars to apply feminist theories of work and family to the issue of water conservation.

Structure and Writing Style

The purpose of a paper in the social sciences designed around a case study is to thoroughly investigate a subject of analysis in order to reveal a new understanding about the research problem and, in so doing, contributing new knowledge to what is already known from previous studies. In general, the structure of a case study research paper is not all that different from a standard college-level research paper. However, there are subtle differences you should be aware of. Here are the key elements to organizing and writing a case study research paper.

I. Introduction

As with any research paper, your introduction should serve as a roadmap for your readers to ascertain the scope and purpose of your study. The introduction to a case study research paper, however, should not only describe the research problem and its significance, but you should also succinctly describe why the case is being used and how it relates to addressing the problem. The two elements should be linked. With this in mind, a good introduction answers these four questions:

1. **What was I studying?** Describe the research problem and describe the subject of analysis you have chosen to address the problem. Explain how they are linked and what elements of the case will help to expand knowledge and understanding about the problem.

2. **Why was this topic important to investigate?** Describe the significance of the research problem and state why a case study design and the subject of analysis that the paper is designed around is appropriate in addressing the problem.

3. **What did we know about this topic before I did this study?** Provide background that helps lead the reader into the more in-depth literature review to follow. If applicable, summarize prior case study research applied to the research problem and why it fails to adequately address the research problem. Describe why your case will be useful. If no prior case studies have been used to address the research problem, explain why you have selected this subject of analysis.

4. **How will this study advance new knowledge or new ways of understanding?** Explain why your case study will be suitable in helping to expand knowledge and understanding about the research problem.

Each of these questions should be addressed in no more than a few paragraphs. Exceptions to this can be when you are addressing a complex research problem or subject of analysis that requires more in-depth background information.

II. Literature Review

The literature review for a case study research paper is generally structured the same as it is for any college-level research paper. The difference, however, is that the literature review is focused on providing background information and enabling historical interpretation of the subject of analysis in relation to the research problem the case is intended to address. This includes synthesizing studies that help to:

- **Place relevant works in the context of their contribution to understanding the case study being investigated.** This would include summarizing studies that have used a similar subject of analysis to investigate the research problem. If there is literature using the same or a very similar case to study, you need to explain why duplicating past research is important [e.g., conditions have changed; prior studies were conducted long ago, etc.].
- **Describe the relationship each work has to the others under consideration that informs the reader why this case is applicable.** Your literature review should include a description of any works that support using the case to study the research problem and the underlying research questions.
- **Identify new ways to interpret prior research using the case study.** If applicable, review any research that has examined the research problem using a different research design. Explain how your case study design may reveal new knowledge or a new perspective or that can redirect research in an important new direction.
- **Resolve conflicts amongst seemingly contradictory previous studies.** This refers to synthesizing any literature that points to unresolved issues of concern about the research problem and describing how the subject of analysis that forms the case study can help resolve these existing contradictions.
- **Point the way in fulfilling a need for additional research.** Your review should examine any literature that lays a foundation for understanding why your case study design and the subject of analysis around which you have designed your study may reveal a new way of approaching the research problem or offer a perspective that points to the need for additional research.
- **Expose any gaps that exist in the literature that the case study could help to fill.** Summarize any literature that not only shows how your subject of analysis contributes to understanding the research problem, but how your case contributes to a new way of understanding the problem that prior research has failed to do.
- **Locate your own research within the context of existing literature [very important!].** Collectively, your literature review should always place your case study within the larger domain of prior research about the problem. The overarching purpose of

reviewing pertinent literature in a case study paper is to demonstrate that you have thoroughly identified and synthesized prior studies in the context of explaining the relevance of the case in addressing the research problem.

III. Method

In this section, you explain why you selected a particular subject of analysis to study and the strategy you used to identify and ultimately decide that your case was appropriate in addressing the research problem. The way you describe the methods used varies depending on the type of subject of analysis that frames your case study.

If your subject of analysis is an incident or event. In the social and behavioral sciences, the event or incident that represents the case to be studied is usually bounded by time and place, with a clear beginning and end and with an identifiable location or position relative to its surroundings. The subject of analysis can be of a rare or critical event or focus on a typical or regular event. The purpose of studying a rare event is to illuminate new ways of thinking about the broader research problem or to test a hypothesis. Critical incident case studies must describe the method by which you identified the event and explain the process by which you determined the validity of this case to inform broader perspectives about the research problem or to reveal new findings. However, the event does not have to be a rare or uniquely significant to support new thinking about the research problem or to challenge an existing hypothesis. For example, Walo, Bull, and Breen conducted a case study to identify and evaluate the direct and indirect economic benefits and costs of a local sports event in the City of Lismore, New South Wales, Australia. The purpose of their study was to provide new insights from measuring the impact of a typical local sports event that prior studies could not measure well because they focused on large "mega-events." Whether the event is rare or not, the methods section should include an explanation of the following characteristics of the event: when did it take place; what were the underlying circumstances leading to the event; what were the consequences of the event

If your subject of analysis is a person. Explain why you selected this particular individual to be studied and describe what experience he or she has had that provides an opportunity to advance new understandings about the research problem. Mention any background about this person which might help the reader understand the significance of his/her experiences that make them worthy of study. This includes describing the relationships this person has had with other people, institutions, and/or events that support using him or her as the subject for a case study research paper. It is particularly important to differentiate the person as the subject of analysis from others and to succinctly explain how the person relates to examining the research problem.

If your subject of analysis is a place. In general, a case study that investigates a place suggests a subject of analysis that is unique or special in some way and that this uniqueness can be used to build new understanding or knowledge about the research problem. A case study of a place must not only describe its various attributes relevant to the research problem [e.g., physical, social, cultural, economic, political, etc.], but you must state the method by which you determined that this place will illuminate new understandings about the research problem. It is also important to articulate why a particular place as the case for study is being used if similar places also exist [i.e., if you are studying patterns of homeless encampments of veterans in open spaces, why study Echo Park in Los Angeles rather than Griffith Park?] and, if applicable, what type of human activity involving this place makes it a good choice to study [prior research reveals Echo Park has more homeless veterans].

If your subject of analysis is a phenomenon. A phenomenon refers to a fact, occurrence, or circumstance that can be studied or observed but with the cause or explanation to be in question. In this sense, a phenomenon that forms your subject of analysis can encompass anything that can be observed or presumed to exist but is not fully understood. In the social and behavioral sciences, the case usually focuses on human interaction within a complex physical, social, economic, cultural, or political system. For example, the phenomenon could be the observation that many vehicles used by ISIS fighters are small trucks with English language advertisements on them. The research problem could be that ISIS fighters are difficult to combat because they are highly mobile. The research questions could be how and by what means are these vehicles used by ISIS being supplied to the militants and how might supply lines to these vehicles be cut? How might knowing the suppliers of these trucks from overseas reveal larger networks of collaborators and financial support? A case study of a phenomenon most often encompasses an in-depth analysis of a cause and effect that is grounded in an interactive relationship between people and their environment in some way.

NOTE: Evidence that supports the method by which you identified and chose your subject of analysis should be linked to the findings from the literature review. Be sure to cite any prior studies that helped you determine that the case you chose was appropriate for investigating the research problem.

IV. Discussion

The main elements of your discussion section are generally the same as any research paper, but centered around interpreting and drawing conclusions about the key findings from your case study. Note that a general social sciences research paper may contain a separate section to report findings. However, in a paper designed around a case study, it is more common to combine a description of the findings with the discussion about their implications. The objectives of your discussion section should include the following:

Reiterate the Research Problem/State the Major Findings

Briefly reiterate the research problem you are investigating and explain why the subject of analysis around which you designed the case study were used. You should then describe the findings revealed from your study of the case using direct, declarative, and succinct proclamation of the study results. Highlight any findings that were unexpected *or* especially profound.

Explain the Meaning of the Findings and Why They are Important

Systematically explain the meaning of your case study findings and why you believe they are important. Begin this part of the section by repeating what you consider to be your most important or surprising finding first, then systematically review each finding. Be sure to thoroughly extrapolate what your analysis of the case can tell the reader about situations or conditions beyond the actual case that was studied while, at the same time, being careful not to misconstrue or conflate a finding that undermines the external validity of your conclusions.

Relate the Findings to Similar Studies

No study in the social sciences is so novel or possesses such a restricted focus that it has absolutely no relation to previously published research. The discussion section should relate your case study results to those found in other studies, particularly if questions raised from prior studies served as the motivation for choosing your subject of analysis. This is important because comparing and contrasting the findings of other studies helps to support the overall importance of your results and it highlights how and in what ways your case study design and the subject of analysis differs from prior research about the topic.

Consider Alternative Explanations of the Findings

It is important to remember that the purpose of social science research is to discover and not to prove. When writing the discussion section, you should carefully consider all possible explanations for the case study results, rather than just those that fit your hypothesis or prior assumptions and biases. Be alert to what the in-depth analysis of the case may reveal about the research problem, including offering a contrarian perspective to what scholars have stated in prior research.

Acknowledge the Study's Limitations

You can state the study's limitations in the conclusion section of your paper but describing the limitations of your subject of analysis in the discussion section provides an opportunity to identify the limitations and explain why they are not significant. This part of the discussion section should also note any unanswered questions or issues your case study could not address. More detailed information about how to document any limitations to your research can be found **here**.

Suggest Areas for Further Research

Although your case study may offer important insights about the research problem, there are likely additional questions related to the problem that remain unanswered or findings that unexpectedly revealed themselves as a result of your in-depth analysis of the case. Be sure that the recommendations for further research are linked to the research problem and that you explain why your recommendations are valid in other contexts and based on the original assumptions of your study.

V. Conclusion

As with any research paper, you should summarize your conclusion in clear, simple language; emphasize how the findings from your case study differs from or supports prior research and why. Do not simply reiterate the discussion section. Provide a synthesis of key findings presented in the paper to show how these converge to address the research problem. If you haven't already done so in the discussion section, be sure to document the limitations of your case study and needs for further research.

The function of your paper's conclusion is to: 1) restate the main argument supported by the findings from the analysis of your case; 2) clearly state the context, background, and necessity of pursuing the research problem using a case study design in relation to an issue, controversy, or a gap found from reviewing the literature; and, 3) provide a place for you to persuasively and succinctly restate the significance of your research problem, given that the reader has now been presented with in-depth information about the topic.

Consider the following points to help ensure your conclusion is appropriate:

1. If the argument or purpose of your paper is complex, you may need to summarize these points for your reader.
2. If prior to your conclusion, you have not yet explained the significance of your findings or if you are proceeding inductively, use the conclusion of your paper to describe your main points and explain their significance.
3. Move from a detailed to a general level of consideration of the case study's findings that returns the topic to the context provided by the introduction or within a new context that emerges from your case study findings.

Note that, depending on the discipline you are writing in and your professor's preferences, the concluding paragraph may contain your final reflections on the evidence presented applied to practice or on the essay's central research problem. However, the nature of being introspective about the subject of analysis you have investigated will depend on whether you are explicitly asked to express your observations in this way.

Problems to Avoid
Overgeneralization

One of the goals of a case study is to lay a foundation for understanding broader trends and issues applied to similar circumstances. However, be careful when drawing conclusions from your case study. They must be evidence-based and grounded in the results of the study; otherwise, it is merely speculation. Looking at a prior example, it would be incorrect to state that a factor in improving girls access to education in Azerbaijan and the policy implications this may have for improving access in other Muslim nations is due to girls access to social media if there is no documentary evidence from your case study to indicate this. There may be anecdotal evidence that retention rates were better for girls who were on social media, but this observation would only point to the need for further research and would not be a definitive finding if this was not a part of your original research agenda.

Failure to Document Limitations

No case is going to reveal all that needs to be understood about a research problem. Therefore, just as you have to clearly state the limitations of a general research study, you must describe the specific limitations inherent in the subject of analysis. For example, the case of studying how women conceptualize the need for water conservation in a village in Uganda could have limited application in other cultural contexts or in areas where fresh water from rivers or lakes is plentiful and, therefore, conservation is understood differently than preserving access to a scarce resource.

Failure to Extrapolate All Possible Implications

Just as you don't want to over-generalize from your case study findings, you also have to be thorough in the consideration of all possible outcomes or recommendations derived from your findings. If you do not, your reader may question the validity of your entire analysis, particularly if you failed to document an obvious outcome from your case study research. For example, in the case of studying the accident at the railroad crossing to evaluate where and what types of warning signals should be located, you failed to take into consideration speed limit signage as well as warning signals. When designing your case study, be sure you have thoroughly addressed all aspects of the problem and do not leave gaps in your analysis.

Organizing Your Social Sciences Research Paper: 18. Writing a Field Report

Definition

The purpose of a field report in the social sciences is to describe the observation of people, places, and/or events and to analyze that observation data in order to identify and categorize common themes in relation to the research problem underpinning the study. The content represents the researcher's interpretation of meaning found in data that has been gathered during one or more observational events.

How to Approach Writing a Field Report

How to Begin

Field reports are most often assigned in disciplines of the applied social sciences [e.g., social work, anthropology, gerontology, criminal justice, education, law, the health care professions] where it is important to build a bridge of relevancy between the theoretical concepts learned in the classroom and the practice of actually doing the work you are being taught to do. Field reports are also common in certain science disciplines [e.g., geology] but these reports are organized differently and serve a different purpose than what is described below.

Professors will assign a field report with the intention of improving your understanding of key theoretical concepts through a method of careful and structured observation of, and reflection about, people, places, or things existing in their natural settings. Field reports facilitate the development of data collection techniques and observation skills and they help you to understand how theory applies to real world situations. Field reports are also an opportunity to obtain evidence through methods of observing professional practice that contribute to or challenge existing theories.

We are all observers of people, their interactions, places, and events; however, your responsibility when writing a field report is to create a research study based on data generated by the act of designing a specific study, deliberate observation, a synthesis of key findings, and an interpretation of their meaning. When writing a field report you need to:

- **Systematically observe and accurately record the varying aspects of a situation**. Always approach your field study with a detailed plan about what you will observe, where you should conduct your observations, and the method by which you will collect and record your data.

- **Continuously analyze your observations**. Always look for the meaning underlying the actions you observe. Ask yourself: What's going on here? What does this observed activity mean? What else does this relate to? Note that this is an on-going process of reflection and analysis taking place for the duration of your field research.

- **Keep the report's aims in mind while you are observing**. Recording what you observe should not be done randomly or haphazardly; you must be focused and pay attention to details. Enter the observation site [i.e., "field"] with a clear plan about what you are intending to observe and record while, at the same time, being prepared to adapt to changing circumstances as they may arise.

- **Consciously observe, record, and analyze what you hear and see in the context of a theoretical framework**. This is what separates data gatherings from simple reporting. The theoretical framework guiding your field research should determine what, when, and how you observe and act as the foundation from which you interpret your findings.

Techniques to Record Your Observations

Although there is no limit to the type of data gathering technique you can use, these are the three most common:

Note Taking

This is the most commonly used and easiest method of recording your observations. Tips for taking notes include: organizing some shorthand symbols beforehand so that recording basic or repeated actions does not impede your ability to observe, using many small paragraphs, which reflect changes in activities, who is talking, etc., and, leaving space on the page so you can write down additional thoughts and ideas about what's being observed, any theoretical insights, and notes to yourself that are set aside for further investigation. See drop-down tab for additional information about note-taking.

Video and Audio Recordings
Video or audio recording your observations has the positive effect of giving you an unfiltered record of the observation event. It also facilitates repeated analysis of your observations. However, these techniques have the negative effect of increasing how intrusive you are as an observer and will often not be practical or even allowed under certain circumstances [e.g., interaction between a doctor and a patient] and in certain organizational settings [e.g., a courtroom].

Illustrations/Drawings
This does not refer to an artistic endeavor but, rather, refers to the possible need, for example, to draw a map of the observation setting or illustrating objects in relation to people's behavior. This can also take the form of rough tables or graphs documenting the frequency and type of activities observed. These can be subsequently placed in a more readable format when you write your field report.

Examples of Things to Document While Observing

- **Physical setting**. The characteristics of an occupied space and the human use of the place where the observation(s) are being conducted.
- **Objects and material culture**. This referes to the presence, placement, and arrangement of objects that impact the behavior or actions of those being observed. If applicable, describe the cultural artifacts representing the beliefs--values, ideas, attitudes, and assumptions--used by the individuals you are observing.
- **Use of language**. Don't just observe but *listen* to what is being said, how is it being said, and, the tone of conversation among participants.
- **Behavior cycles**. This refers to documenting when and who performs what behavior or task and how often they occur. Record at which stage is this behavior occurring within the setting.
- **The order in which events unfold**. Note sequential patterns of behavior or the moment when actions or events take place and their significance.
- **Physical characteristics of subjects.** If relevant, note age, gender, clothing, etc. of individuals being observed.
- **Expressive body movements**. This would include things like body posture or facial expressions. Note that it may be relevant to also assess whether expressive body movements support or contradict the language used in conversation [e.g., detecting sarcasm].

Brief notes about all of these examples contextualize your observations; however, your observation notes will be guided primarily by your theoretical framework, keeping in mind that your observations will feed into and potentially modify or alter these frameworks.

Sampling Techniques

Sampling refers to the process used to select a portion of the population for study. Qualitative research, of which observation is one method, is generally based on non-probability and purposive sampling rather than probability or random approaches characteristic of quantitatively-driven studies. Sampling in observational research is flexible and often continues until no new themes emerge from the data, a point referred to as data saturation.

All sampling decisions are made for the explicit purpose of obtaining the richest possible source of information to answer the research questions. Decisions about sampling assumes you know what you want to observe, what behaviors are important to record, and what research problem you are addressing before you begin the study. These questions determine what sampling technique you should use, so be sure you have adequately answered them before selecting a sampling method.

Ways to sample when conducting an observation include:

Ad Libitum Sampling -- this approach is not that different from what people do at the zoo--observing whatever seems interesting at the moment. There is no organized system of recording the observations; you just note whatever seems relevant at the time. The advantage of this method is that you are often able to observe relatively rare or unusual behaviors that might be missed by more deliberate sampling methods. This method is also useful for obtaining preliminary observations that can be used to develop your final field study. Problems using this method include the possibility of inherent bias toward conspicuous behaviors or individuals and that you may miss brief interactions in social settings.

Behavior Sampling -- this involves watching the entire group of subjects and recording each occurance of a specific behavior of interest and with reference to which individuals were involved. The method is useful in recording rare behaviors missed by other sampling methods and is often used in conjunction with focal or scan methods. However, sampling can be biased towards particular conspicuous behaviors.

Continuous Recording -- provides a faithful record of behavior including frequencies, durations, and latencies [the time that elapses between a stimulus and the response to it]. This is a very demanding method because you are trying to record everything within the setting and, thus, measuring reliability may be sacrificed. In addition, durations and latencies are only reliable if subjects remain present throughout the collection of data. However, this method facilitates analyzing sequences of behaviors and ensures obtaining a wealth of data about the observation site and the people within it. The use of audio or video recording is most useful with this type of sampling.

Focal Sampling -- this involves observing one individual for a specified amount of time and recording all instances of that individual's behavior. Usually you have a set of predetermined categories or types of behaviors that you are interested in observing [e.g., when a teacher walks around the classroom] and you keep track of the duration of those behaviors. This approach doesn't tend to bias one behavior over another and provides significant detail about a individual's behavior. However, with this method, you likely have to conduct a lot of focal samples before you have a good idea about how group members interact. It can also be difficult within certain settings to keep one individual in sight for the entire period of the observation.

Instantaneous Sampling -- this is where observation sessions are divided into short intervals divided by sample points. At each sample point the observer records if predetermined behaviors of interest are taking place. This method is not effective for recording discrete events of short duration and, frequently, observers will want to record novel behaviors that occur slightly before or after the point of sampling, creating a sampling error. Though not exact, this method does give you an idea of durations and is relatively easy to do. It is also good for recording behavior patterns occurring at a specific instant, such as, movement or body positions.

One-Zero Sampling -- this is very similar to instantaneous sampling, only the observer records if the behaviors of interest have occurred at any time during an interval instead of at the instant of the sampling point. The method is useful for capturing data on behavior patterns that start and stop repeatedly and rapidly, but that last only for a brief period of time. The disadvantage of this approach is that you get a dimensionless score for an entire recording session, so you only get one one data point for each recording session.

Scan Sampling -- this method involves taking a census of the entire observed group at predetermined time periods and recording what each individual is doing at that moment. This is useful for obtaining group behavioral data and allows for data that are evenly representative across individuals and periods of time. On the other hand, this method may be biased towards more conspicuous behaviors and you may miss a lot of what is going on between observations, especially rare or unusual behaviors. It is also difficult to record more than a few individuals in a group setting without missing what each individual is doing at each predetermined moment in time [e.g., children sitting at a table during lunch at school].

Structure and Writing Style

How you choose to format your field report is determined by the research problem, the theoretical perspective that is driving your analysis, the observations that you make, and/or specific guidelines established by your professor. Since field reports do not have a standard format, it is worthwhile to determine from your professor what the preferred organization should be before you begin to write. Note that field reports should be written in the past tense. With this in mind, most field reports in the social sciences include the following elements:

I. Introduction

The introduction should describe the research problem, the specific objectives of your research, and the important theories or concepts underpinning your field study. The introduction should describe the nature of the organization or setting where you are conducting the observation, what type of observations you have conducted, what your focus was, when you observed, and the methods you used for collecting the data. You should also include a review of pertinent literature related to the research problem, particularly if similar methods were used in prior studies. Conclude your introduction with a statement about how the rest of the paper is organized.

II. Description of Activities

Your readers only knowledge and understanding of what happened will come from the description section of your report because they have not been witness to the situation, people, or events that you are writing about. Given this, it is crucial that you provide sufficient details to place the analysis that will follow into proper context; don't make the mistake of providing a description without context. The description section of a field report is similar to a well written piece of journalism. Therefore, a helpful approach to systematically describing the varying aspects of an observed situation is to answer the "Five W's of Investigative Reporting." These are:

- **What** -- describe what you observed. Note the temporal, physical, and social boundaries you imposed to limit the observations you made. What were your general impressions of the situation you were observing. For example, as a student teacher, what is your impression of the application of iPads as a learning device in a history class; as a cultural anthropologist, what is your impression of women's participation in a Native American religious ritual?

- **Where** -- provide background information about the setting of your observation and, if necessary, note important material objects that are present that help contextualize the observation [e.g., arrangement of computers in relation to student engagement with the teacher].
- **When** -- record factual data about the day and the beginning and ending time of each observation. Note that it may also be necessary to include background information or key events which impact upon the situation you were observing [e.g., observing the ability of teachers to re-engage students after coming back from an unannounced fire drill].
- **Who** -- note background and demographic information about the individuals being observed e.g., age, gender, ethnicity, and/or any other variables relevant to your study]. Record who is doing what and saying what, as well as, who is not doing or saying what. If relevant, be sure to record who was missing from the observation.
- **Why** -- why were you doing this? Describe the reasons for selecting particular situations to observe. Note why something happened. Also note why you may have included or excluded certain information.

III. Interpretation and Analysis

Always place the analysis and interpretations of your field observations within the larger context of the theories and issues you described in the introduction. Part of your responsibility in analyzing the data is to determine which observations are worthy of comment and interpretation, and which observations are more general in nature. It is your theoretical framework that allows you to make these decisions. You need to demonstrate to the reader that you are looking at the situation through the eyes of an informed viewer, not as a lay person.

Here are some questions to ask yourself when analyzing your observations:

- What is the meaning of what you have observed?
- Why do you think what you observed happened? What evidence do you have for your reasoning?
- What events or behaviors were typical or widespread? If appropriate, what was unusual or out of ordinary? How were they distributed among categories of people?
- Do you see any connections or patterns in what you observed?
- Why did the people you observed proceed with an action in the way that they did? What are the implications of this?
- Did the stated or implicit objectives of what you were observing match what was achieved?
- What were the relative merits of the behaviors you observed?

- What were the strengths and weaknesses of the observations you recorded?
- Do you see connections between what you observed and the findings of similar studies identified from your review of the literature?
- How do your observations fit into the larger context of professional practice? In what ways have your observations possibly changed or affirmed your perceptions of professional practice?
- Have you learned anything from what you observed?

NOTE: Only base your interpretations on what you have actually observed. Do not speculate or manipulate your observational data to fit into your study's theoretical framework.

IV. Conclusion and Recommendations

The conclusion should briefly recap of the entire study, reiterating the importance or significance of your observations. Avoid including any new information. You should also state any recommendations you may have. Be sure to describe any unanticipated problems you encountered and note the limitations of your study. The conclusion should not be more than two or three paragraphs.

V. Appendix

This is where you would place information that is not essential to explaining your findings, but that supports your analysis [especially repetitive or lengthy information], that validates your conclusions, or that contextualizes a related point that helps the reader understand the overall report. Examples of information that could be included in an appendix are figures/ tables/ charts/ graphs of results, statistics, pictures, maps, drawings, or, if applicable, transcripts of interviews. There is no limit to what can be included in the appendix or its format [e.g., a DVD recording of the observation site], provided that it is relevant to the study's purpose and reference is made to it in the report. If information is placed in more than one appendix ["appendices"], the order in which they are organized is dictated by the order they were first mentioned in the text of the report.

VI. References

List all sources that you consulted and obtained information from while writing your field report. Note that field reports generally do not include further readings or an extended bibliography. However, consult with your professor concerning what your list of sources should be included. Be sure to write them in the preferred citation style of your discipline [i.e., APA, Chicago, MLA, etc.].

1

Organizing Your Social Sciences Research Paper: About Informed Consent

Definition

Informed consent is the process through which a researcher obtains, as well as maintains, the permission of a person or a person's authorized representative to participate in a research study. Informed consent is achieved when a subject of your study receives full disclosure of the research plan and its intent, understands all of the information that is disclosed to him or her, voluntarily consents to participate in the study and is competent to do so, and understand they may withdraw from the study at any time.

Obtaining Informed Consent

One of the most important ethical rules governing qualitative research is that individuals must voluntarily give their informed consent before participating in a study. However, the conditions under which you may be required to obtain permission from those being observed varies. For example, observations taking place in open, public spaces, such as in a park or at the beach, usually does not require informed consent because there is no expection that you cannot be observed. However, there is likely an expectation of obtaining consent in a bounded observational space, such as, a classroom, a homeless shelter, or a hospital emergency room.

In most cases, you will need to obtain informed consent from those you are studying. According to the U.S. Office for Human Research Protections, the Code of Federal Regulations requires that specific information be provided to research subjects before they participate in a study. Rules related to conducting qualitative research in the social sciences [rather than in the medical sciences] at USC are governed by the University Park Institutional Review Board [IRB]. If you are asked to write a field report involving methods of observation, be sure you speak with your professor about the preferred process for obtaining consent, if needed, and that you understand the required procedures for obtaining informed consent.

Guidelines for writing an informed consent for to be signed by each participant generally includes the following:

1. A statement that the study involves research, an explanation of the purposes of the research, the expected duration of the subject's participation, and a description of the research procedures that will followed.

2. A description of any reasonably and foreseeable risks or discomforts to the subject [e.g., if an embarrassing incident occurs during an observation, you may be obligated to document it].

3. A description of any benefits to the subject which may reasonably be expected from the research. This would include any incentives [financial or otherwise] used to encourage people to participate or the benefits may be stated generally within the context of contributing to a finite but growing literature about your research problem and prompting other researchers to conduct similar studies.

4. A disclosure of appropriate alternative procedures, if any, that might be advantageous to the subject.

5. A statement describing the extent to which confidentiality of records identifying the subject will be maintained [e.g., .pseudonyms will be used]

6. A description of the level of risk to the subject. For most observational studies, the level of participatory risk would be minimal. A risk is considered "minimal" when the probability and magnitude of harm or discomfort anticipated in the proposed research are not greater, in and of themselves, than those ordinarily encountered in daily life.

7. An explanation of whom to contact for answers to pertinent questions about the research and research subjects' rights [i.e., if a person under observation believes you are not conducting the study in the way each of you agreed to, who can they contact? In most cases, this would be your professor].

8. A statement that participation is voluntary, refusal to participate will involve no penalty, and the subject may discontinue participation at any time without penalty. This would also include a statement that you reserve the right to remove a participant from the study if you so choose.

NOTE: The informed consent forms that you and your research subjects must sign have to be written in plain language. In addition, the form should not contain any exculpatory language. That is, subjects should not be asked to waive [or appear to waive] any of their legal rights, nor should they be asked to release the investigator or the university from liability for negligence.

2

Organizing Your Social Sciences Research Paper: Writing Field Notes

Definition
Refers to notes created by the researcher during the act of qualitative fieldwork to remember and record the behaviors, activities, events, and other features of an observation. Field notes are intended to be read by the researcher as evidence to produce meaning and an understanding of the culture, social situation, or phenomenon being studied. The notes may constitute the whole data collected for a research study [e.g., an observational project] or contribute to it, such as when field notes supplement conventional interview data.

How to Approach Writing Field Notes
The ways in which you take notes during an observational study is very much a personal decision developed over time as you become more experienced in observing. However, all field notes generally consist of two parts:
1. **Descriptive information**, in which you attempt to accurately document factual data [e.g., date and time] and the settings, actions, behaviors, and conversations that you observe; and,
2. **Reflective information**, in which you record your thoughts, ideas, questions, and concerns as you are conducting the observation.

Field notes should be fleshed out as soon as possible after an observation is completed. Your initial notes may be recorded in cryptic form and, unless additional detail is added as soon as possible after the observation, important facts and opportunities for fully interpreting the data may be lost.

Characteristics of Field Notes
- **Be accurate.** You only get one chance to observe a particular moment in time so, before you conduct your observations, practice taking notes in a setting that is similar to your observation site in regards to number of people, the environment, and social dynamics.

This will help you develop your own style of transcribing observations quickly and accurately.

- **Be organized**. Taking accurate notes while you are actively observing can be difficult. It is therefore important that you plan ahead how you will document your observation study [e.g., strictly chronologically or according to specific prompts]. Notes that are disorganized will make it more difficult for you to interpret the data.
- **Be descriptive**. Use descriptive words to document what you observe. For example, instead of noting that a classroom appears "comfortable," state that the classroom includes soft lighting and cushioned chairs that can be moved around by the study participants. Being descriptive means supplying yourself with enough factual evidence that you don't end up making assumptions about what you meant when you write the final report.
- **Focus on the research problem**. Since it's impossible to document everything you observe, include the greatest detail about aspects of the research problem and the theoretical constructs underpinning your research; avoid cluttering your notes with irrelevant information. For example, if the purpose of your study is to observe the discursive interactions between nursing home staff and the family members of residents, then it would only be necessary to document the setting in detail if it in some way directly influenced those interactions [e.g., there is a private room available for discussions between staff and family members].
- **Record insights and thoughts**. As you observe, be thinking about the underlying meaning of what you observe and record your thoughts and ideas accordingly. This will help if you to ask questions or seek clarification from participants after the observation. To avoid any confusion, subsequent comments from participants should be included in a separate, reflective part of your field notes and not merged with the descriptive notes.

General Guidelines for the Descriptive Content
- Describe the physical setting.
- Describe the social environment and the way in which participants interacted within the setting. This may include patterns of interactions, frequency of interactions, direction of communication patterns [including non-verbal communication], and patterns of specific behavioral events, such as, conflicts, decision-making, or collaboration.
- Describe the participants and their roles in the setting.

- Describe, as best you can, the meaning of what was observed from the perspectives of the participants.
- Record exact quotes or close approximations of comments that relate directly to the purpose of the study.
- Describe any impact you might have had on the situation you observed [important!].

General Guidelines for the Reflective Content

- Note ideas, impressions, thoughts, and/or any criticisms you have about what you observed.
- Include any unanswered questions or concerns that have arisen from analyzing the observation data.
- Clarify points and/or correct mistakes and misunderstandings in other parts of field notes.
- Include insights about what you have observed and speculate as to why you believe specific phenomenon occurred.
- Recond thoughts that you may have regarding any future observations.

NOTE: Analysis of your field notes should occur as they are being written and while you are conducting your observations. This is important for at least two reasons. First, preliminary analysis fosters self-reflection, and self-reflection is crucial for understanding and meaning-making in any research study. Second, preliminary analysis reveals emergent themes. Identifying emergent themes while observing allows you to shift your attention in ways that can foster a more developed investigation.

Organizing Your Social Sciences Research Paper: 19. Writing a Policy Memo

Definition
A policy memo is a practical and professionally written document that can vary in length from one page to over one hundred pages. It provides analysis and/or recommendations directed to a predetermined audience regarding a specific situation or topic. A well-written policy memo reflects attention to the research problem. It is well organized and structured in a clear and concise style that assumes the reader possesses limited knowledge of, as well as little time to conduct research about, the issue of concern. There is no thesis statement or overall theoretical framework underpinning the document; the focus is on describing one or more specific policy recommendations and their supporting action items.

How to Approach Writing a Policy Memo
Policy memo writing assignments are intended to promote the following learning outcomes:
- Help students learn how to write academically rigorous, persuasive papers about a specific "real-world" issue,
- Learn how to choose and craft a document's content based on the needs of a particular audience [rather than for a general readership],
- Prepare students about how to write effectively in non-academic settings,
- Teach students to be client-oriented and to better anticipate the assumptions and concerns of their targeted readership, and
- Enable students to create original work that synthesizes their research into a succinctly written document advocating change or a specific course of action.

You should not approach writing a policy memo like you would an academic research paper. Yes, there are certain commonalities in how the content is presented [e.g., a well-written problem statement], but the overarching objective of a policy memo is not to discover or create new knowledge. It is focused on providing a pre-determined group of readers the rationale for choosing a particular policy alternative or specific course of action. In this sense, most policy memos possess a component of advocacy and policy advice intended to promote evidence-based dialogue about an issue.

Given these intended learning outcomes, keep in mind the following:

Focus and Objectives

The overall content of your memo should be strategically aimed at achieving the following goal: convincing your target audience about the accuracy of your analysis and, by extension, that your policy recommendations are valid. Avoid lengthy digressions and superfluous narration that can distract the reader from understanding the policy problem.

Professionally Written

Always keep in mind that a policy memorandum is a tool for decision-making. Keep it professional and avoid hyperboles that could undermine the credibility of your document. The presentation and content of the memo should be polished, easy to understand, and free of jargon. Writing professionally does not imply that you can't be passionate about your topic, but your policy recommendations should be grounded in solid reasoning and a succinct writing style.

Evidence-based

A policy memo is not an argumentative debate paper. The reader should expect your recommendations to be based upon evidence that the problem exists and of the consequences [both good and bad] of adopting particular policy alternatives. To address this, policy memos include a clear cost-benefit analysis that considers anticipated outcomes, the potential impact on stakeholder groups you have identified, clear and quantifiable performance goals, and how success is to be measured.

Accessibility

A policy memo requires clear and simple language that avoids unnecessary jargon and concepts of an academic discipline. Do not skip around. Use one paragraph to develop one idea or argument and make that idea or argument explicit within the first one or two sentences. Your memo should have a straightforward, explicit organizational structure that provides well-explained arguments arranged within a logical sequence of reasoning [think in terms of an if/then logic model--if this policy recommendation, then this action; if this benefit, then this potential cost].

Presentation Style
The visual impact of your memo affects the reader's ability to grasp your ideas quickly and easily. Include a table of contents and list of figures and charts, if necessary. Subdivide the text using clear and descriptive headings to guide the reader. Incorporate devices such as capitalization, bold text, and bulleted items but be consistent, and don't go crazy; the purpose is to facilitate access to specific sections of the paper for successive readings. If it is difficult to find information in your document, policy makers will not use it.

Practical and Feasible
Your memorandum should provide a set of actions based on what is actually happening in reality. The purpose is never to base your policy recommendations on future scenarios that are unlikely to occur or that do not appear realistic to your targeted readers. Here again, your cost-benefit analysis can be essential to validating the practicality and feasibility to your recommendations.

Explicit Transparency
Provide specific criteria to assess either the success or failure of the policies you are recommending. As much as possible, this criteria should be derived from your cost/benefit analysis. Do not hide or under-report information that does not support your policy recommendations. Just as you should note limitations in an original research study, a policy memo should describe the weaknesses of your analysis. Be straightforward about it because doing so strengthens your arguments and it will help the reader to assess the overall impact of recommended policy changes.

NOTE: Technically, your policy memo could argue for maintaining the status quo. However, the general objective of policy memos is to examine opportunities for change and describe the risks of on-going complacency. If you choose to argue for maintaining the current policy trajectory, be concise in identifying and systematically refuting all relevant policy options. Summarize why the outcomes of maintaining the status quo are preferable to any alterative policy options.

Structure and Writing Style

The contents of a policy memo can be organized in a variety of ways. Below is a general template adapted from the "Policy Memo Requirements and Guidelines, 2012-2013 edition" published by the Institute for Public Policy Studies at the University of Denver and from suggestions made in the book, *A Practical Guide for Policy Analysis: The Eightfold Path to More Effective Problem-Solving* [Eugene Bardach. 4th edition. Thousand Oaks, CA: Sage, 2012] . Both provide useful approaches to writing a policy memo should your professor not provide you with specific guidance. The tone of your writing should be formal but assertive. Note that the most important consideration in terms of writing style is professionalism, not creativity.

I. Cover Page

Provide a complete and informative cover page that includes the document title, date, the full names and titles of the writer or writers [i.e., Joe Smith, Student, Department of Political Science, University of Southern California]. The title of the policy memo should be formally written and specific to the policy issue [e.g., "Charter Schools, Fair Housing, and Legal Standards: A Call for Equal Treatment"]. For longer memos, consider including a brief executive summary that highlights key findings and recommendations.

II. Introduction and Problem Definition

A policy memorandum should begin with a short summary introduction that defines the policy problem, provides important contextual background information, and explains what issues the memo covers. This is followed by a short justification for writing the memo, why a decision needs to be made [answering the "So What?" question], and an outline of the recommendations you make or key themes the reader should keep in mind. Summarize your main points in a few sentences, then conclude with a description of how the remainder of the memo is organized.

III. Methods

This is usually where other research about the problem or issue of concern is summarized. Describe how you plan to identify and locate the information on which your policy memo is based. This may include peer-reviewed journals and books as well as possible professionals you interviewed, databases and websites you explored, or legislative histories or relevant case law that you used. Remember this is not intended to be a thorough literature review; only choose sources that persuasively support your position or that helps lay a foundation for understanding why actions need to be taken.

IV. Issue Analysis

This section is where you explain in detail how you examined the issue and, by so doing, persuade the reader of the appropriateness of your analysis. This is followed by a description of how your analysis contributes to the current policy debate. It is important to demonstrate that the policy issue may be more complex than a basic pro versus con debate. Very few public policy debates can be reduced to this type of rhetorical dichotomy. Be sure your analysis is thorough and takes into account all factors that may influence possible strategies that could advance a recommended set of solutions.

V. Proposed Solutions

Write a brief review of the specific solutions you evaluated, noting the criteria by which you examined and compared different proposed policy alternatives. Identify the stakeholders impacted by the proposed solutions and describe in what ways the stakeholders benefit from your proposed solution. Focus on identifying solutions that have not been proposed or tested elsewhere. Offer a contrarian viewpoint that challenges the reader to take into account a new perspective on the research problem. Note that you can propose solutions that may be considered radical or unorthodox, but they must be realistic and politically feasible.

VI. Strategic Recommendations

Solutions are just opinions until you provide a path that delineates how to get from where you are to where you want to go. Describe what you believe are the best recommended courses of action ["action items"]. In writing this section, state the broad approach to be taken, with specific practical steps or measures that should be implemented. Be sure to also state by whom and within what time frame these actions should be taken. Conclude by highlighting the consequences of maintaining the status quo [or if supporting the status quo, why change at this time would be detrimental]. Also, clearly explain why your strategic recommendations are best suited for addressing the current policy situation.

VI. Limitations

As in any academic paper, you must describe limitations to your analysis. In particular, ask yourself if each of your recommendations are realistic, feasible, and sustainable, and in particular, that they can be implemented within the current bureaucratic, economic, political, cultural, or other type of contextual climate in which they reside. If not, you should go back and clarify your recommendations or provide further evidence as to why the recommendation is most appropriate for addressing the issue. If the limitation cannot be overcome, it does not necessarily undermine the overall recommendations of your study, but you must clearly acknowledge it. Place the limitation within the context of a critical issue that needs further study in concurrance with possible implementation [i.e., findings indicate service learning promotes civic engagement, but.there is a lack of data on the types of service learning programs that exist among higth schools in Los Angeles].

248 :: How to write a research proposal, paper or thesis

VII. Cost-Benefit Analysis

This section may be optional but some policy memos benefit by having an explicit summary analysis of the costs and benefits of each strategic recommendation. If you include a separate cost-benefit analysis, be concise and brief. Most policy memos do not have a formal conclusion, therefore, the cost-benefit analysis can act as your conclusion by summarizing key differences among policy alternatives.

Proofreading the Memo
Problems to Avoid

The style and arrangement of an effectively written memo can differ because no two policies, nor their intended audience of readers, are exactly the same. Nevertheless, before you submit your policy memo, be sure you proofread the document in order to avoid these common problems. **If you identify one or more of them, you should rewrite or re-organize the content accordingly.**

1. Acknowledge the law of unintended consequences -- no policy analysis is complete until you have identified for whom the policy is supposed to benefit as well as identify what groups may be impacted by the consequences of implementation. Review your memo and make sure you have clearly delineated who could be helped and who could be potentially harmed or excluded from benefitting from your recommended policy actions. As noted by Wilcoxen, this is also important because describing who benefits and who may not can help you anticipate which stakeholder groups will support your policy recommendations and which groups will likely oppose it. Calculating potential winners and losers will help reveal how much it may cost to compensate those groups excluded from benefitting. By building this compensation into your policy recommendations, you are better able to show the reader how to reduce political obstacles.

2. Anticipate the reader's questions -- examine your recommended courses of action and identify any open-ended, declarative, or ambiguous statements that could lead the reader to have to ask further questions. For example, you declare that the most important factor supporting school choice among parents is distance from home. Without clarification or additional information, a reader may question why or by what means do you know this, or what distance is considered to be too far? Or, what factors contribute to parent's decision about school choice and distance from schools? What age group does this most apply to? Clarify these types of open-ended statements so that your policy can be more fully understood.

3. Be concise -- being succinct in your writing does not relate to the overall length of the policy memo or the amount of words you use. It relates to an ability to provide a lot of information clearly and without superfluous detail. Strategies include reviewing long paragraphs and breaking them up into parts, looking for long sentences and eliminating unnecessary qualifiers and modifiers, and deleting prepositional phrases in favor of adjectives or adverbs. The overarching goal is to be thorough and precise in how you present ideas and to avoid writing that uses too many words or excessively technical expressions.

4. Focus on the results -- while it's important that your memo describe the methods by which you gathered and analyzed the data informing your policy recommendations, the content should focus on explaining the results of your analysis and the logic underpinning your recommendations. Remember your audience. The reader is presumably a decision-maker with limited knowledge of the issue and with little time to contemplate the methods of analysis. The validity of your findings will be determined primarily by your reader's determination that your policy recommendations and supporting action items are realistic and rooted in sound reasoning. Review your memo and make sure the statement about how you gathered the data is brief and concise. If necessary, technical issues or raw data can be included as an appendix.

5. Minimize subjective reasoning -- avoid emphasizing your personal opinion about the topic. A policy memo should be written in a professional tone with recommendations based upon empirical reasoning while, at the same time, reflecting a level of passion about your topic. However, being passionate does not imply being opinionated. The memo should emphasize presenting all of the facts a reader would need to reach his or her own conclusions about the validity of your recommendations.

6. Use of non-textual elements -- review all tables, charts, figures, graphs, or other non-textual elements and make sure they are labelled correctly. Examine each in relation to the text and make sure they are described adequately and relate to the overall content of your memo. If these elements are located in appendices, make sure references to them within the text is correct [i.e., reference to Figure 2 is actually the table you want the reader to look at].

Organizing Your Social Sciences Research Paper: 20. Writing a Research Proposal

Definition

The goal of a research proposal is to present and justify the need to study a research problem and to present the practical ways in which this research should be conducted. The design elements and procedures for conducting the research are governed by standards within the predominant discipline in which the problem resides, so guidelines for research proposals are more exacting and less formal than a general project proposal. Research proposals contain extensive literature reviews. They must provide persuasive evidence that a need exists for the proposed study. In addition to providing a rationale, a proposal describes detailed methodology for conducting the research consistent with requirements of the professional or academic field and a statement on anticipated outcomes and/or benefits derived from the study's completion.

How to Approach Writing a Research Proposal

Your professor may assign the task of writing a research proposal for the following reasons:

- Develop your skills in thinking about and designing a comprehensive research study;
- Learn how to conduct a comprehensive review of the literature to ensure a research problem has not already been answered [or you may determine the problem has been answered ineffectively] and, in so doing, become better at locating scholarship related to your topic;
- Improve your general research and writing skills;
- Practice identifying the logical steps that must be taken to accomplish one's research goals; and,
- Nurture a sense of inquisitiveness within yourself and to help see yourself as an active participant in the process of doing scholarly research.

A proposal should contain all the key elements involved in designing a completed research study, with sufficient information that allows readers to assess the validity and usefulness of your proposed study. The only elements missing from a research proposal are the results of the study and your analysis of those results. Finally, an effective proposal is judged on the quality of your writing and, therefore, it is important that your writing is coherent, clear, and compelling.

Regardless of the research problem you are investigating and the methodology you choose, all research proposals must address the following questions:

1. **What do you plan to accomplish?** Be clear and succient in defining the research problem and what it is you are proposing to research.
2. **Why do you want to do it?** In addition to detailing your research design, you also must conduct a thorough review of the literature and provide convincing evidence that it is a topic worthy of study. Be sure to answer the "So What?" question.
3. **How are you going to do it?** Be sure that what you propose is doable. If you're having trouble formulating a research problem to propose investigating, **go here**.

Common Mistakes to Avoid

- Failure to be concise; being "all over the map" without a clear sense of purpose.
- Failure to cite landmark works in your literature review.
- Failure to delimit the contextual boundaries of your research [e.g., time, place, people, etc.].
- Failure to develop a coherent and persuasive argument for the proposed research.
- Failure to stay focused on the research problem; going off on unrelated tangents.
- Sloppy or imprecise writing, or poor grammar.
- Too much detail on minor issues, but not enough detail on major issues.

Structure and Writing Style
Beginning the Proposal Process

As with writing a traditional research paper, research proposals are generally organized the same way throughout most social science disciplines. Proposals vary between ten and twenty pages in length. However, before you begin, read the assignment carefully and, if anything seems unclear, ask your professor whether there are any specific requirements for organizing and writing the proposal.

A good place to begin is to ask yourself a series of questions:

- What do I want to study
- Why is the topic important?
- How is it significant within the subject areas covered in my class?
- What problems will it help solve?
- How does it build upon [and hopefully go beyond] research already conducted on the topic?
- What exactly should I plan to do, and can I get it done in the time available?

In the end, your research proposal should document your knowledge of the topic and highlight enthusiasm for conducting the study. Approach it with the intention of leaving your readers feeling like--"Wow, that's an exciting idea and I can't wait to see how it turns out!"

In general your proposal should include the following sections:

I. Introduction

In the real world of higher education, a research proposal is most often written by scholars seeking grant funding for a research project or it's the first step in getting approval to write a doctoral dissertation. Even if this is just a course assignment, treat your introduction as the initial pitch of an idea. After reading the introduction, your readers should not only have an understanding of what you want to do, but they should also be able to sense your passion for the topic and be excited about the study's possible outcomes.

Think about your introduction as a narrative written in one to three paragraphs that succinctly answers the following four questions:

1. What is the central research problem?
2. What is the topic of study related to that problem?
3. What methods should be used to analyze the research problem?
4. Why is this important research, and why should someone reading the proposal care about the outcomes from the study?

II. Background and Significance

This section can be melded into your introduction or you can create a separate section to help with the organization and flow of your proposal. This is where you explain the context of your study proposal and outline why it's important. Approach writing this section with the thought that you can't assume your readers will know as much about the research problem as you do. Note that this section is not an essay going over everything you have learned about the research problem; instead, you must choose what is relevant to help explain the goals for your study.

To that end, while there are no hard and fast rules, you should attempt to deal with some or all of the following:

- State the research problem and give a more detailed explaination about the purpose of the study than what you stated in the introduction. This is particularly important if the problem is complex or multifaceted.
- Present the rationale of your proposed study and clearly indicate why it is worth doing. Answer the "So What? question [i.e., why should anyone care].
- Describe the major issues or problems to be addressed by your research.
- Explain how you plan to go about conducting your research. Clearly identify the key sources you intend to use and explain how they will contribute to your analysis of the topic.
- Set the boundaries of your proposed research in order to provide a clear focus.
- If necessary, provide definitions of key concepts or terms.

III. Literature Review

Connected to the background and significance of your study is a more deliberate review and synthesis of prior studies related to the research problem under investigation. The purpose here is to place your project within the larger whole of what is currently being explored, while demonstrating to your readers that your work is original and innovative. Think about what questions other researchers have asked, what methods they have used, and what is your understanding of their findings. Assess what you believe is still missing, and state how previous research has failed to examine the issue that your study addresses.

Since a literature review is information dense, it is crucial that this section is intelligently structured to enable a reader to grasp the key arguments underpinning your study in relation to that of other researchers. A good strategy is to break the literature into "conceptual categories" [themes] rather than systematically describing groups of materials one at a time.

To help frame your proposal's literature review, here are the "five C's" of writing a literature review:

1. **Cite**: keep the primary focus on the literature pertinent to your research problem.

2. **Compare** the various arguments, theories, methodologies, and findings expressed in the literature: what do the authors agree on? Who applies similar approaches to analyzing the research problem?

3. **Contrast** the various arguments, themes, methodologies, approaches and controversies expressed in the literature: what are the major areas of disagreement, controversy, or debate?

4. **Critique** the literature: Which arguments are more persuasive, and why? Which approaches, findings, methodologies seem most reliable, valid, or appropriate, and why? Pay attention to the verbs you use to describe what an author says/does [e.g., asserts, demonstrates, etc.].

5. **Connect** the literature to your own area of research and investigation: how does your own work draw upon, depart from, or synthesize what has been said in the literature?

IV. Research Design and Methods

This section must be well-written and logically organized because you are not actually doing the research. As a consequence, the reader will never have a study outcome from which to evaluate whether your methodological choices were the correct ones. The objective here is to convince the reader that your overall research design and methods of analysis will correctly address the research problem. Your design and methods should be unmistakably tied to the specific aims of your study.

Describe the overall research design by building upon and drawing examples from your review of the literature. Be specific about the methodological approaches you plan to undertake to gather information, about the techniques you would use to analyze it, and about the tests of external validity to which you commit yourself [i.e., the trustworthiness by which you can generalize from your study to other people, places, or times].

When describing the methods you will use, be sure to cover these issues:

- Specify the research operations you will undertake and the way you will interpret the results of these operations in relation to your research problem. Don't just describe what you intend to achieve from applying the methods you choose, but state how you will spend your time while applying these methods [e.g., coding text from interviews to find statements about changes to school curriculum].

- Keep in mind that a methodology is not just a list of tasks; it is an argument as to why these tasks add up to the best way to investigate the research problem. This is an important point because the mere listing of tasks to be performed does not demonstrate that they add up to the best feasible approach.

- Be sure to anticipate and acknowledge any potential barriers and pitfalls in carrying out your research design and explain how you plan to address them.

V. Preliminary Suppositions and Implications

Just because you don't have to actually conduct the study and analyze the results, this doesn't mean that you can skip talking about the analytical process and potential implications. The purpose of this section is to argue how and in what ways you believe your research will refine, revise, or extend existing knowledge in the subject area under investigation. Depending on the aims and objectives of your study, describe how the anticipated results of your study will impact future scholarly research, theory, practice, forms of interventions, or policy. Note that such discussions may have either substantive [a potential new policy], theoretical [a potential new understanding], or methodological [a potential new way of analyzing] significance.

When thinking about the potential implications of your study, ask the following questions:
- What might the results mean in regards to the theoretical framework that underpins the study?
- What suggestions for subsequent research could arise from the potential outcomes of the study?
- What will the results mean to practitioners in the natural settings of their workplace?
- Will the results influence programs, methods, and/or forms of intervention?
- How might the results contribute to the solution of social, economic, or other types of problems?
- Will the results influence policy decisions?
- In what way do individuals or groups benefit should your study be pursued?
- What will be improved or changed as a result of the proposed research?
- How will the results of the study be implemented, and what innovations will come about?

VI. Conclusion

The conclusion reiterates the importance or significance of your proposal and provides a brief summary of the entire study. This section should be only one or two paragraphs long, emphasizing why the research problem is worth investigating, why your research study is unique, and how it advances knowledge.

Someone reading this section should come away with an understanding of:

- Why the study was done,
- The specific purpose of the study and the research questions it attempted to answer,
- The research design and methods used,
- The potential implications emerging from your proposed study of the research problem, and
- A sense of how your study fits within the broader scholarship about the research problem.

VII. Citations

As with any scholarly research paper, you must cite the sources you used in composing your proposal. In a standard research proposal, this section can take two forms, so consult with your professor about which one is preferred.

1. **References** -- lists only the literature that you actually used or cited in your proposal.
2. **Bibliography** -- lists everything you used or cited in your proposal with additional citations to any key sources relevant to understanding the research problem.

In either case, this section should testify to the fact that you did enough preparatory work to make sure the project will complement and not duplicate the efforts of other researchers. Start a new page and use the heading "References" or "Bibliography" centered at the top of the page. Cited works should always use a standard format that follows the writing style advised by the discipline of your course [i.e., education=APA; history=Chicago, etc]. This section normally does not count towards the total length of your proposal.

Organizing Your Social Sciences Research Paper:21.Acknowledgements

Sources Consulted

There are a tremendous number of books, journal and trade magazine articles, and commercial and non-commercial web sites offering advice about how to write a college-level research paper. In particular, the web sites linked below were consulted while developing this research guide. To facilitate further access to information about writing papers and completing related assignments in social sciences coursework, most text boxes include a bibliography of links to these sites, other online resources active at the time the page was written, and selected print sources. Suggestions for additional bibliographic sources or feedback concerning improvements to the guide are welcomed and can be sent directly to the author at labaree@usc.edu.

Academic Skills Program, **University of Canberra**

Department of Psychology Writing Center, **University of Washington**

Political Science/Law, Societies, and Justice/Jackson School of International Studies Writing Center, University of Washington

"How to Write a Paper in Scientific Journal Style and Format." Greg Anderson, Department of Biology, Bates College

The Institute for Writing and Rhetoric, **Dartmouth College**

The OWL (Online Writing Lab). Purdue University.

The Reading/Writing Center, Hunter College.

The Waldin Writing Center, Waldin University.

Web Center for Social Research Methods, Cornell University Office for Rsearch on Evaluation

Writing@CSU. Colorado State University.

The Writing Center. University of Kansas.

The Writing Center. University of North Carolina, Chapel Hill.

The Writing Center. University of Wisconsin, Madison.
Writing Guide, Department of English, George Mason University.
Writing at the University of Toronto.
Writing Tutorial Services, **Indiana University**

Organizing Your Social Sciences Research Paper: Glossary of Research Terms

Glossary of Research Terms

This glossary is intended to assist you in understanding commonly used terms and concepts when reading, interpreting, and evaluating scholarly research in the social sciences. Also included are general words and phrases defined within the context of how they apply to research in the social and behavioral sciences.

- **Acculturation** -- refers to the process of adapting to another culture, particularly in reference to blending in with the majority population [e.g., an immigrant adopting American customs]. However, acculturation also implies that both cultures add something to one another, but still remain distinct groups unto themselves.
- **Accuracy** -- a term used in survey research to refer to the match between the target population and the sample.
- **Affective Measures** -- procedures or devices used to obtain quantified descriptions of an individual's feelings, emotional states, or dispositions.
- **Aggregate** -- a total created from smaller units. For instance, the population of a county is an aggregate of the populations of the cities, rural areas, etc. that comprise the county. As a verb, it refers to total data from smaller units into a large unit.
- **Anonymity** -- a research condition in which no one, including the researcher, knows the identities of research participants.
- **Baseline** -- a control measurement carried out before an experimental treatment.

262 :: How to write a research proposal, paper or thesis

- **Behaviorism** -- school of psychological thought concerned with the observable, tangible, objective facts of behavior, rather than with subjective phenomena such as thoughts, emotions, or impulses. Contemporary behaviorism also emphasizes the study of mental states such as feelings and fantasies to the extent that they can be directly observed and measured.
- **Beliefs** -- ideas, doctrines, tenets, etc. that are accepted as true on grounds which are not immediately susceptible to rigorous proof.
- **Benchmarking** -- systematically measuring and comparing the operations and outcomes of organizations, systems, processes, etc., against agreed upon "best-in-class" frames of reference.
- **Bias** -- a loss of balance and accuracy in the use of research methods. It can appear in research via the sampling frame, random sampling, or non-response. It can also occur at other stages in research, such as while interviewing, in the design of questions, or in the way data are analyzed and presented. Bias means that the research findings will not be representative of, or generalizable to, a wider population.
- **Case Study** -- the collection and presentation of detailed information about a particular participant or small group, frequently including data derived from the subjects themselves.
- **Causal Hypothesis** -- a statement hypothesizing that the independent variable affects the dependent variable in some way.
- **Causal Relationship** -- the relationship established that shows that an independent variable, and nothing else, causes a change in a dependent variable. It also establishes how much of a change is shown in the dependent variable.
- **Causality** -- the relation between cause and effect.
- **Central Tendency** -- any way of describing or characterizing typical, average, or common values in some distribution.
- **Chi-square Analysis** -- a common non-parametric statistical test which compares an expected proportion or ratio to an actual proportion or ratio.
- **Claim** -- a statement, similar to a hypothesis, which is made in response to the research question and that is affirmed with evidence based on research.
- **Classification** -- ordering of related phenomena into categories, groups, or systems according to characteristics or attributes.
- **Cluster Analysis** -- a method of statistical analysis where data that share a common trait are grouped together. The data is collected in a

way that allows the data collector to group data according to certain characteristics.

- **Cohort Analysis** -- group by group analytic treatment of individuals having a statistical factor in common to each group. Group members share a particular characteristic [e.g., born in a given year] or a common experience [e.g., entering a college at a given time].
- **Confidentiality** -- a research condition in which no one except the researcher(s) knows the identities of the participants in a study. It refers to the treatment of information that a participant has disclosed to the researcher in a relationship of trust and with the expectation that it will not be revealed to others in ways that violate the original consent agreement, unless permission is granted by the participant.
- **Confirmability Objectivity** -- the findings of the study could be confirmed by another person conducting the same study.
- **Construct** -- refers to any of the following: something that exists theoretically but is not directly observable; a concept developed [constructed] for describing relations among phenomena or for other research purposes; or, a theoretical definition in which concepts are defined in terms of other concepts. For example, intelligence cannot be directly observed or measured; it is a construct.
- **Construct Validity** -- seeks an agreement between a theoretical concept and a specific measuring device, such as observation.
- **Constructivism** -- the idea that reality is socially constructed. It is the view that reality cannot be understood outside of the way humans interact and that the idea that knowledge is constructed, not discovered. Constructivists believe that learning is more active and self-directed than either behaviorism or cognitive theory would postulate.
- **Content Analysis** -- the systematic, objective, and quantitative description of the manifest or latent content of print or nonprint communications.
- **Context Sensitivity** -- awareness by a qualitative researcher of factors such as values and beliefs that influence cultural behaviors.
- **Control Group** -- the group in an experimental design that receives either no treatment or a different treatment from the experimental group. This group can thus be compared to the experimental group.
- **Controlled Experiment** -- an experimental design with two or more randomly selected groups [an experimental group and control group] in which the researcher controls or introduces the independent variable and measures the dependent variable at least two times [pre- and post-test measurements].

- **Correlation** -- a common statistical analysis, usually abbreviated as r, that measures the degree of relationship between pairs of interval variables in a sample. The range of correlation is from -1.00 to zero to +1.00. Also, a non-cause and effect relationship between two variables.
- **Covariate** -- a product of the correlation of two related variables times their standard deviations. Used in true experiments to measure the difference of treatment between them.
- **Credibility** -- a researcher's ability to demonstrate that the object of a study is accurately identified and described based on the way in which the study was conducted.
- **Critical Theory** -- an evaluative approach to social science research, associated with Germany's neo-Marxist "Frankfurt School," that aims to criticize as well as analyze society, opposing the political orthodoxy of modern communism. Its goal is to promote human emancipatory forces and to expose ideas and systems that impede them.
- **Data** -- factual information [as measurements or statistics] used as a basis for reasoning, discussion, or calculation.
- **Data Mining** -- the process of analyzing data from different perspectives and summarizing it into useful information, often to discover patterns and/or systematic relationships among variables.
- **Data Quality** -- this is the degree to which the collected data [results of measurement or observation] meet the standards of quality to be considered valid [trustworthy] and reliable [dependable].
- **Deductive** -- a form of reasoning in which conclusions are formulated about particulars from general or universal premises.
- **Dependability** -- being able to account for changes in the design of the study and the changing conditions surrounding what was studied.
- **Dependent Variable** -- a variable that varies due, at least in part, to the impact of the independent variable. In other words, its value "depends" on the value of the independent variable. For example, in the variables "gender" and "academic major," academic major is the dependent variable, meaning that your major cannot determine whether you are male or female, but your gender might indirectly lead you to favor one major over another.
- **Deviation** -- the distance between the mean and a particular data point in a given distribution.
- **Discourse Community** -- a community of scholars and researchers in a given field who respond to and communicate to each other through published articles in the community's journals and

presentations at conventions. All members of the discourse community adhere to certain conventions for the presentation of their theories and research.

- **Discrete Variable** -- a variable that is measured solely in whole units, such as, gender and number of siblings.
- **Distribution** -- the range of values of a particular variable.
- **Effect Size** -- the amount of change in a dependent variable that can be attributed to manipulations of the independent variable. A large effect size exists when the value of the dependent variable is strongly influenced by the independent variable. It is the mean difference on a variable between experimental and control groups divided by the standard deviation on that variable of the pooled groups or of the control group alone.
- **Emancipatory Research** -- research is conducted on and with people from marginalized groups or communities. It is led by a researcher or research team who is either an indigenous or external insider; is interpreted within intellectual frameworks of that group; and, is conducted largely for the purpose of empowering members of that community and improving services for them. It also engages members of the community as co-constructors or validators of knowledge.
- **Empirical Research** -- the process of developing systematized knowledge gained from observations that are formulated to support insights and generalizations about the phenomena being researched.
- **Epistemology** -- concerns knowledge construction; asks what constitutes knowledge and how knowledge is validated.
- **Ethnography** -- method to study groups and/or cultures over a period of time. The goal of this type of research is to comprehend the particular group/culture through immersion into the culture or group. Research is completed through various methods but, since the researcher is immersed within the group for an extended period of time, more detailed information is usually collected during the research.
- **Expectancy Effect** -- any unconscious or conscious cues that convey to the participant in a study how the researcher wants them to respond. Expecting someone to behave in a particular way has been shown to promote the expected behavior. Expectancy effects can be minimized by using standardized interactions with subjects, automated data-gathering methods, and double blind protocols.
- **External Validity** -- the extent to which the results of a study are generalizable or transferable.

- **Factor Analysis** -- a statistical test that explores relationships among data. The test explores which variables in a data set are most related to each other. In a carefully constructed survey, for example, factor analysis can yield information on patterns of responses, not simply data on a single response. Larger tendencies may then be interpreted, indicating behavior trends rather than simply responses to specific questions.
- **Field Studies** -- academic or other investigative studies undertaken in a natural setting, rather than in laboratories, classrooms, or other structured environments.
- **Focus Groups** -- small, roundtable discussion groups charged with examining specific topics or problems, including possible options or solutions. Focus groups usually consist of 4-12 participants, guided by moderators to keep the discussion flowing and to collect and report the results.
- **Framework** -- the structure and support that may be used as both the launching point and the on-going guidelines for investigating a research problem.
- **Generalizability** -- the extent to which research findings and conclusions conducted on a specific study to groups or situations can be applied to the population at large.
- **Grounded Theory** -- practice of developing other theories that emerge from observing a group. Theories are grounded in the group's observable experiences, but researchers add their own insight into why those experiences exist.
- **Group Behavior** -- behaviors of a group as a whole, as well as the behavior of an individual as influenced by his or her membership in a group.
- **Hypothesis** -- a tentative explanation based on theory to predict a causal relationship between variables.
- **Independent Variable** -- the conditions of an experiment that are systematically manipulated by the researcher. A variable that is not impacted by the dependent variable, and that itself impacts the dependent variable. In the earlier example of "gender" and "academic major," (see Dependent Variable) gender is the independent variable.
- **Individualism** -- a theory or policy having primary regard for the liberty, rights, or independent actions of individuals.
- **Inductive** -- a form of reasoning in which a generalized conclusion is formulated from particular instances.

- **Inductive Analysis** -- a form of analysis based on inductive reasoning; a researcher using inductive analysis starts with answers, but formulates questions throughout the research process.
- **Insiderness** -- a concept in qualitative reserch that refers to the degree to which a researcher has access to and an understanding of persons, places, or things within a group or community based on being a member of that group or community.
- **Internal Consistency** -- the extent to which all questions or items assess the same characteristic, skill, or quality.
- **Internal Validity** -- the rigor with which the study was conducted [e.g., the study's design, the care taken to conduct measurements, and decisions concerning what was and was not measured]. It is also the extent to which the designers of a study have taken into account alternative explanations for any causal relationships they explore. In studies that do not explore causal relationships, only the first of these definitions should be considered when assessing internal validity.
- **Life History** -- a record of an event/events in a respondent's life told [written down, but increasingly audio or video recorded] by the respondent from his/her own perspective in his/her own words. A life history is different from a "research story" in that it covers a longer time span, perhaps a complete life, or a significant period in a life.
- **Margin of Error** -- the permittable or acceptable deviation from the target or a specific value. The allowance for slight error or miscalculation or changing circumstances in a study.
- **Measurement** -- process of obtaining a numerical description of the extent to which persons, organizations, or things possess specified characteristics.
- **Meta-Analysis** -- an analysis combining the results of several studies that address a set of related hypotheses.
- **Methodology** -- a theory or analysis of how research does and should proceed.
- **Methods** -- systematic approaches to the conduct of an operation or process. It includes steps of procedure, application of techniques, systems of reasoning or analysis, and the modes of inquiry employed by a discipline.
- **Mixed-Methods** -- a research approach that uses two or more methods from both the quantitative and qualitative research categories. It is also referred to as blended methods, combined methods, or methodological triangulation.

- **Modeling** -- the creation of a physical or computer analogy to understand a particular phenomenon. Modeling helps in estimating the relative magnitude of various factors involved in a phenomenon. A successful model can be shown to account for unexpected behavior that has been observed, to predict certain behaviors, which can then be tested experimentally, and to demonstrate that a given theory cannot account for certain phenomenon.
- **Models** -- representations of objects, principles, processes, or ideas often used for imitation or emulation.
- **Naturalistic Observation** -- observation of behaviors and events in natural settings without experimental manipulation or other forms of interference.
- **Norm** -- the norm in statistics is the average or usual performance. For example, students usually complete their high school graduation requirements when they are 18 years old. Even though some students graduate when they are younger or older, the norm is that any given student will graduate when he or she is 18 years old.
- **Null Hypothesis** -- the proposition, to be tested statistically, that the experimental intervention has "no effect," meaning that the treatment and control groups will not differ as a result of the intervention. Investigators usually hope that the data will demonstrate some effect from the intervention, thus allowing the investigator to reject the null hypothesis.
- **Ontology** -- a discipline of philosophy that explores the science of what is, the kinds and structures of objects, properties, events, processes, and relations in every area of reality.
- **Panel Study** -- a longitudinal study in which a group of individuals is interviewed at intervals over a period of time.
- **Participant** -- individuals whose physiological and/or behavioral characteristics and responses are the object of study in a research project.
- **Peer-Review** -- the process in which the author of a book, article, or other type of publication submits his or her work to experts in the field for critical evaluation, usually prior to publication. This is standard procedure in publishing scholarly research.
- **Phenomenology** -- a qualitative research approach concerned with understanding certain group behaviors from that group's point of view.
- **Philosophy** -- critical examination of the grounds for fundamental beliefs and analysis of the basic concepts, doctrines, or practices that express such beliefs.

- **Phonology** -- the study of the ways in which speech sounds form systems and patterns in language.
- **Policy** -- governing principles that serve as guidelines or rules for decision making and action in a given area.
- **Policy Analysis** -- systematic study of the nature, rationale, cost, impact, effectiveness, implications, etc., of existing or alternative policies, using the theories and methodologies of relevant social science disciplines.
- **Population** -- the target group under investigation. The population is the entire set under consideration. Samples are drawn from populations.
- **Position Papers** -- statements of official or organizational viewpoints, often recommending a particular course of action or response to a situation.
- **Positivism** -- a doctrine in the philosophy of science, positivism argues that science can only deal with observable entities known directly to experience. The positivist aims to construct general laws, or theories, which express relationships between phenomena. Observation and experiment is used to show whether the phenomena fit the theory.
- **Predictive Measurement** -- use of tests, inventories, or other measures to determine or estimate future events, conditions, outcomes, or trends.
- **Principal Investigator** -- the scientist or scholar with primary responsibility for the design and conduct of a research project.
- **Probability** -- the chance that a phenomenon will occur randomly. As a statistical measure, it is shown as p [the "p" factor].
- **Questionnaire** -- structured sets of questions on specified subjects that are used to gather information, attitudes, or opinions.
- **Random Sampling** -- a process used in research to draw a sample of a population strictly by chance, yielding no discernible pattern beyond chance. Random sampling can be accomplished by first numbering the population, then selecting the sample according to a table of random numbers or using a random-number computer generator. The sample is said to be random because there is no regular or discernible pattern or order. Random sample selection is used under the assumption that sufficiently large samples assigned randomly will exhibit a distribution comparable to that of the population from which the sample is drawn. The random assignment of participants increases the probability that differences observed

between participant groups are the result of the experimental intervention.

- **Reliability** -- the degree to which a measure yields consistent results. If the measuring instrument [e.g., survey] is reliable, then administering it to similar groups would yield similar results. Reliability is a prerequisite for validity. An unreliable indicator cannot produce trustworthy results.
- **Representative Sample** -- sample in which the participants closely match the characteristics of the population, and thus, all segments of the population are represented in the sample. A representative sample allows results to be generalized from the sample to the population.
- **Rigor** -- degree to which research methods are scrupulously and meticulously carried out in order to recognize important influences occurring in an experimental study.
- **Sample** -- the population researched in a particular study. Usually, attempts are made to select a "sample population" that is considered representative of groups of people to whom results will be generalized or transferred. In studies that use inferential statistics to analyze results or which are designed to be generalizable, sample size is critical, generally the larger the number in the sample, the higher the likelihood of a representative distribution of the population.
- **Sampling Error** -- the degree to which the results from the sample deviate from those that would be obtained from the entire population, because of random error in the selection of respondent and the corresponding reduction in reliability.
- **Saturation** -- a situation in which data analysis begins to reveal repetition and redundancy and when new data tend to confirm existing findings rather than expand upon them.
- **Semantics** -- the relationship between symbols and meaning in a linguistic system. Also, the cuing system that connects what is written in the text to what is stored in the reader's prior knowledge.
- **Social Theories** -- theories about the structure, organization, and functioning of human societies.
- **Sociolinguistics** -- the study of language in society and, more specifically, the study of language varieties, their functions, and their speakers.
- **Standard Deviation** -- a measure of variation that indicates the typical distance between the scores of a distribution and the mean; it is determined by taking the square root of the average of the squared

deviations in a given distribution. It can be used to indicate the proportion of data within certain ranges of scale values when the distribution conforms closely to the normal curve.

- **Statistical Analysis** -- application of statistical processes and theory to the compilation, presentation, discussion, and interpretation of numerical data.

- **Statistical Bias** -- characteristics of an experimental or sampling design, or the mathematical treatment of data, that systematically affects the results of a study so as to produce incorrect, unjustified, or inappropriate inferences or conclusions.

- **Statistical Significance** -- the probability that the difference between the outcomes of the control and experimental group are great enough that it is unlikely due solely to chance. The probability that the null hypothesis can be rejected at a predetermined significance level [0.05 or 0.01].

- **Statistical Tests** -- researchers use statistical tests to make quantitative decisions about whether a study's data indicate a significant effect from the intervention and allow the researcher to reject the null hypothesis. That is, statistical tests show whether the differences between the outcomes of the control and experimental groups are great enough to be statistically significant. If differences are found to be statistically significant, it means that the probability [likelihood] that these differences occurred solely due to chance is relatively low. Most researchers agree that a significance value of .05 or less [i.e., there is a 95% probability that the differences are real] sufficiently determines significance.

- **Subcultures** -- ethnic, regional, economic, or social groups exhibiting characteristic patterns of behavior sufficient to distinguish them from the larger society to which they belong.

- **Testing** -- the act of gathering and processing information about individuals' ability, skill, understanding, or knowledge under controlled conditions.

- **Theory** -- a general explanation about a specific behavior or set of events that is based on known principles and serves to organize related events in a meaningful way. A theory is not as specific as a hypothesis.

- **Treatment** -- the stimulus given to a dependent variable.

- **Trend Samples** -- method of sampling different groups of people at different points in time from the same population.

- **Triangulation** -- a multi-method or pluralistic approach, using different methods in order to focus on the research topic from different viewpoints and to produce a multi-faceted set of data. Also used to check the validity of findings from any one method.

- **Unit of Analysis** -- the basic observable entity or phenomenon being analyzed by a study and for which data are collected in the form of variables.
- **Validity** -- the degree to which a study accurately reflects or assesses the specific concept that the researcher is attempting to measure. A method can be reliable, consistently measuring the same thing, but not valid.
- **Variable** -- any characteristic or trait that can vary from one person to another [race, gender, academic major] or for one person over time [age, political beliefs].
- **Weighted Scores** -- scores in which the components are modified by different multipliers to reflect their relative importance.
- **White Paper** -- an authoritative report that often states the position or philosophy about a social, political, or other subject, or a general explanation of an architecture, framework, or product technology written by a group of researchers. A white paper seeks to contain unbiased information and analysis regarding a business or policy problem that the researchers may be facing.

About the author

ROBERT V. LABAREE, Ed.D. is the Political Science/International Relations Librarian at the University of Southern California. He has maintained collections, provided information literacy instruction, and provided research methods consultation to students and faculty in international relations, political science, and related areas of study since his arrival at USC in 1995. His scholarly interests include applying qualitative research methods to the study of library practice and investigating the changing role of academic libraries to support student learning in a technology-enriched environment. Recent publications include an analysis of the ethical and methodological dilemmas of conducting insider participant observation research and co-authoring a study that developed a framework for addressing philosophical problems of truth in librarianship. His current research includes a co-authored investigation of efforts by world governments to control access to information in direct opposition to Article 19 of the United Nations Universal Declaration on Human Rights and a study of the philosophical constructs of not knowing in library practice. Dr. Labaree received a Bachelor's of Arts degree in History from the University of Nebraska, Lincoln and a Master's degree in Library Science from Louisiana State University. He received his doctorate in Higher Education Leadership from the USC Rossier School of Education in 2004.

About the compiler

Dr Azadeh Nemati is an Assistant Professor in Iran, majoring in ELT. She is the member of Network of Women Scientists of the Islamic world and also the editor in chief of some international journals. She has already published + 10 books and + 30 articles nationally and internationally. She has presented in many international conferences and also supervised some MA theses. In 2010, 2012 and 2014 she was selected as distinguished researcher in the University.

She is the author of the following books:

English-Persian Dictionary of body Idioms, English-Persian Dictionary of color Idioms, English-Persian Dictionary of animal Idioms, English through games (Persian edition), A collection of practical questionnaires for ELT researchers, Principles of writing resume (Persian Edition), Aspects of Language Learning Strategies (LLS): Focus on vocabulary learning strategies (VLS), Special English for the students of midwifery, Special English for the students of biology. Skills: How to be a better student and language learner by learning techniques (Persian Edition). The Impact of Vocabulary Strategies on Short and long Term, Tear and tea, A span between the moon and me and some more books.

She can be reached at her website: WWW.BaNarvan.com

www.ingramcontent.com/pod-product-compliance
Lightning Source LLC
Chambersburg PA
CBHW070353270326
41926CB00014B/2530